IMAGES
of America

WINSTON-SALEM'S HISTORIC SALEM CEMETERY

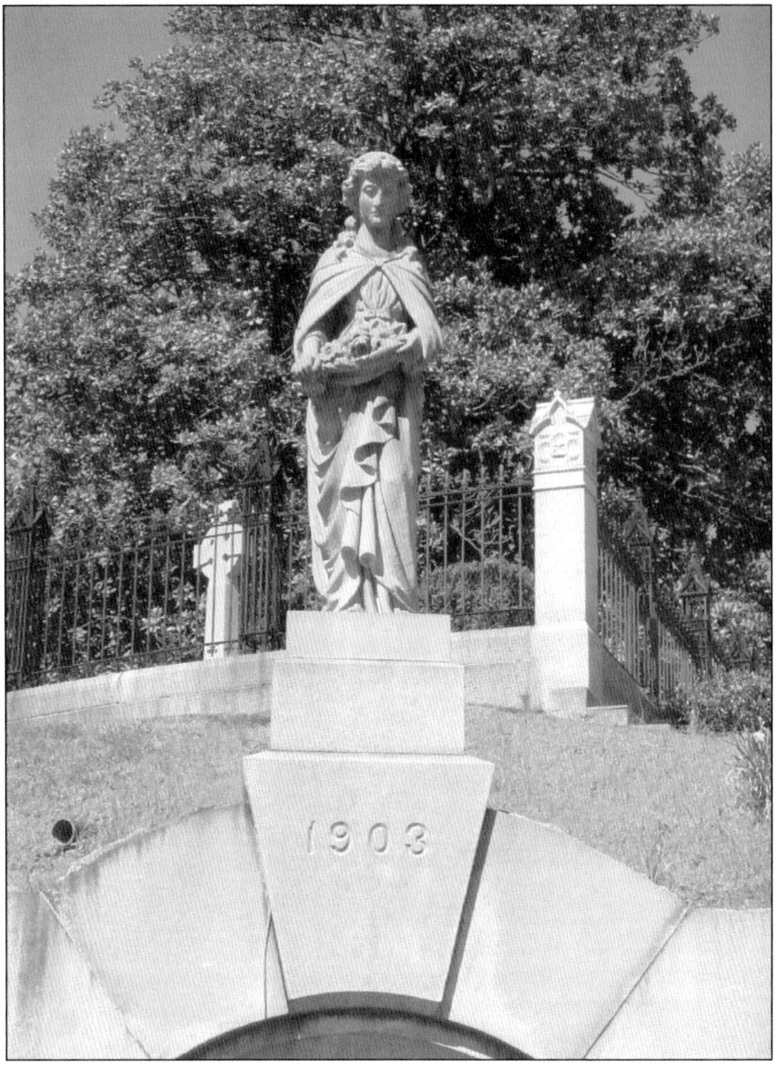

SALEM CEMETERY. Alice Warren Winkler published a 93-page booklet in 1890 titled *Souvenir of the Twin Cities of North Carolina, Winston-Salem, Forsyth County, Descriptive and Historical*. She covered in detail the city's history, businesses, churches, and associations. She described Salem Academy and the Moravian graveyard and also had a little to say about Salem Cemetery. "The grounds are reached by a rustic bridge spanning a ravine and are laid off with some attention to modern landscape gardening; the sections sold to individuals. Some of the monuments are handsome, with two private vaults above one of which stands a life-size marble figure of Hope guarding the entrance." It is not known if the statue shown here is the same as in Winkler's description, but this statue towers over the P.N. Bailey vault and could indeed symbolize hope. (MGR.)

ON THE COVER: The Rufus Patterson family plot is situated on a hill near the vaults and fairly close to Cemetery Street. Mary Louise Morehead Patterson died in 1862, so the family plot is one of the oldest in the cemetery. The ornate cast-iron fence that surrounds the Patterson family plot includes a tall gate with the Patterson name outlined in iron. The tall, decorative Celtic cross is located in the center of the family plot. Read more about the Patterson family on pages 90 and 91. (MGR.)

IMAGES
of America

WINSTON-SALEM'S HISTORIC SALEM CEMETERY

Molly Grogan Rawls

ARCADIA
PUBLISHING

ISBN 978-1-4671-1525-4

Published by Arcadia Publishing
Charleston, South Carolina

Printed in the United States of America

Library of Congress Control Number: 2015949529

For all general information, please contact Arcadia Publishing:
Telephone 843-853-2070
Fax 843-853-0044
E-mail sales@arcadiapublishing.com
For customer service and orders:
Toll-Free 1-888-313-2665

Visit us on the Internet at www.arcadiapublishing.com

As we gratefully honor the past and those who came before us, we also acknowledge the impact of present and future generations. We dedicate this book to the newest member of our family, Chloe Leigh Rawls, with thankfulness to God for the blessing of new life.

—Molly and Jeffrey Rawls

Contents

ACKNOWLEDGMENTS

Salem Cemetery is a beautiful and sacred place in Winston-Salem. While some people may think it is an unusual topic for a book, it is a topic that I have enjoyed researching and learning about for several years. My family connection to the cemetery includes two uncles and an aunt, plus a group of distantly related family members. As a second-generation Winston-Salem native, I also feel a strong connection to the cemetery, because I recognize individual and family names that play such a prominent part in the city's history.

I appreciate the support and indulgence of my husband, Jeffrey D. Rawls, who spent countless hours with me as we walked throughout the cemetery. We explored during every season, always admiring the rolling terrain and the varying landscape that makes Salem Cemetery so unique. Jeffrey was patient as I recorded names and dates and recounted what I knew about this person and that family. He also read the manuscript, made beneficial comments, and helped me prepare the digital images for publication.

My friend Carol Carter Matthieu provided information about the Joseph Worth Bacon family. Saundra Grogan and my aunt Jean Shoemaker Grogan helped provide a photograph of my uncle John G. Grogan.

Unless otherwise noted, the photographs in this book came from the Forsyth County Public Library Photograph Collection, where I work as photograph archivist. When photographs are used from other sources, they are indicated in the courtesy line as Molly Grogan Rawls (MGR), Jeffrey D. Rawls (JDR), Wayne and Louise Biby (WLB), and Jean Shoemaker Grogan (JSG).

I thank the Forsyth County Genealogy Society for its cemetery inventory that was published in 1978. Since that time, some of the tombstone information has deteriorated and markers have broken, so the written record provides names and dates that can no longer be read.

Introduction

You can learn a lot of life lessons from visiting a cemetery. Some are hard, in that life is too short and often ends quickly and tragically. Some are bittersweet, in that even after lengthy, fulfilling lives, loved ones are still mourned. And some are universal, in that death is inevitable, but how one's life is lived makes each person's story unique.

My first experience reading Shakespeare was in my sophomore English class at North Forsyth High School. Ruth McClaren, my English teacher, introduced me to the play *Julius Caesar.* I remember a line from that play, uttered by Marc Antony during Caesar's funeral oration: "The evil that men do lives after them; the good is oft interred with their bones." It struck me then as such a sad comment on a person's life. The purpose of this book is to introduce the reader to some of the many people who helped grow and shape Winston-Salem. They gave their time and resources to build schools, hospitals, businesses, churches, and good homes, so that later residents could benefit from their work and their lives. The good that they did for all should not be buried or forgotten.

In conjunction with my work in the North Carolina Room of the Forsyth County Public Library and with identifying and locating photographs, I often needed to learn about the people who lived and worked in Winston-Salem and Forsyth County. One project involved locating information on Winston-Salem mayors, and I noticed that many of them were buried in Salem Cemetery. The cemetery records were a valuable resource for finding birth and death dates and enabled me to search newspapers on microfilm to locate obituaries. I also noticed that many of the city's leaders, business owners, professionals, and their families were buried in Salem Cemetery. When I located the obituaries, I created a research file that grew to fill many notebooks with articles, obituaries, notes, and photographs. This book is a product of the information that I accumulated over the years from many different sources.

Salem Cemetery is located within a mile of downtown Winston-Salem and near the restored Moravian town of Old Salem. While Salem Cemetery is adjacent to the Moravian graveyard, God's Acre, they are separate entities. Salem Cemetery is privately owned. In recent years, a columbarium and a mausoleum were constructed.

The act to incorporate Salem Cemetery was ratified on January 24, 1857, by the General Assembly of North Carolina. The first president of the cemetery company was Elias A. Vogler, and Henry W. Fries was secretary-treasurer. The board of managers consisted of Francis Fries, Thomas J. Wilson, Robert Gray, William Barrow, and Rufus L. Patterson. A 1927 *Winston-Salem Journal* article gave a good historical account of the cemetery, which started on 10 acres. The original prices were 10¢ per square foot for lots located on the outside margin of the grounds and 12.5¢ per square foot for the remaining lots, except those within the oval center plot, which were 15¢ per square foot. By 1927, the prices had risen to 75¢ and upwards of $6 per square foot.

Walking the paths of Salem Cemetery, one can read the names on the tombstones and immediately feel connected to Winston-Salem's history. Since the cemetery was chartered in 1857, families and individuals have chosen this site as their final resting place. The first burial in the cemetery was one-year-old John Barrow. He was the son of William Barrow, a local magistrate and member of the Salem Cemetery Board of Managers who later became mayor of Winston. The child's mother died just a few months later and is buried in the family plot. Enclosed by a black iron fence, the Barrow plot also includes William, his second wife Mary Jane, and their children.

For the purposes of this book, the cemetery is divided into three sections: the hilltop, the vaults, and the large section called "the garden" that comprises the majority of the cemetery. Some individuals are buried singly on the hilltop, which was once referred to as the "stranger's graveyard." Women and infants who died in childbirth are buried on the hilltop. People who were passing through town and children whose families did not remain in town were also often buried on the hilltop.

The majority of the vaults are concentrated in a semi-circular area at the base of a hill in the oldest section of the cemetery. There are also some scattered stand-alone vaults. The facades of the vaults are all different and reflect the personal tastes of the families. One family vault contains a stained-glass window that is illuminated by the outside light.

The garden mostly consists of family plots, with a wide range of monument styles and sizes. Many of the family plots are landscaped with shrubbery, and others began with small trees that now tower over the grounds. The tombstones are mostly unsigned, but many were likely crafted by local monument companies. Some of these companies are highlighted in Chapter One. Some individuals selected the white, flat stones that are common in God's Acre, adjacent to Salem Cemetery. One Moravian family, wanting to be buried in a family plot, selected a location at the edge of Salem Cemetery and chose the white, recumbent stones. Many of the tombstones contain favorite Bible verses or personal reminiscences.

The name "Snookie Dyer" caught my attention from the Forsyth County Genealogy Society's inventory for Salem Cemetery. I noticed that she was just two years old when she died. Wanting to know more about Snookie, I searched for her obituary in the local newspaper, but did not find a Snookie Dyer. The only child mentioned during that time was a little girl named Virginia Bell Vanden Boom, and she was not included in the Salem Cemetery listing. Over the last several years, I have visited the cemetery, walked the paths, admired the beautiful Easter flowers, studied the names on tombstones, and recalled people I have known and others that I know only by name. I always looked for Snookie's grave.

In 2013, I drove to the cemetery to photograph a February snowfall. With snow covering the grass, I stepped carefully. Standing beside the Shaffner vault, I spotted the "Dyer" tombstone. Off to the side, I saw a smaller stone that read "Snookie." The stone was by itself but faced a very large tombstone with the name "Vanden Boom." On the other side of the Vanden Boom tombstone was a stone with the name "Adrian" and another stone with the name "Virginia Humphrey," which included dates. Virginia Bell Vanden Boom, nicknamed "Snookie," was the daughter of Adrian and Virginia Vanden Boom. She was listed with the Dyers because her stone did not include a last name. Read more about the Vanden Booms on page 12.

Confined to a limited number of pages with a limited amount of space for each caption, I could not include everyone or say everything. In addition to the people mentioned in the caption titles, others are mentioned within the captions, with their birth and deaths dates in parentheses. The majority of these people, with few exceptions, are also buried in Salem Cemetery. Some of the people mentioned in this book—and others who are not in the book—are profiled on my website, www.winstonsalemtimetraveler.com.

One

Salem Cemetery

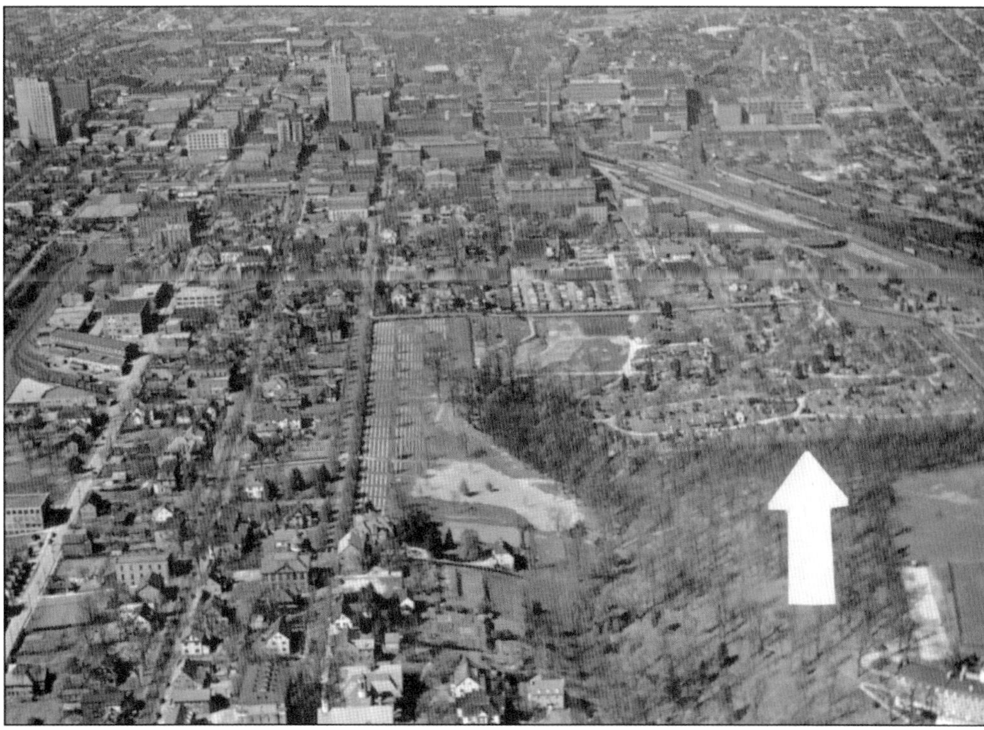

Aerial of Salem Cemetery, 1938. Situated just south of downtown, to the east of the Moravian graveyard, Salem Cemetery is indicated in this photograph with an arrow. Its winding paths that look white in the photograph are visible from the air. The forest that surrounds the cemetery on two sides will eventually come down, providing more useable land for both the cemetery and the graveyard.

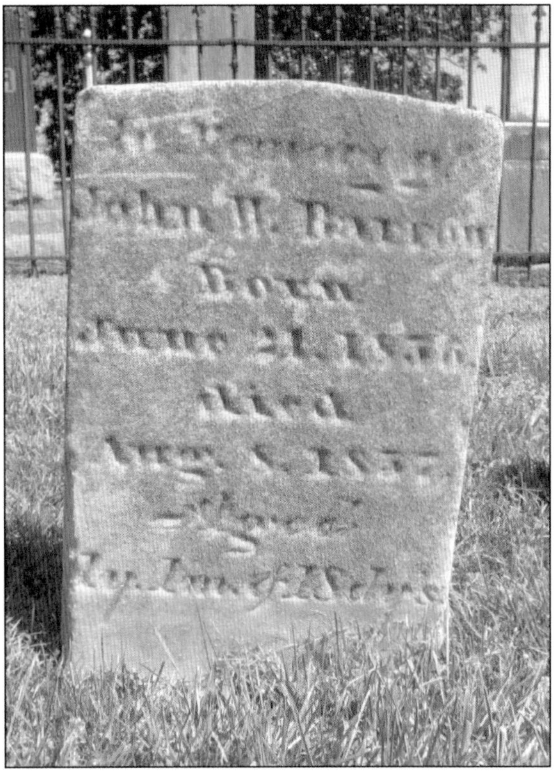

JOHN WILLIAM BARROW (1856–1857). John, the only son of William Barrow (1826–1901) and Abigail Saunders Barrow (1821–1857), was the first burial in Salem Cemetery, following an illness. His mother's burial came about three months later. William Barrow was a justice of the peace. He was elected county trustee in 1858 and the first mayor of Winston in 1859. His second wife was Mary Jane Barrow (1837–1889). (MGR.)

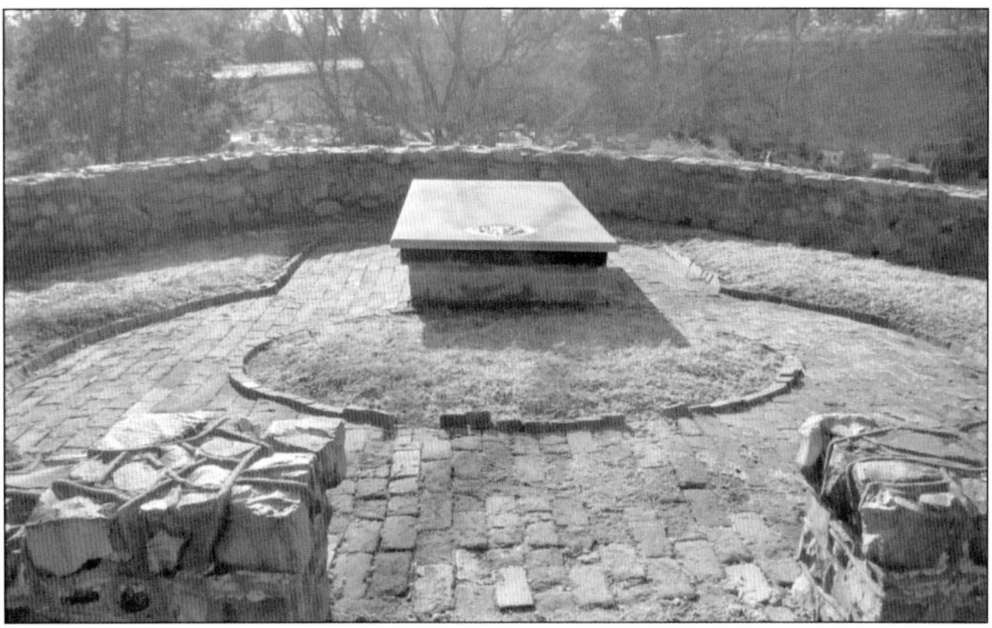

ELIAS ALEXANDER VOGLER (1825–1876). Born in Salem, Elias was the son of John and Christina Spach Vogler. He married Emma Antoinette Reich (1828–1883). Elias was a talented man, much like his father. He was an artist, merchant, architect, and surveyor. He served as justice of the peace and mayor of Salem. Elias was the first president of the Salem Cemetery Company after it was organized in 1857. (MGR.)

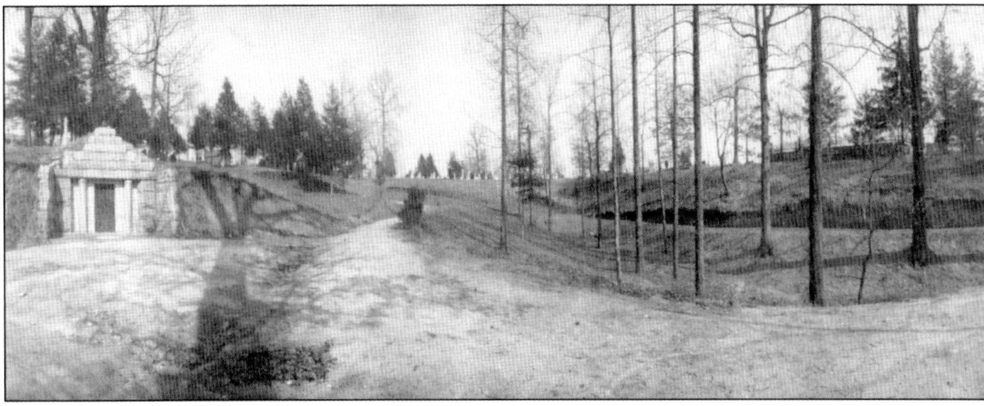

EARLY VIEWS OF SALEM CEMETERY. The cemetery was mentioned in the 1888 booklet *Descriptive Sketch of Winston-Salem*: "Crossing a ravine to the eastward from [God's Acre] is found among the original forest trees the peoples' cemetery. This has a number of handsome monuments, and could be made an attractive spot, but as yet has had little care bestowed upon its surroundings. Those having the matter in charge would do well to spend a little more towards beautifying this sacred spot." Henry Simmons Foy, hired as cemetery superintendent in 1898, became the first groundskeeper. He recalled that the "weeds were three and four feet high in all parts of the grounds, that there were only a few gravel walks laid off, and trees and shrubbery were in a dilapidated condition." Under Foy's supervision and guidance, the grounds were beautified and the gravesites were regularly maintained.

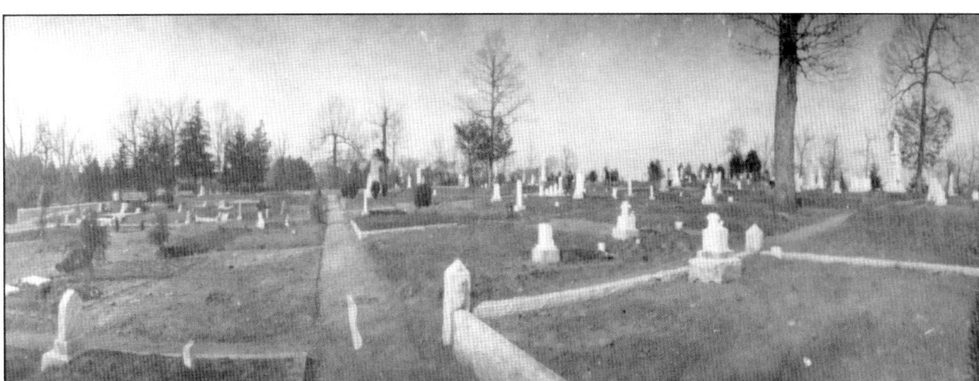

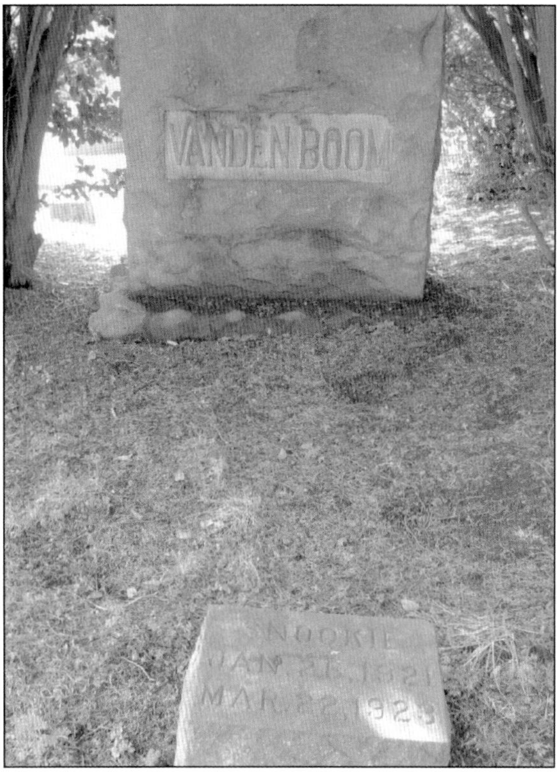

Vanden Boom Family. Adrian Vanden Boom (1892–1922) was born in Kampen, Holland, and came to the United States about 1910. He settled in Walnut Cove about 1917 and organized the American Collapsible Box Company. He married Virginia Woodruff (1894–1952), and they were parents of Virginia Bell "Snookie" Vanden Boom (1921–1923). Apparently, Virginia Woodruff Vanden Boom remarried, as her marker includes the name "Humphrey." (MGR.)

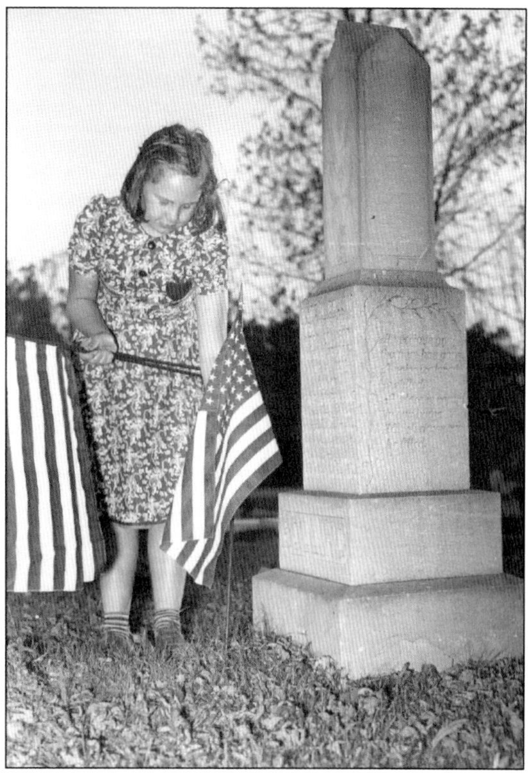

Pvt. Clyde W. Bolling (1897–1918). Clyde was a Winston-Salem native, son of Charles Welborn Bolling (1859–1949) and Mary Miranda Webster Bolling (1865–1944). Clyde enlisted in the 18th Infantry during World War I and was the first local soldier killed in France. Forsyth County American Legion Post No. 55 was named in his memory. Clyde's body was returned to Winston-Salem for burial in 1921, and a memorial tablet was erected bearing the names of 69 Forsyth County men who died in World War I. Carroll Gray marked Clyde's grave with a flag during the 1938 Veterans Day observance.

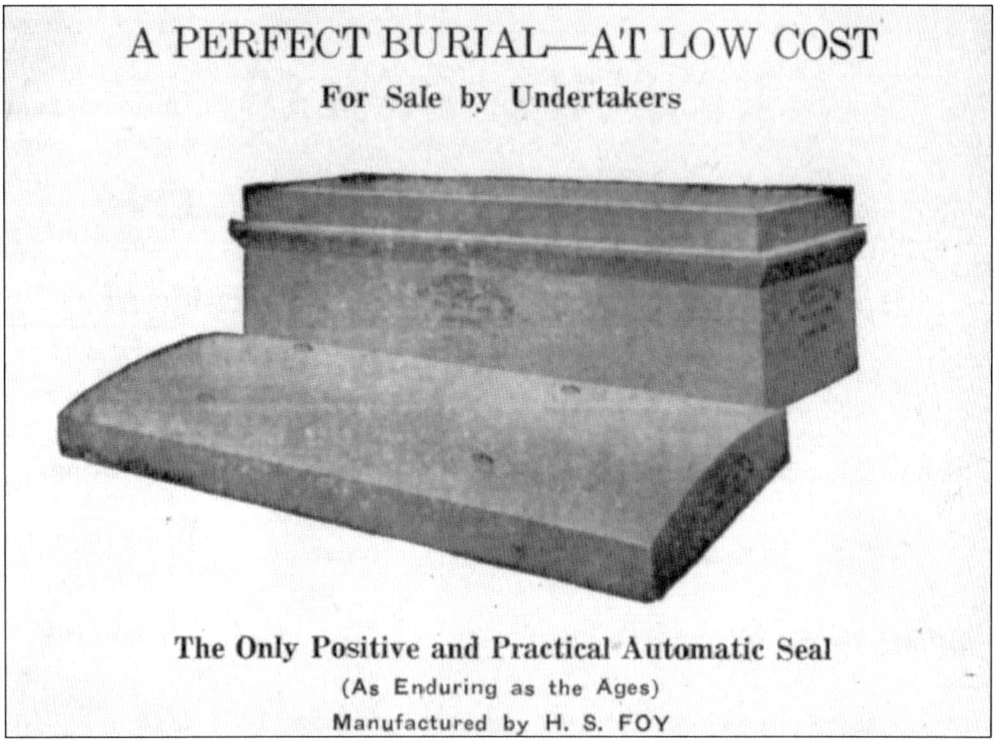

Henry Simmons Foy Sr. (1853–1935). A native of Pender County, Henry came to Winston-Salem in 1879. He engaged in the plug and twist tobacco business and operated a livery stable. In 1898, he became superintendent of Salem Cemetery Company and held the position for 28 years. He also made caskets, as shown in this 1926 advertisement. Henry was married first to Molly Frances White Foy (1861–1897) and secondly to Louise Scott Foy (1867–1959).

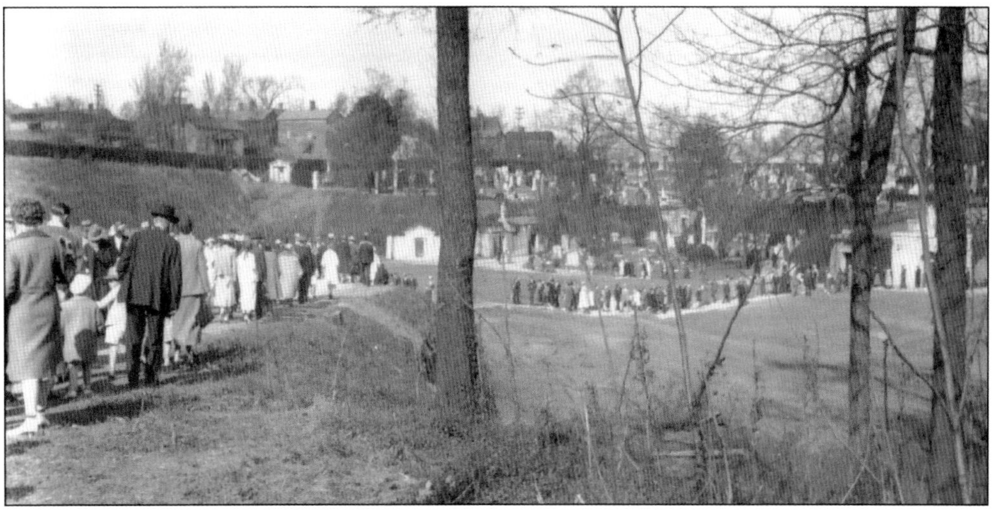

Easter Sunrise Service, 1936. The wettest spring in a decade brought floods and crippled train and automobile traffic, but the sun shone on Easter Sunday in April 1936. Christ's resurrection was proclaimed for the 165th time in Old Salem when Bishop J. Kenneth Pfohl addressed the assembly at Home Moravian Church and led the throngs to God's Acre, the Moravian graveyard. This photograph shows the crowds that spilled into Salem Cemetery.

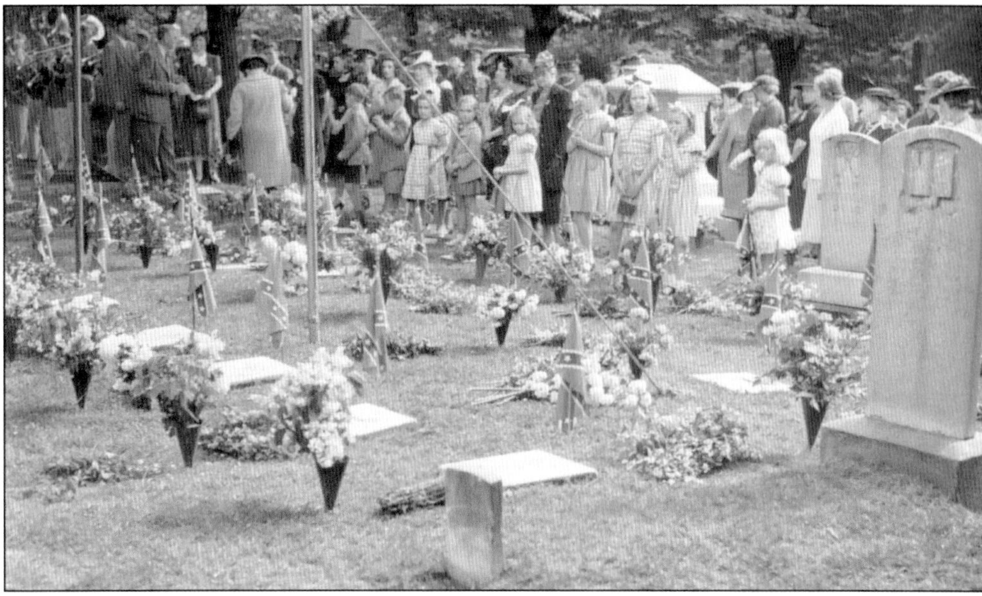

Confederate Memorial Day Observances in 1939 and 1953. "Both pride and gratitude forbids our losing them from off the pages of our memory." So began the address by Dr. John R. Cunningham in 1939 to descendants of the Confederate soldiers who are buried in Salem Cemetery. "These are the men in gray who fought for an ideal when a nation was divided against itself 73 years ago." David Settle Reid, the last living Confederate veteran in Forsyth County, was present at the ceremonies. Flowers and a flag were placed on each grave in the special "Our Confederate Dead" section of the cemetery. The photograph above shows some of the attendees. Members of the James B. Gordon Chapter of the United Daughters of the Confederacy adorned each grave with a flag for the ceremony in 1953, pictured below.

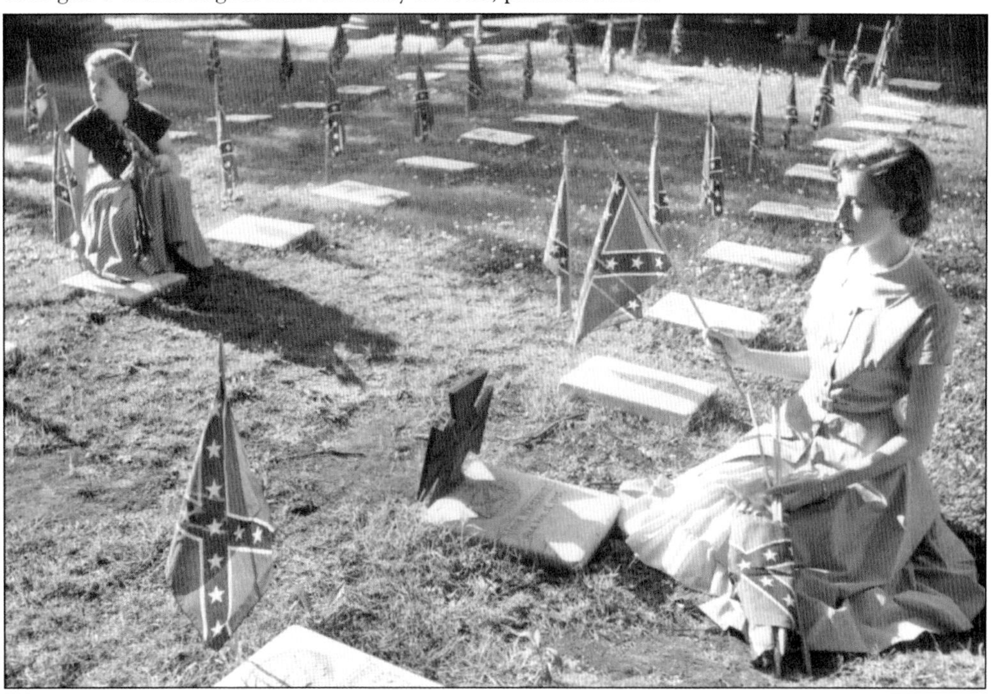

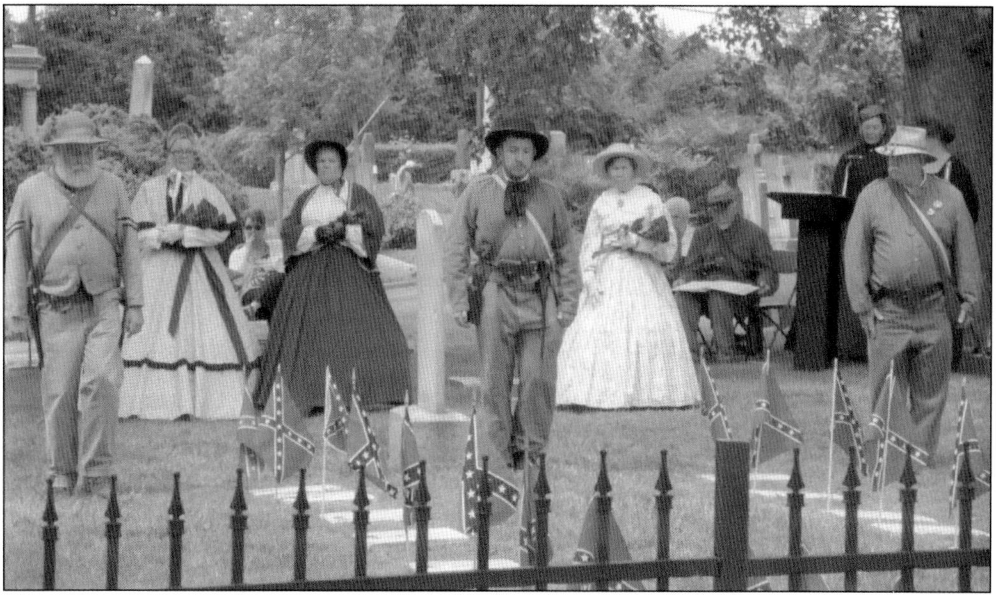

CONFEDERATE MEMORIAL DAY OBSERVANCE, 2015. The James B. Gordon Chapter of the United Daughters of the Confederacy was chartered in March 1898. Two months later, the first Confederate Memorial Day was observed by the Norfleet Camp of Confederate Veterans. Several hundred veterans from Forsyth and adjoining counties, led by the Salem Band, marched from downtown to Salem Cemetery while singing Moravian funeral hymns. They gathered around the graves of Confederate soldiers and offered prayers, with a gun salute and a bugle call. The Confederate Monument was presented to the veterans, funded by members of the United Daughters of the Confederacy. The 117th observance of Confederate Memorial Day, pictured, occurred in 2015. Women wearing period clothing placed a rose and a flag on each grave as the costumed men recited the names, followed by a gun salute. (Both, MGR.)

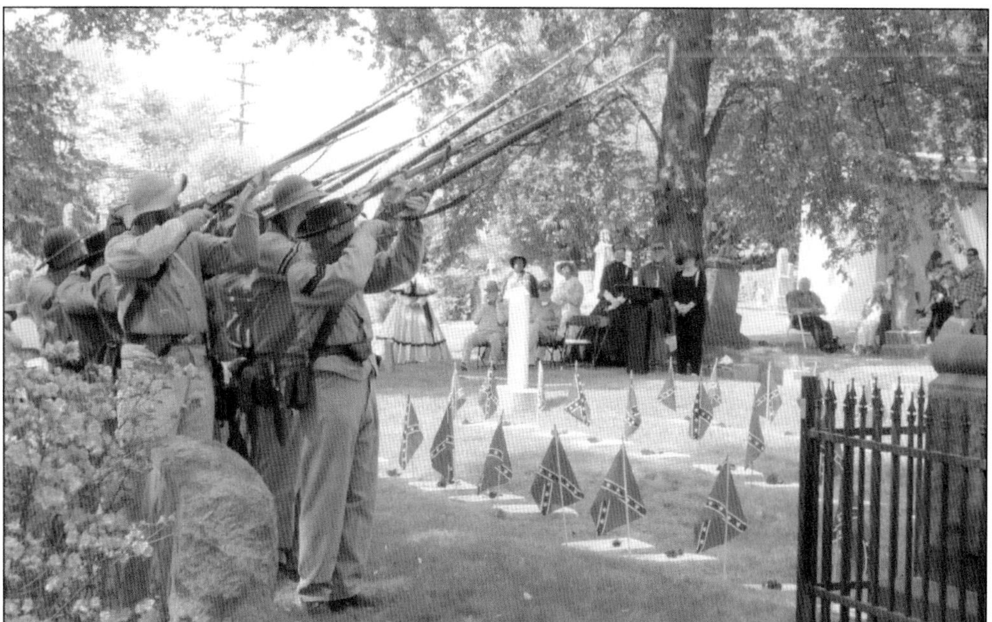

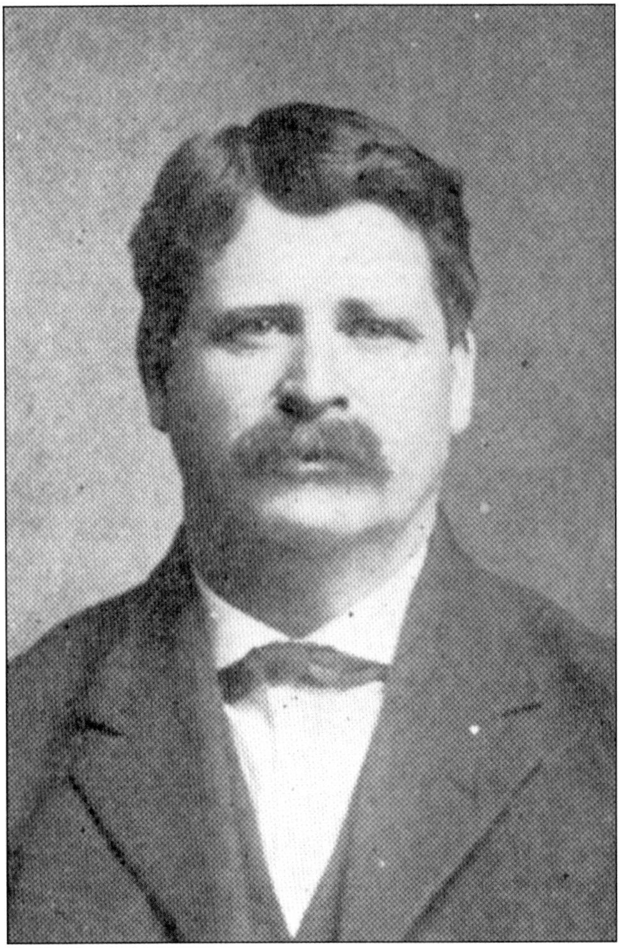

CAMERON ALEX MCGALLIARD (1857–1922). Cameron was born in Morganton and came to Winston-Salem around 1877. He founded his marble and granite monument business in 1880 and was engaged in this occupation until his death in 1922. The business was located at 1522 North Liberty Street, which was also where he and his family lived. Cameron had a reputation for "executing the rarest design and most artistic lettering, carving, and polishing." Cameron married Emma Adelaide Pitts (1860–1943) in 1881, and they had three children. Their daughter Ethel McGalliard (1892–1972) was a graduate of Salem College and a music teacher.

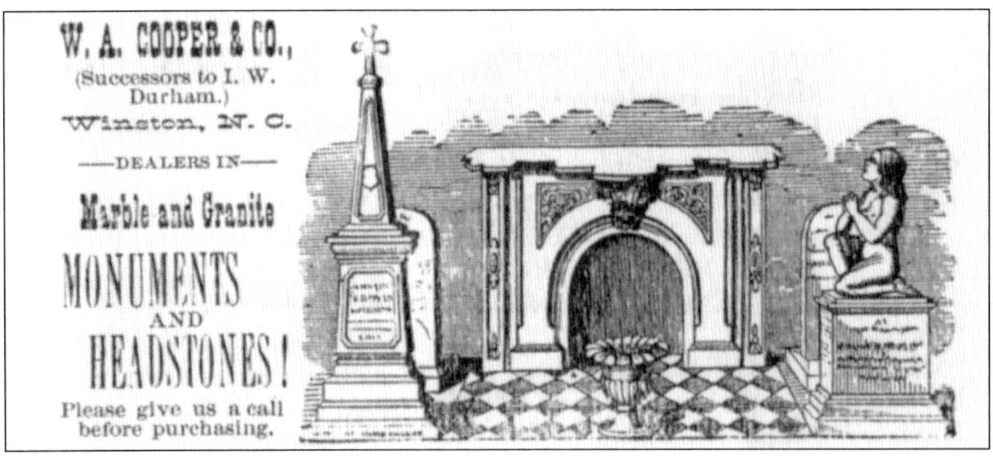

W.A. COOPER & COMPANY. I.W. Durham learned the marble-cutting trade in Charlotte. He came to Winston-Salem around 1876 and established a monument and gravestone business. William Alexander Cooper Sr. (1868–1930), a Forsyth County native, worked as an apprentice for I.W. Durham and bought the business when Durham returned to Charlotte. Cooper and his two brothers moved to Raleigh in 1894 and established Cooper Brothers, a monument company.

J.A. WALL & SON. James Alford "J.A." Wall (1856–1937) and his son Wesley Lucian Wall (1883–1952) organized their monument and tombstone business in 1905. The accompanying advertisement shows the marble yards of the company in 1913. The business was located at Liberty and Balsey (Fifteenth) Streets. Two men, possibly J.A. and Wesley, stand in the doorway of the business. A 1910 account of the business states that James was involved with company sales, while Wesley was the monument engraver and designer. This company exists today as Wall Monument Company and is located on Indiana Avenue.

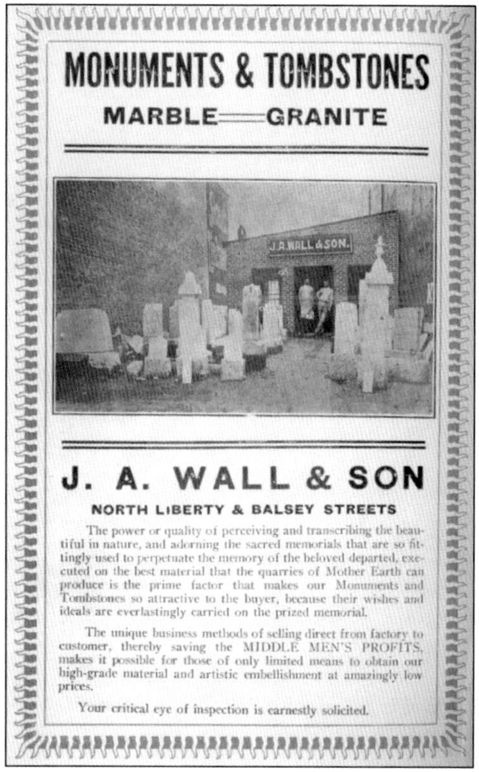

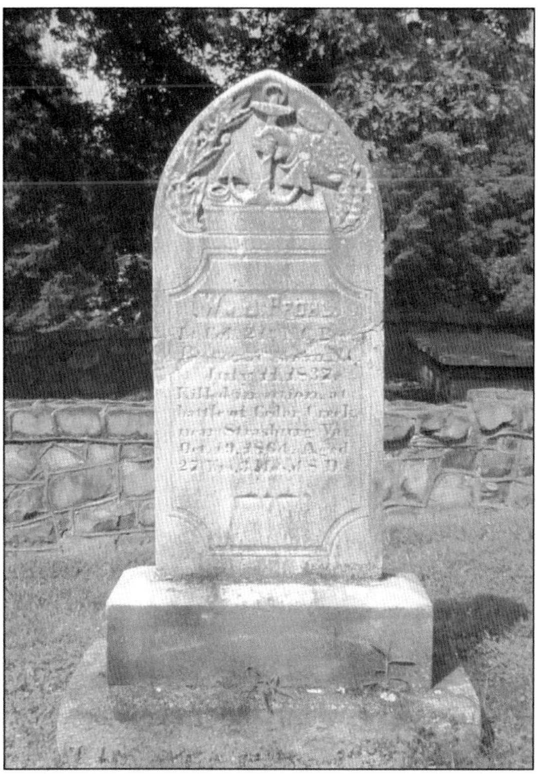

WILLIAM JACOB PFOHL (1837–1864). William Jacob was the son of Theodore Christian and Anna Susanna Pfohl. He and his brother Edward Alexander Pfohl (1834–1896) fought in the Civil War with the 21st Regiment of the North Carolina Troops. William Jacob was a major, and Edward was a first sergeant. William Jacob was killed in action at the battle of Cedar Creek near Strasburg, Virginia, as noted on his tombstone. His headstone is also marked with "Leak & Wilson," making it one of few that identifies the stone maker. Leak & Wilson was operated by D.R. Leak and T.A. Wilson. (MGR.)

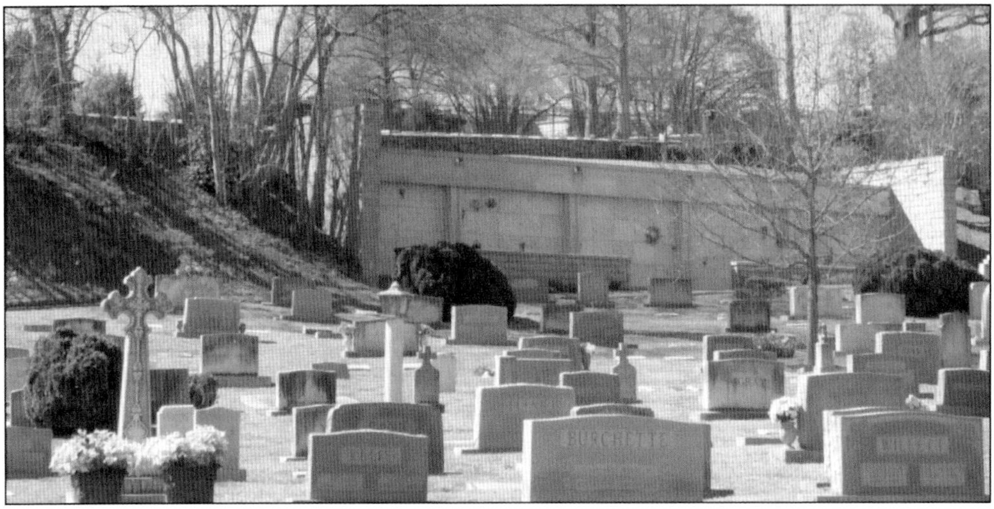

Current Views of Salem Cemetery. Even the casual cemetery visitor notices that a lot of work goes into keeping the grounds mowed and maintained. The work that Superintendent Foy began in the late 1890s continues on a regular basis. Foy voiced concern in 1927 about the gradual deterioration of the marble and granite tombstones by smoke from the nearby railroad yards, which erased inscriptions and harmed the vegetation. The 1989 tornado wreaked havoc throughout the cemetery, taking down limbs and trees and upsetting tombstones. Landscaping is an ongoing project, with lot owners adding personal touches to family plots, such as shrubbery and birdhouses. In the springtime, dogwood and cherry trees burst forth and flowering bulbs and azaleas add color throughout. Two fairly new structures at the cemetery are the mausoleum (above) and the columbarium (below). (Both, MGR.)

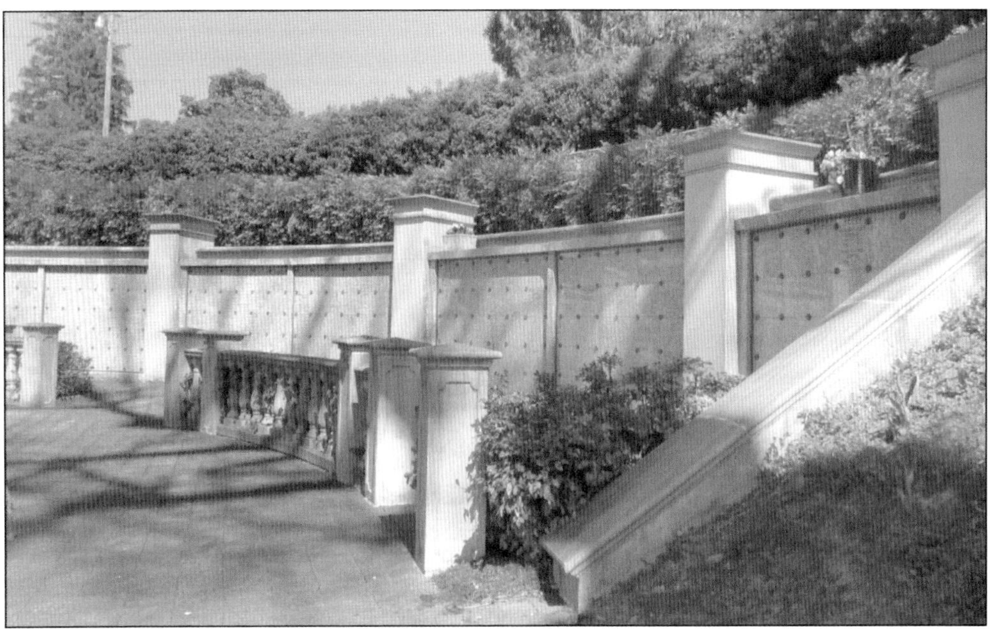

Two

The Hilltop

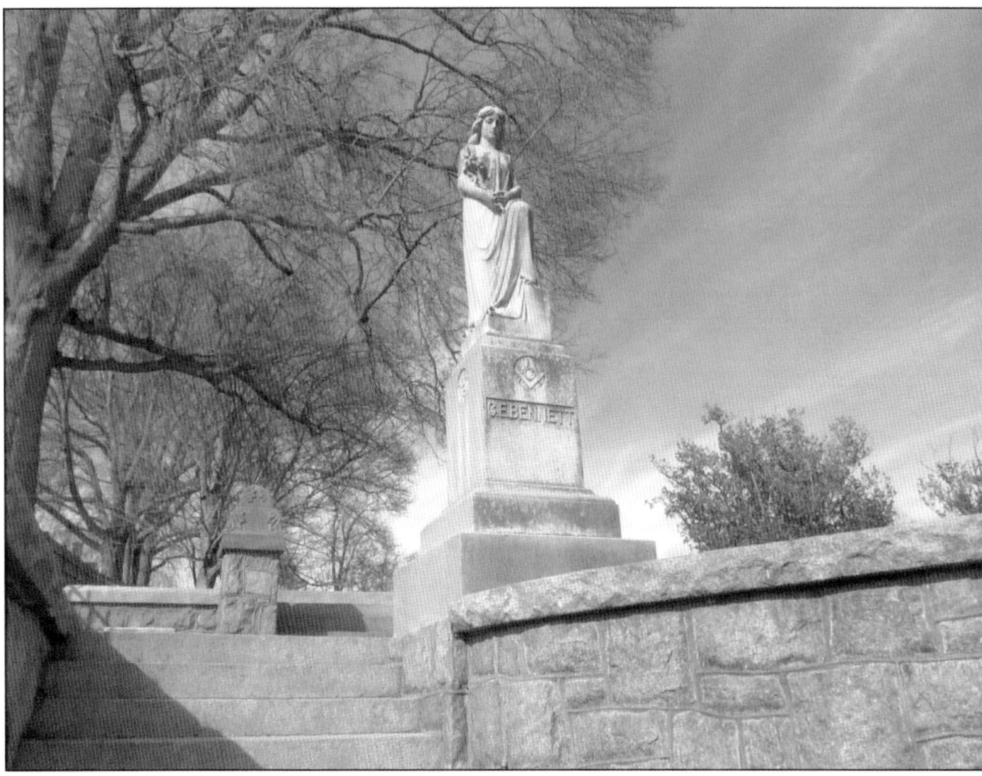

Bennett Family Plot. Directly adjacent to God's Acre are the stairs that lead to the hilltop section of the cemetery. Beside the stairs is a large statue of a woman that bears the name "C.E. Bennett," indicating the Bennett family plot. Edward Bennett (1826–1870) was the patriarch of the family, and he was married to Tabitha Knott Bennett (1837–1929). Edward came to the United States from England. (MGR.)

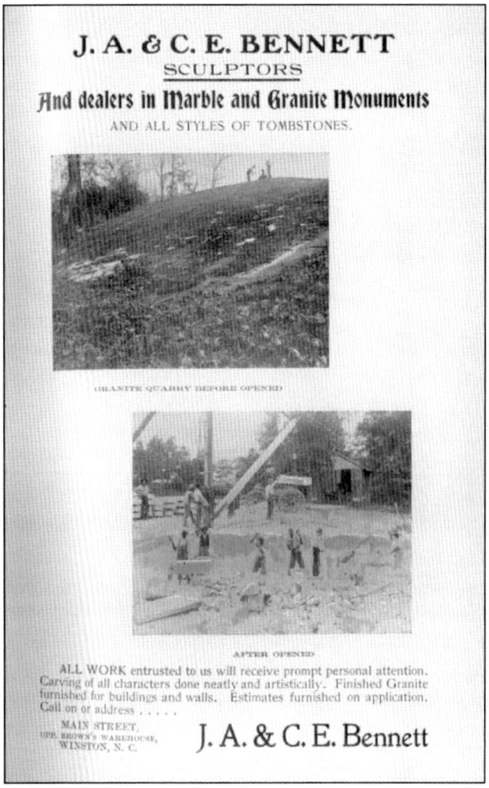

CHARLES EDWARD BENNETT (1860–1937). Charles was born in Winston-Salem to Edward and Tabitha Knott Bennett. Charles and his brother John operated the J.A. and C.E. Bennett Marble and Granite Works. Also called Winston-Salem Granite Works, the business was located at 430 North Main Street. The brothers also operated the Winston-Salem Bottling Works at that address. Charles was called to jury duty for a 1932 murder trial in Forsyth Superior Court. After stating his occupation as head of a monument plant, Defense Attorney Slawter removed him from the jury pool, indicating that his business interest in the trial outcome might override his objectivity. Charles married Emma Holt Axsom (1868–1934) in 1888.

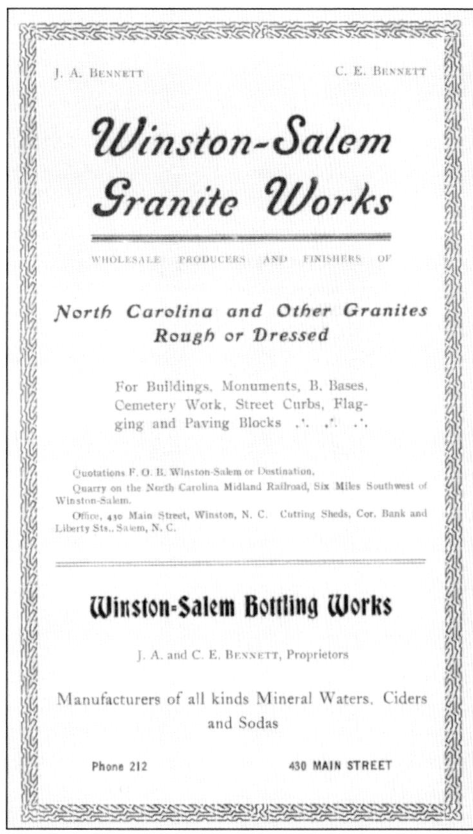

FAMILY OF CHARLES EDWARD BENNETT. Charles and his wife, Emma, were parents of 13 children. The oldest child, John Edgar Bennett (1889–1956), worked with his father in the monument business. Another son, Clyde Edward Bennett (1891–1953), worked as a carpenter and was married to Cora Longworth Bennett (1894–1982). Daughter Nellie Bennett Bates (1893–1966) attended Salem College. Son William Axsom Bennett (1911–1944) enlisted in military service in 1943 and served in Company C, 807th Tank Destroyer Battalion. Youngest child, Harry Eugene Bennett (1915–2000), worked for Quality Oil Company and married Margaret Walker Bennett (1914–2003).

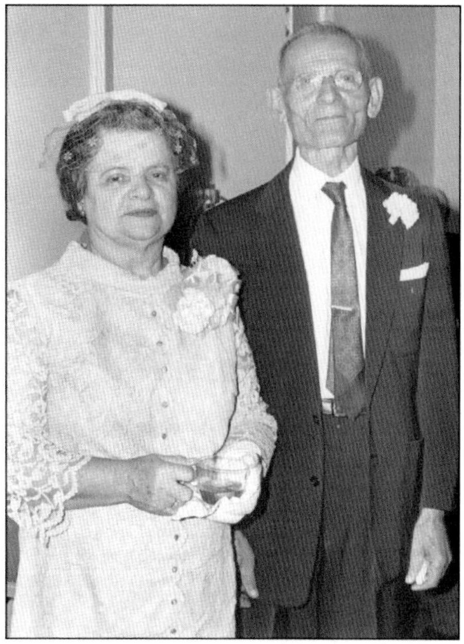

Chrisoula Simmons Hondros (1902–1995) and Arthur Konstantine Hondros (1886–1981). Natives of Greece, Chrisoula and Arthur married in 1919. They were the first couple to be married in Winston-Salem under Greek Orthodox Church rites. Arthur was the founder of the local Greek Orthodox Church, and Chrisoula was a founder of the church's Ladies Philoptochos Society. Arthur owned and operated the Piedmont Café on North Trade Street and the Shell Grill on North Marshall Street. Son George Arthur Hondros (1927–1988) worked with his father in the restaurants.

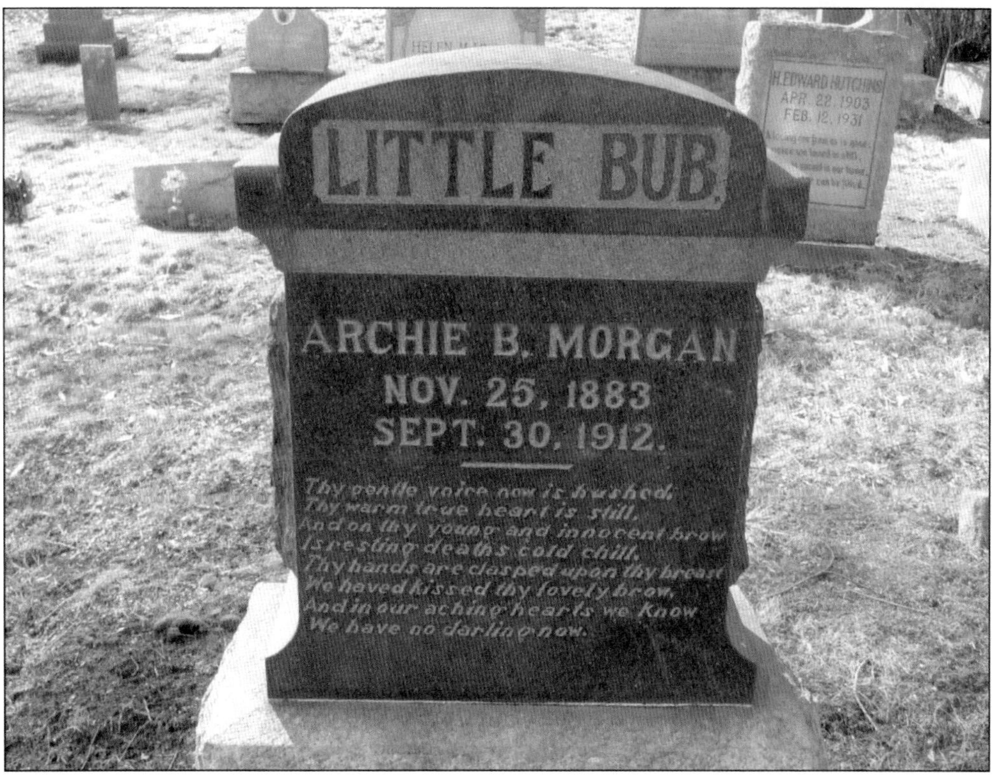

Archie B. Morgan (1883–1912). Archie was the oldest child of William L. and Matilda Foltz Morgan. At the top of his marker are the words, "Little Bub," an affectionate nickname for the 28-year-old who died tragically from an assault by two attackers when he was walking home from the fairgrounds. Archie was employed as a yard conductor with the Norfolk & Western Railway Company. (MGR.)

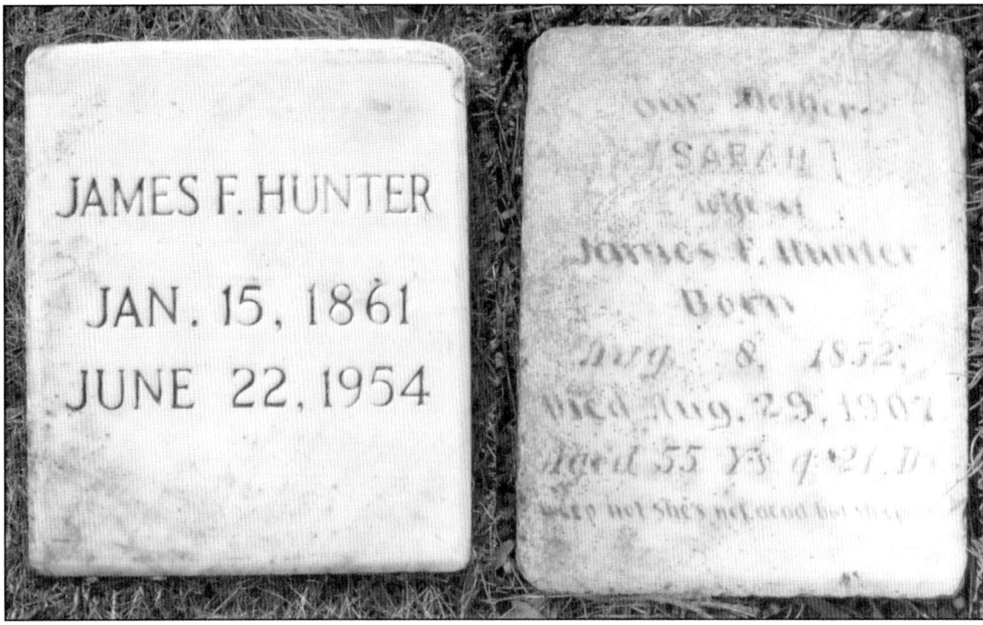

JAMES FRANKLIN HUNTER (1861–1954) AND SARAH HARVEL HUNTER (1852–1907). James was born in Yadkin County to Major Washington and Sarah Gough Hunter. James worked for the Fries Woolen Mill and P.H. Hanes Knitting Mill. In 1882, he married Sarah Harvel, daughter of Tyre and Elizabeth Harvel, and they had seven children. After Sarah's death, James married Octavia Rogers Edwards (1874–1956), daughter of George and Emily Rogers, in 1912. (MGR.)

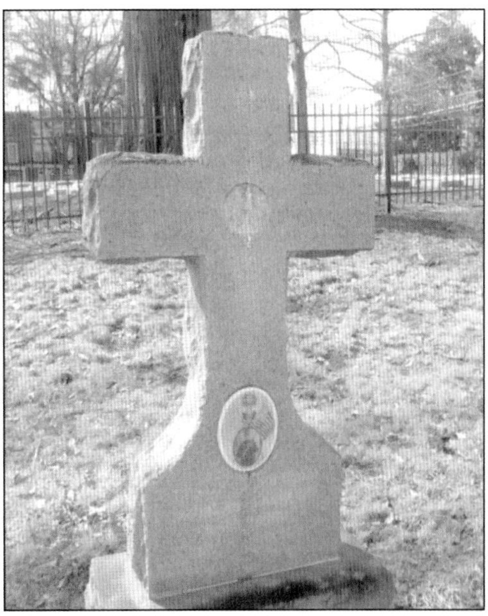

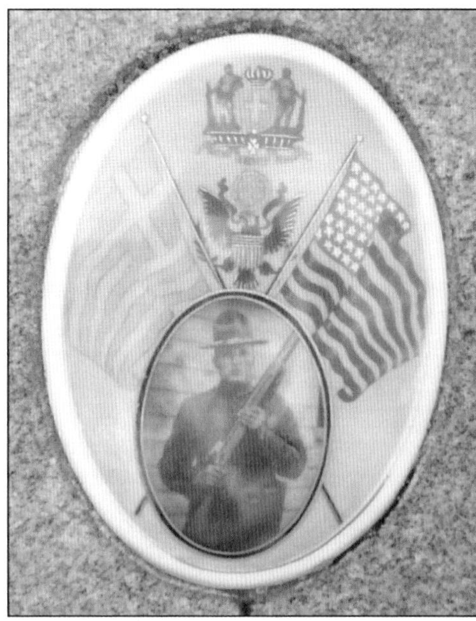

COSMAS ABRAHAM (1896–1931). A native of Turkey, Cosmas came to the United States around 1913. He served during the Balkan Wars and in the US Army during World War I. He and his brother Paul operated the Center Café on Waughtown Street. Cosmas was fatally injured in an automobile accident in 1931, and Paul continued to operate the café for a few more years. Cosmas's monument features a photograph of him in uniform. (MGR.)

THOMAS "TOM" CHRISTIAN HEGE (1871–1923). Tom was the son of Zacharias George Hege (1837–1890) and Sarah Amanda Lash Hege (1846–1916). Zacharias operated a general mercantile business and was a furniture-maker. Tom was born into a Moravian family, but he forged his own career path and chose his own religion. He worked as a photographer and a repair shop operator. Tom was reported to be the first person in Winston-Salem to embrace the Seventh-day Adventist religion. Tom caused a stir in town when he insisted on conducting business on Sunday, which was against town ordinances.

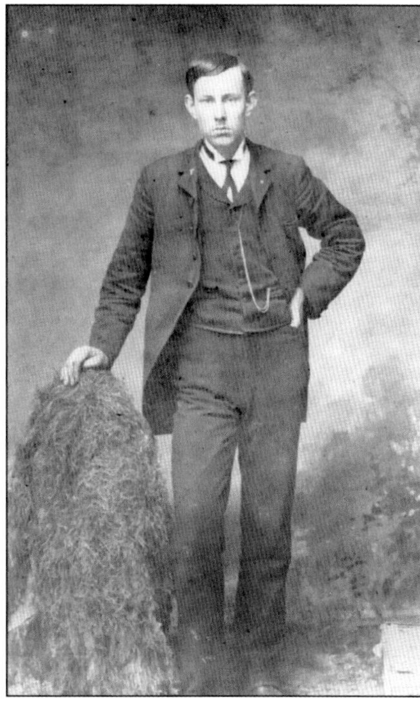

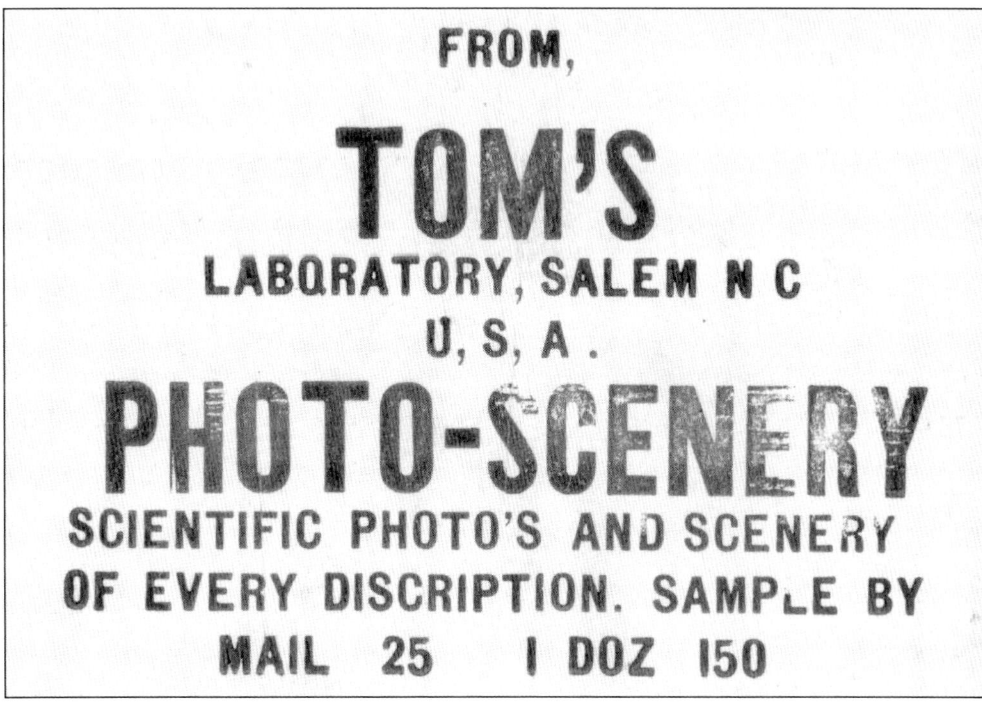

TOM HEGE, PHOTOGRAPHER. Tom's photography shop opened in Salem in 1894 as Tom Hege Photo and Stock Company. He advertised "scientific laboratory and photographic work," and his name appeared in huge letters above the door. Tom carried a variety of goods, and his workshop was located in the back of the shop. Some of his images survived and were collected by his nephew, local newspaper photographer Frank B. Jones Jr.

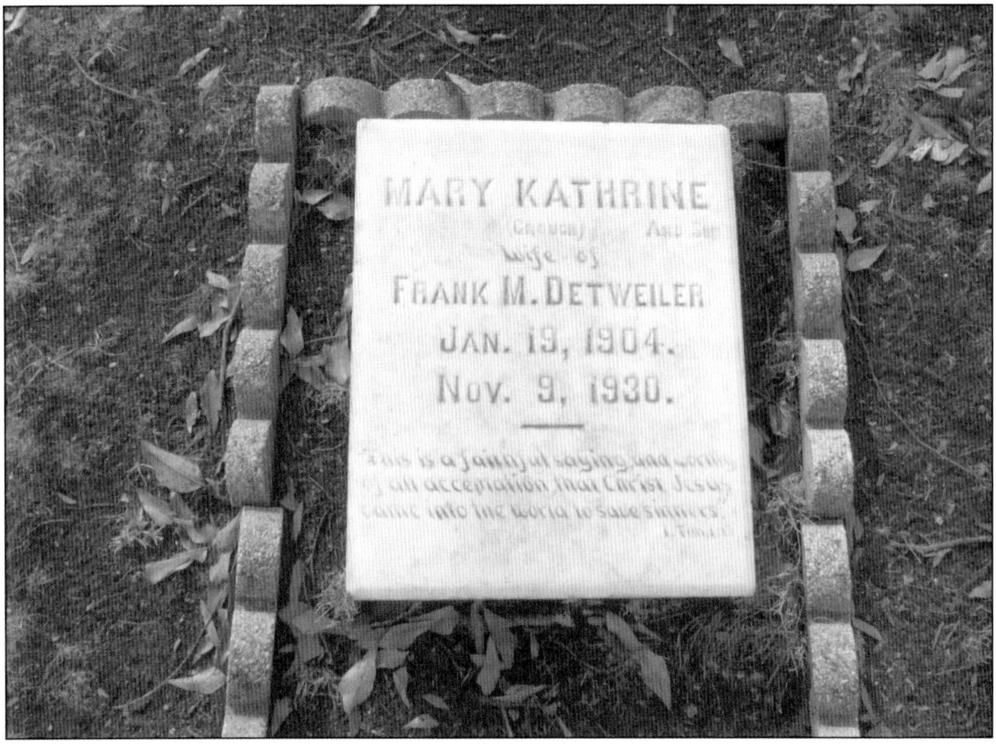

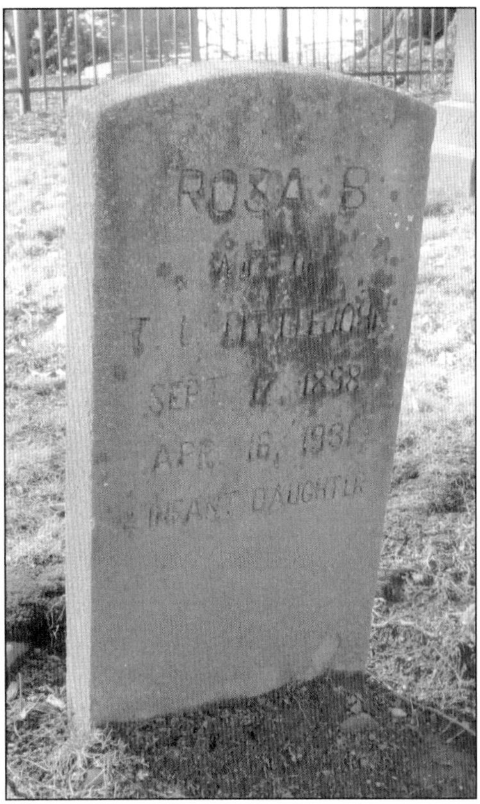

MARY KATHRINE CROUCH DETWEILER (1904–1930) AND INFANT SON DETWEILER (1930). Mary Kathrine was born in Forsyth County to Rev. James Parmonia and Ida Bell Beckel Crouch. Reverend Crouch, a teacher and rural mail carrier, was also a lay pastor who became an ordained Moravian minister. Mary Kathrine attended Salem College before marrying Rev. Frank M. Detweiler in 1929. She was living in Marion when she and her infant son passed away. (MGR.)

ROSA BELLVE GRAY LITTLEJOHN (1898–1931) AND INFANT DAUGHTER LITTLEJOHN (1931). Rosa was born in Dare County to William Winston Gray (1874–1948) and Ida Williams Gray (1874–1898). Rosa's mother died when she was two months old, and her father later married Carrie O'Neal. Rosa married Thomas Lester Littlejohn (1899–1949) and came to Forsyth County around 1921. They were parents to Thomas Welton Littlejohn. Rosa and their four-day-old daughter succumbed to pneumonia. (MGR.)

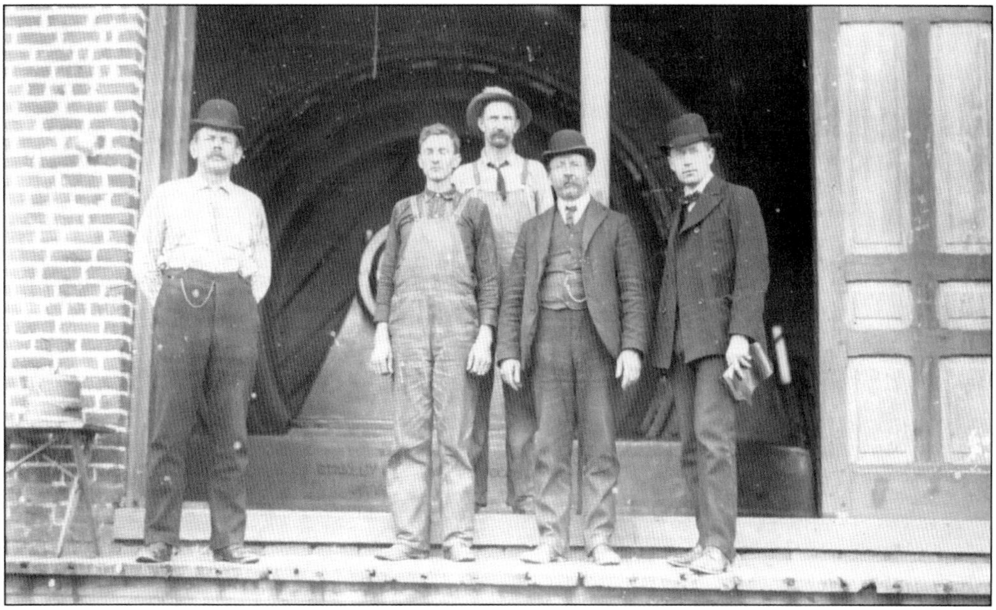

CAPT. JOHN JACOB SIGG (C. 1854–1926). John was born in Switzerland and came to the United States around 1873. He worked as superintendent of the Standard Woolen Mills in Philadelphia. When the company decided to operate the mills day and night, light machines were installed and John took charge of the electrical machinery. He studied electricity at night and later worked for several electrical companies, where he earned a reputation as an excellent electrical engineer. John came to Winston-Salem in 1901 to work for the Fries Manufacturing and Power Company. He is shown at the company in the above photograph (second from right). He also managed Nissen Park, owned by Fries Manufacturing, and introduced the first moving pictures at the park. He was an expert botanist and is shown in the photograph below in the Nissen Park botanical garden.

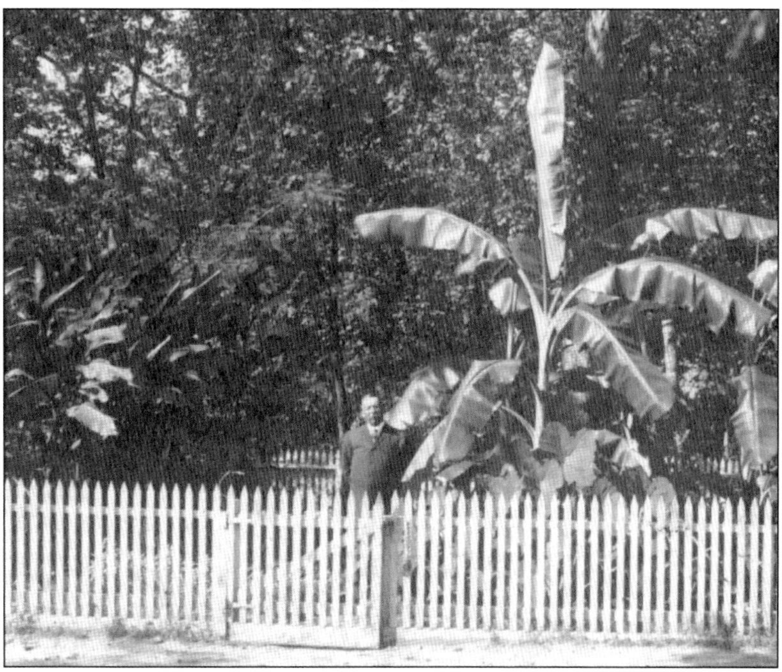

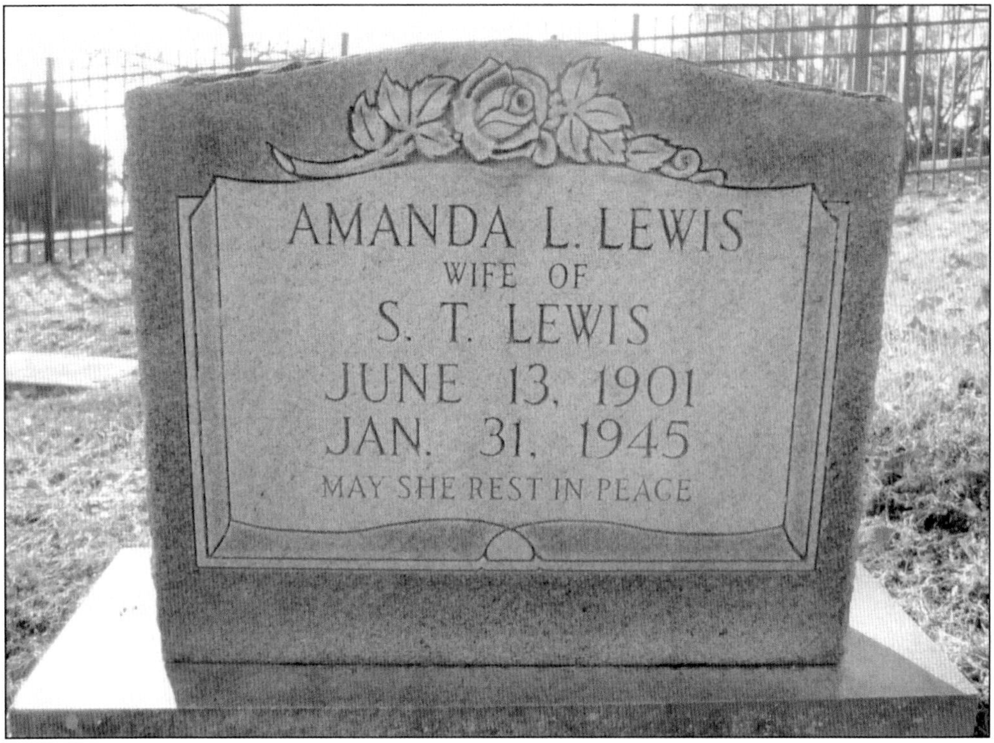

AMANDA L. TRIPLETT LEWIS (1901–1945). Amanda, or "Mandy," was born in Forsyth County to Marcus Rufus Triplett (1869–1948) and Luzetta Jarvis Triplett (1880–1937). She married Sidney Thomas Lewis (1894–1961) in 1915, and they were the parents of six children. Mandy worked for R.J. Reynolds Tobacco Company, as did her husband before he went to work for Pleasants Hardware Company. (MGR.)

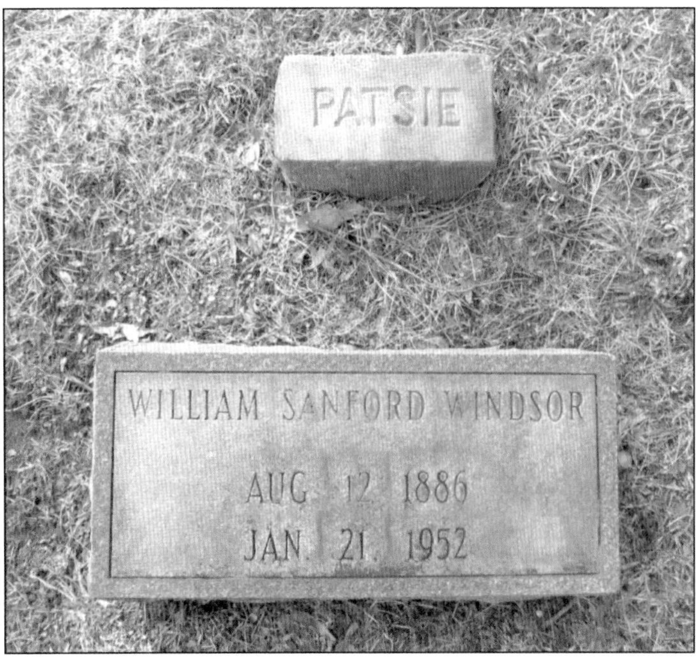

WILLIAM SANFORD WINDSOR (1886–1952). William was a native of Iredell County but lived most of his life in Forsyth County. He worked as an interior decorator and contractor and married Violet Combs (1887–1963) in 1907. Daughter Patsie Bill Windsor (1912–1927) was a schoolgirl when she was injured in an automobile accident that later resulted in her death. Another daughter, Ruth Windsor Caudle (1909–1950), married Lester Gray Caudle in 1926. (MGR.)

Three

The Vaults

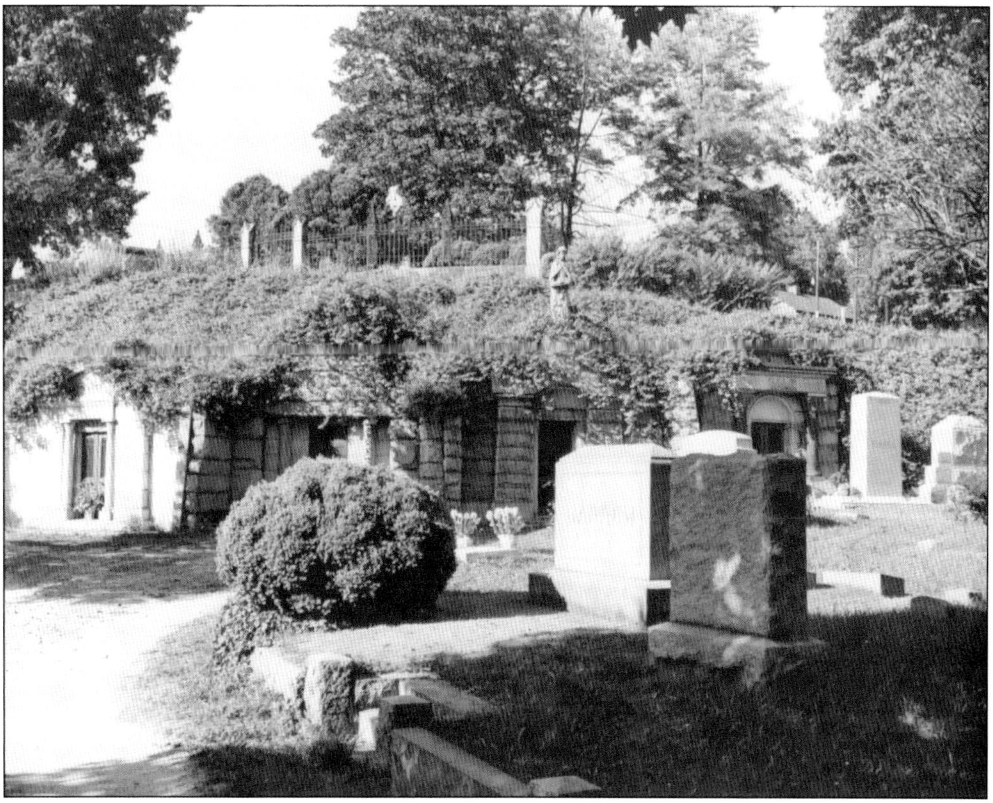

Salem Cemetery Vaults. Francis L. Fries began construction of the Fries family vault in 1858. Apparently, the rugged terrain in an area called "Stony-Point" made excavation and construction a challenge, but the rocks provided a firm foundation. Eight family vaults are built into the hillside in a horseshoe shape, some visible in this photograph. There are also stand-alone family vaults scattered throughout the cemetery.

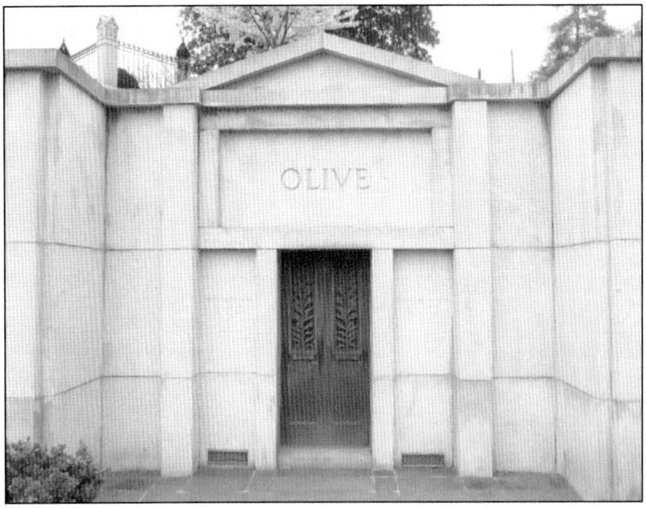

AGNES MAKELY OLIVE (1884–1965) AND JOHN HARRY OLIVE (1916–1967). Agnes Makely Olive was born in Hyde County to Metra and Mary McBurney Makely. She married Dr. William Wade Olive Sr. and lived in Durham, where he practiced medicine. Shortly after his death in 1922, Agnes and her two sons, John Harry and William Wade Jr., moved to Winston-Salem. William Wade Jr. later relocated to Edenton. (MGR.)

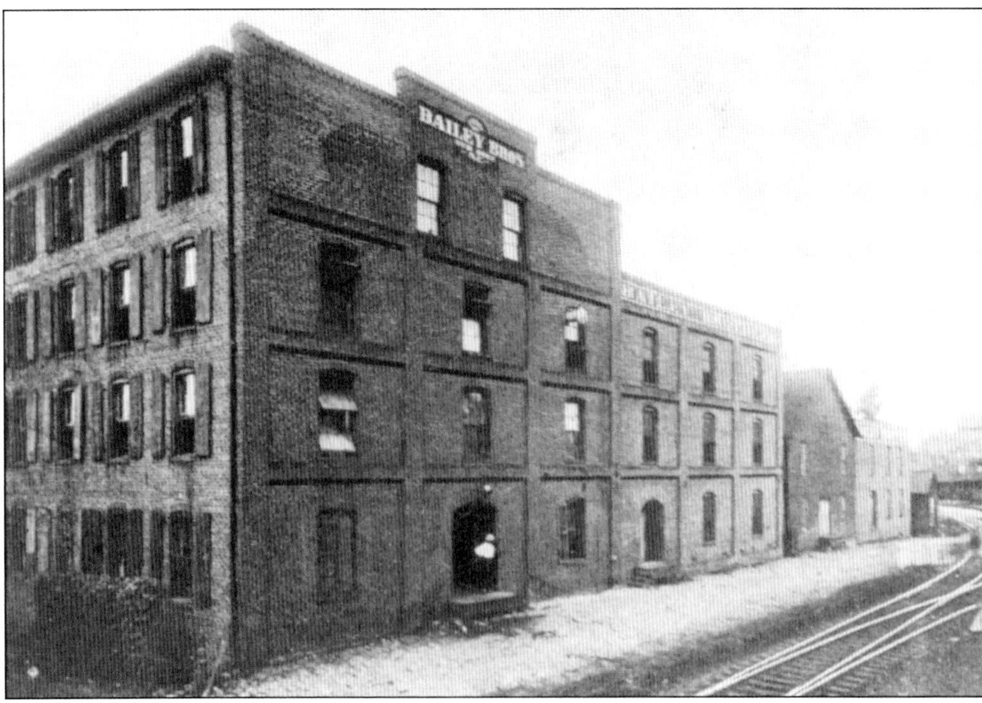

PHILLIP NATHANIEL "P.N." BAILEY (1849–1905) AND LAURA BENTON BAILEY (1856–1937). P.N. Bailey was born in Davie County and moved to Statesville with his family around 1870. P.N. and his brother Mumford DeJournett (1846–1929) began manufacturing tobacco and moved their business, Bailey Brothers, to Forsyth County in 1880. P.N. married Laura Benton in 1885, served as an alderman for Winston, and was an advocate for good streets.

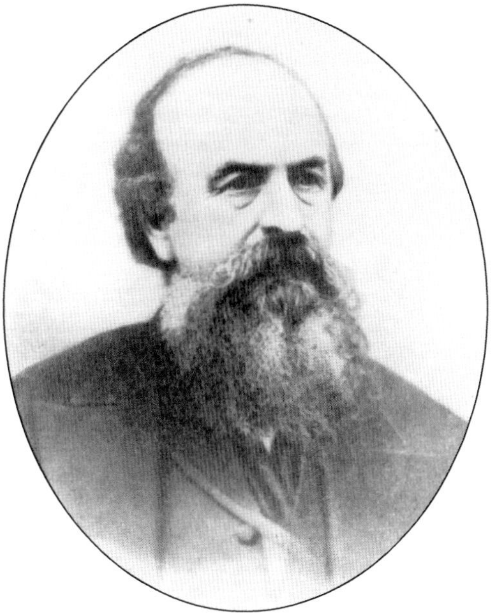

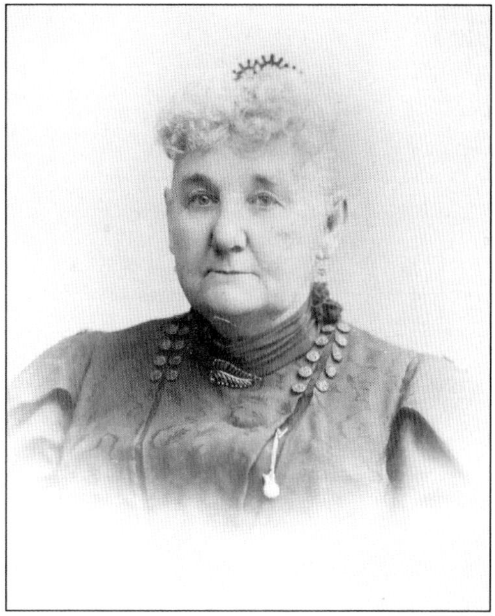

EDWIN THEODORE CLEMMONS (1826–1896) AND HARRIET "HATTIE" BUTNER CLEMMONS (1829–1910). Hattie Butner was born in Salem, where her parents ran the Butner Hotel from 1850 to 1884. She married Edwin (sometimes listed as Edward) in 1858. He drove a stagecoach, named the *Hattie Butner* for his wife, from High Point through Salem to Wytheville, Virginia. When the stagecoach business declined in Forsyth County, Edwin and Hattie moved to Asheville in 1874 to manage the Eagle Hotel. Edwin made provisions in his will to establish a school at Clemmons. The *Hattie Butner* stagecoach was moved to the Wachovia Museum in 1937 and is pictured below. Today, the restored stagecoach resides in the Village Hall of Clemmons, the town named for Edwin's family.

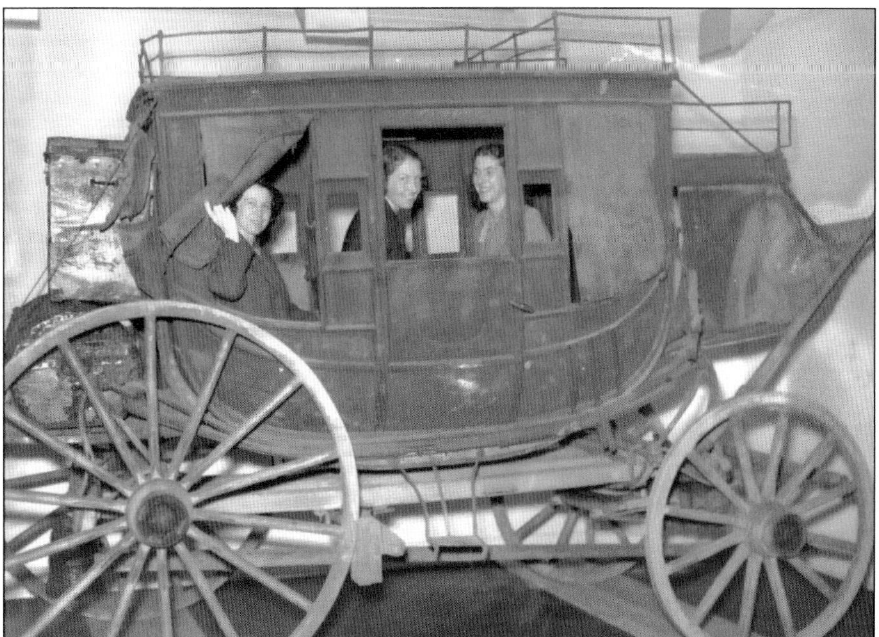

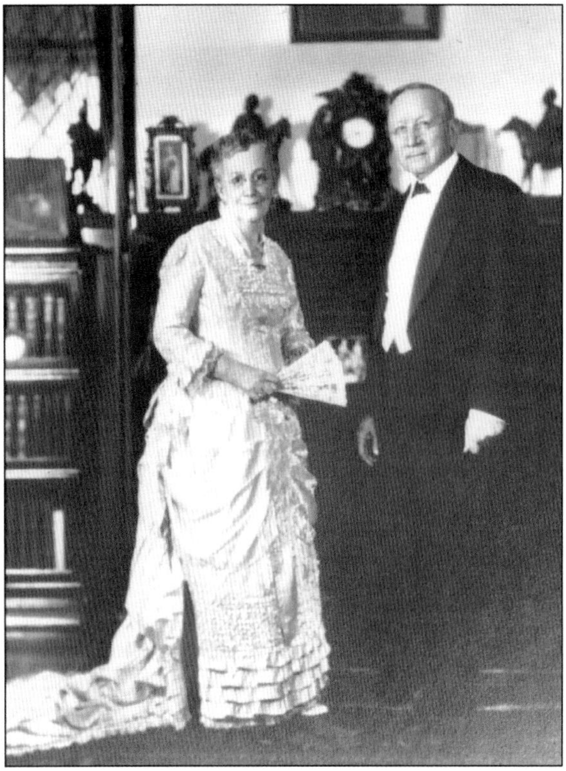

Rosa Elvira Mickey Fries (1860–1938) and Henry Elias Fries (1857–1949). Wearing their wedding attire, Rosa and Henry celebrated their 50th wedding anniversary at a reception in 1931. Rosa and Henry were born into long-established Salem families. Rosa was the daughter of Julius E. and Lavinia Vogler Mickey, and Henry was the son of Francis Levin and Lisetta Maria Vogler Fries. Henry was manager of Wachovia Mills and founded the Fries Manufacturing and Power Company. He was also active in politics, transportation, and education. Rosa organized the first wheat fair, which was the forerunner of the local agricultural fair.

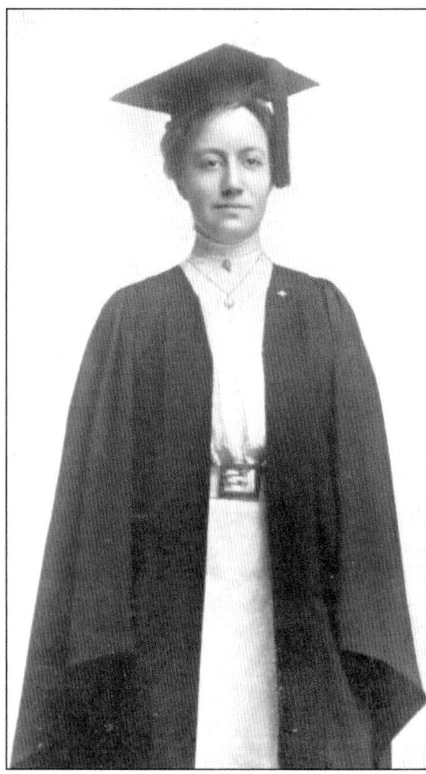

Anna Marguerite Fries (1892–1916). Anna Marguerite was the only child of Rosa and Henry Fries. She attended Salem Academy and College, graduating in 1911. Following graduation, Anna Marguerite and her parents traveled to several European countries. A member of Home Moravian Church, Anna Marguerite taught a Sunday school class of young women at Fries Memorial Church, which was named in honor of her parents and their long years of service to the Moravian Church. Anna Marguerite succumbed to scarlet fever, one of 50 cases that prompted the closing of local schools. Shortly before her death, Anna Marguerite wrote a poem on "Jesse Franklin's Ride" that was published in the *Winston-Salem Journal* and reprinted in other North Carolina newspapers.

FRANCIS LEVIN FRIES (1812–1863). Francis was born in Salem to John Christian William and Johanna Nissen Fries. His father was a cabinetmaker from Germany, and Francis attended school locally and in Pennsylvania. He taught at the Salem Boys' School for a few years and then traveled north to learn about manufacturing. He supervised the building of Salem Manufacturing Company's plant. Francis married Lisetta Marie Vogler (1820–1903), daughter of John and Christina Spach Vogler. Francis and his father built a wool-spinning mill run by steam power. When his brother Henry joined the firm, it became F. & H. Fries Company.

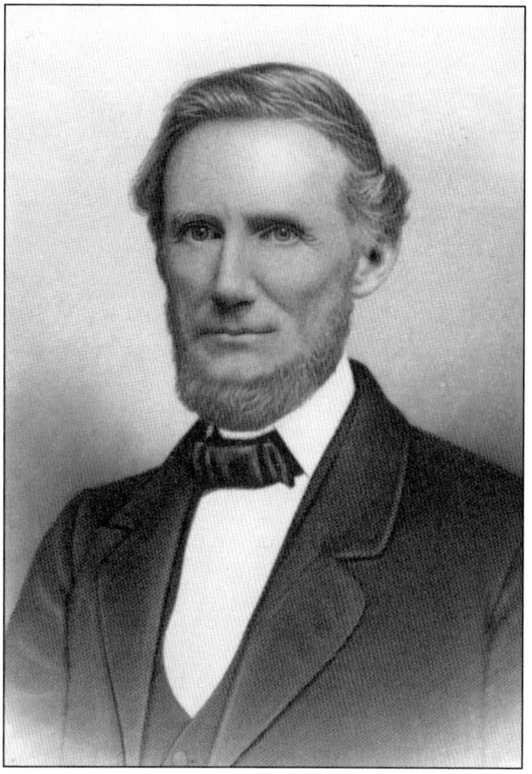

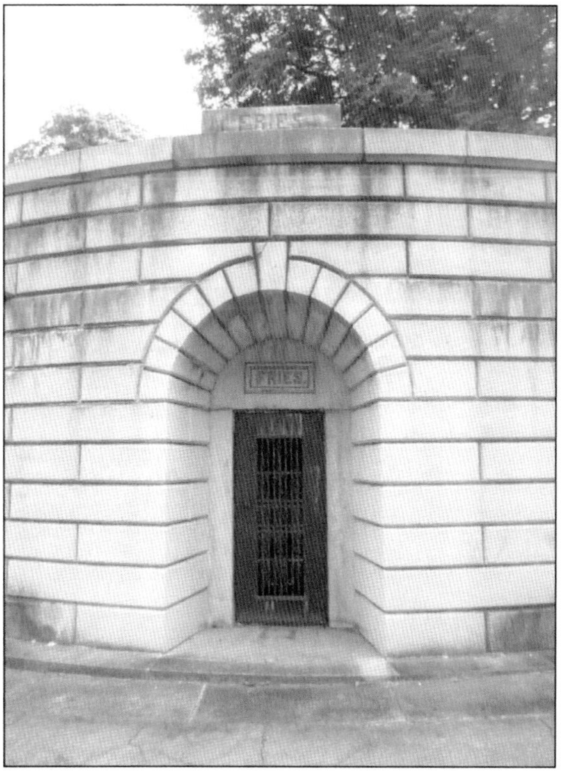

FRIES VAULT. Francis Fries added a cotton mill to the family business, which was later converted to a woolen mill. He designed Main Hall for Salem Girls' School and selected the site and designed the first Forsyth County courthouse. He also designed the Fries vault, a new feature for the cemetery. He selected the hill formerly known as Stony-Point for his lot. The inner vault was divided into three apartments, one above the other, which were supported and enclosed by arches. The entrance to the vault was closed with an iron door, above which "Fries" appears in raised letters on marble. (MGR.)

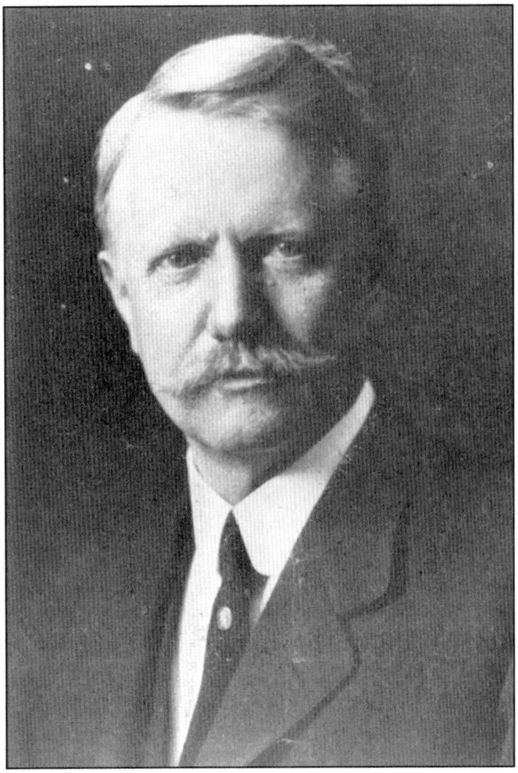

COL. FRANCIS "FRANK" HENRY FRIES (1855–1931). The son of Frances L. and Lisetta Vogler Fries, Frank became a partner in the F. & H. Fries Company when he turned 21 in 1876. He built Arista Mills and Indera Mills as well as founded other mills that were consolidated into Washington Mills at Fries, Virginia. Frank built the Roanoke & Southern Railway to connect Winston and Salem to Roanoke. He later built a line from Winston and Salem to Wadesboro. He was president of Wachovia Bank and Trust Company. Frank was married first to Letitia Walker Patterson (1860–1884) and secondly to Anna Paulina deSchweinitz (1860–1934).

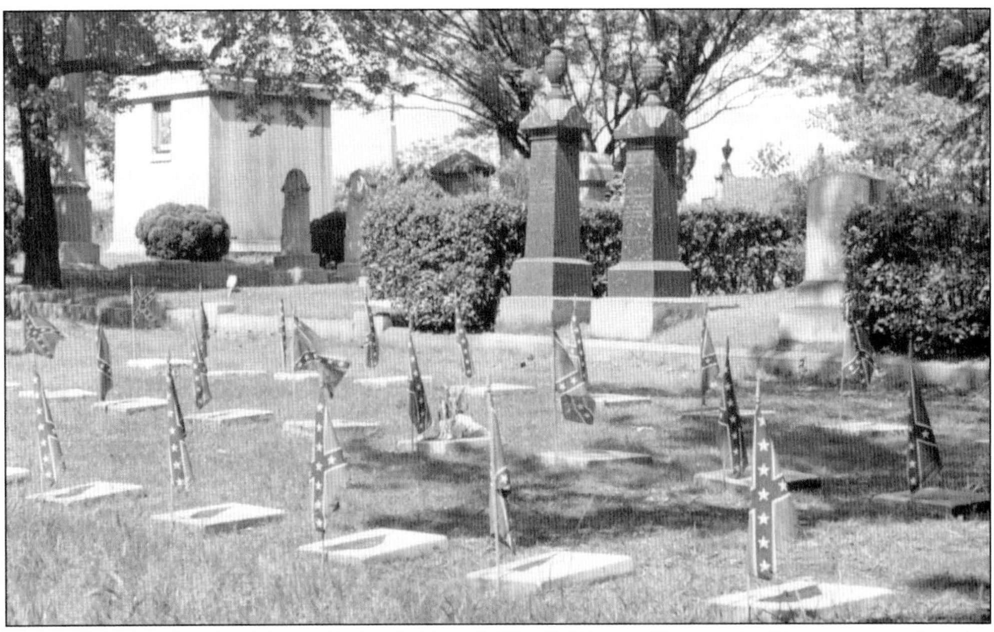

JACOB CICERO TISE (1855–1917). Jacob Tise (1817–1904) was Winston's oldest citizen when he died in 1904. He manufactured wagons, ran a mercantile business, and was mayor of Winston. Son Jacob Cicero also ran a mercantile establishment and a real estate business. In 1900, Jacob Cicero purchased Vade Mecum Springs, which he improved and beautified. His will provided funds for a cottage at the Children's Home and a vault, pictured at a distance.

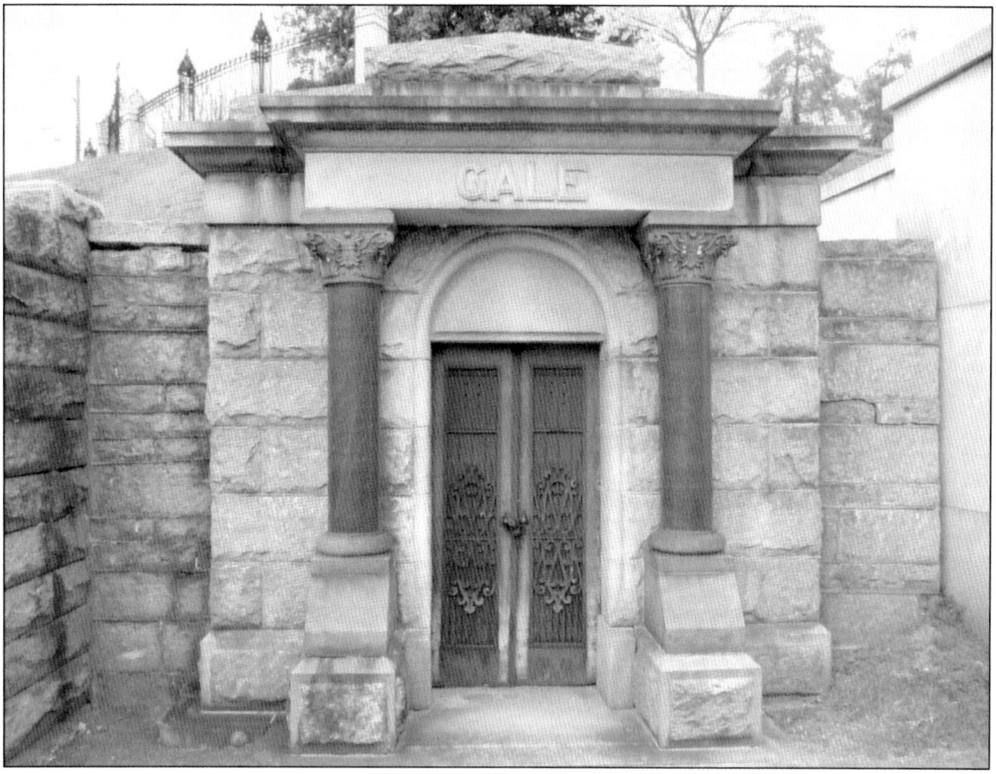

GALE VAULT. Capt. Alfred John "A.J" Gale (1852–1906) was a native of England. In 1880, he married Nancy "Nannie" Fisher (1855–1918), the daughter of Robert Fisher (1821–1905) and Amey Rachel Samuels Fisher (1823–1911). After the death of Captain Gale, Nancy married John R. Brown in 1912. Nancy was a member of Calvary Moravian and Home Moravian Churches and had a special interest in decorating and beautifying the churches for special occasions. (MGR.)

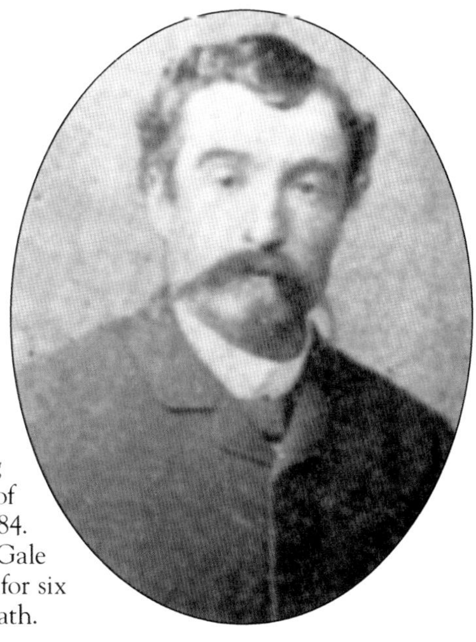

CAPT. ALFRED JOHN "A.J." GALE (1852–1906). A.J. Gale came to the United States from England in 1872. He worked as a building contractor in New York City, New York; Chicago, Illinois; Williamsport, Pennsylvania; and Elmira, New York. He arrived in North Carolina in 1876 and worked on the federal building in Raleigh before coming to Winston-Salem. Gale was a charter member of Fire Company No. 1 and was elected captain in 1884. When Chief John B. McCreary resigned in 1904, Gale was elected chief. He also served as an alderman for six years. The Gale vault was built shortly after his death.

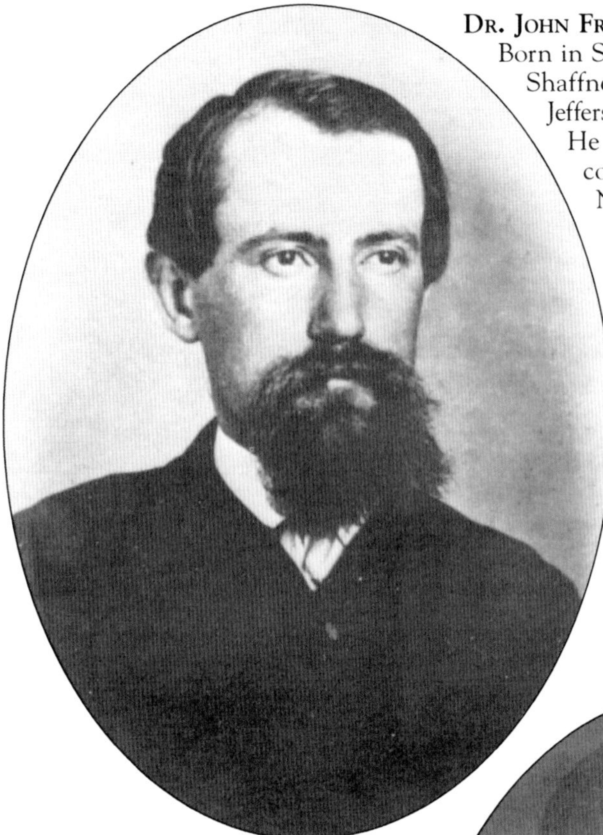

Dr. John Francis Shaffner Sr. (1838–1908). Born in Salem to Henry and Levinia Hauser Shaffner, John Francis Sr. graduated from Jefferson Medical College in Philadelphia. He volunteered for Capt. A.H. Belo's company in the 21st Regiment of the North Carolina Troops and served as surgeon in the Confederate army until Robert E. Lee's surrender at Appomattox. John Sr. (pictured) married Caroline "Carrie" Louise Fries (1839–1922) in 1865. He was a medical practitioner, druggist, mayor of Salem, and president of Salem Water Supply Company. Carrie taught at Salem Academy and was active in benevolent community organizations.

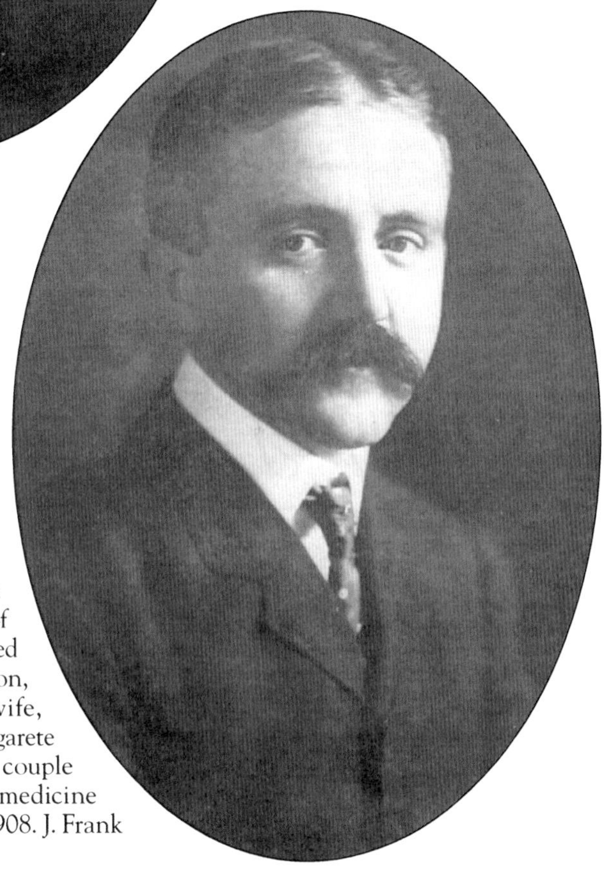

Dr. John Francis "J. Frank" Shaffner Jr. (1874–1910). J. Frank was born in Salem to Dr. John Francis Sr. and Carrie Shaffner. He attended Salem Boys' School and the University of North Carolina and received his medical training at the University of Pennsylvania. J. Frank (pictured) served his residency at the hospital in Easton, Pennsylvania, where he met his wife, Margarete Schroeder (1874–1952). Margarete was a German-born nurse, and the couple married in 1901. J. Frank practiced medicine with his father until John Sr. died in 1908. J. Frank passed away two years later.

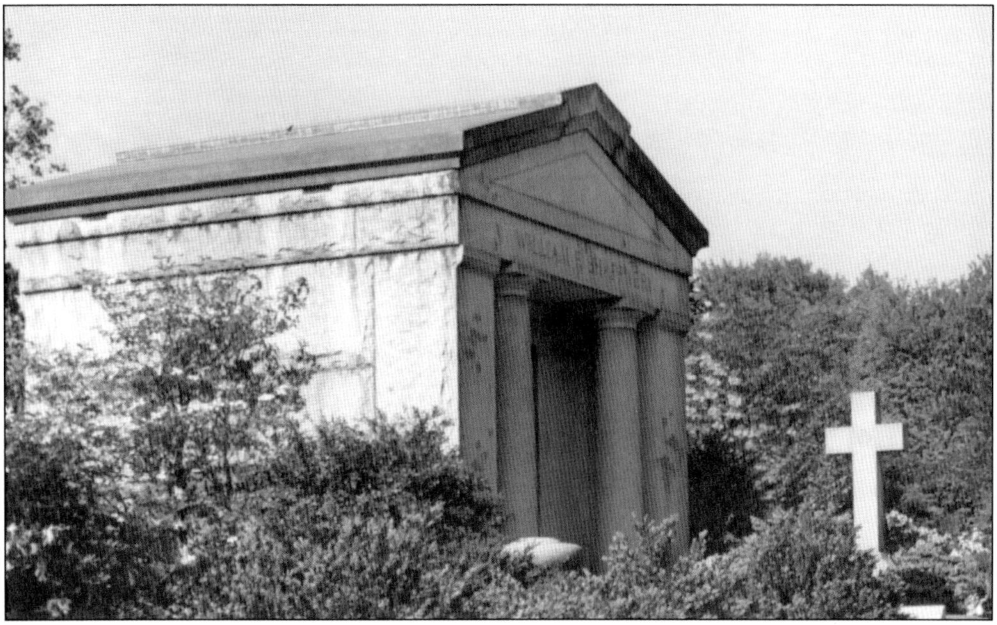

William Francis Shaffner Sr. (1869–1944). Salem native William Francis Sr. was the son of Dr. John Francis Sr. and Carrie Shaffner. William Francis Sr. married Virginia Trice Richardson (1871–1909) in 1902. Virginia died in 1909, leaving two young children. Shaffner and William C. Briggs invented a cigarette-making machine and organized the Briggs-Shaffner Company. He was involved in banking and real estate and helped develop Carolina Beach.

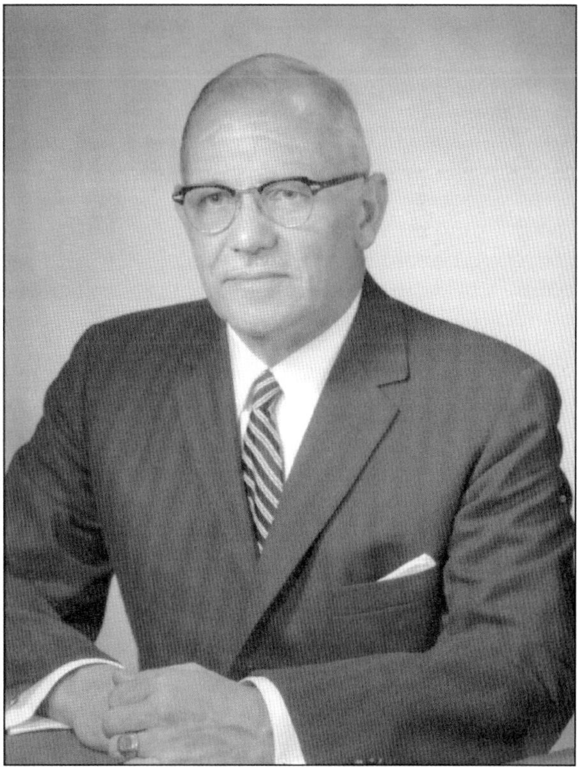

William Francis Shaffner Jr. (1907–1971). William Francis Jr. followed in his father's footsteps with involvement in the Pilot Real Estate Company and the Briggs-Shaffner Company. Elected to the board of aldermen, William Francis Jr. served terms before and after he participated in the US Navy during World War II. He held several offices in city government during the city's postwar growth phase. He married Louella Spaugh Nissen (1910–1970), the widow of Richard Wray Nissen (1906–1940), in 1947. The Shaffner family donated part of their farm for the Silas Creek Parkway right-of-way and for Shaffner Park.

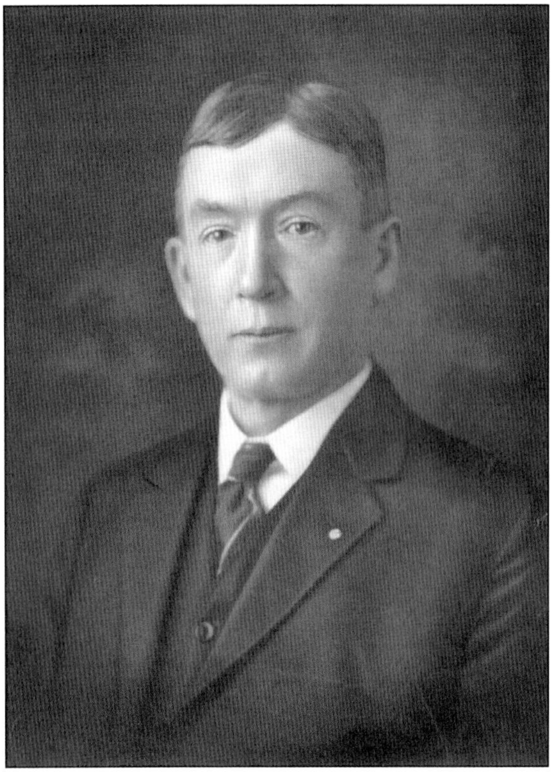

Messick-Moore Vault. Born in Pamlico County, Erastus Radford Messick (1864–1927) studied business and worked in the grocery trade. He came to Winston-Salem in 1890 and married Rebecca Jane Stone (1874–1933) in 1891. Erastus (pictured) was a Bible scholar and was active in his church, Fourth Street Church of Christ. He founded a wholesale grocery and produce commission business in 1897, which he operated until he sold it and retired in 1920. Their daughter Nellie Elmere Messick (1895–1982) was a schoolteacher and married Dr. Robert Alexander Moore (1886–1970), who was director of orthopedics at Bowman Gray School of Medicine.

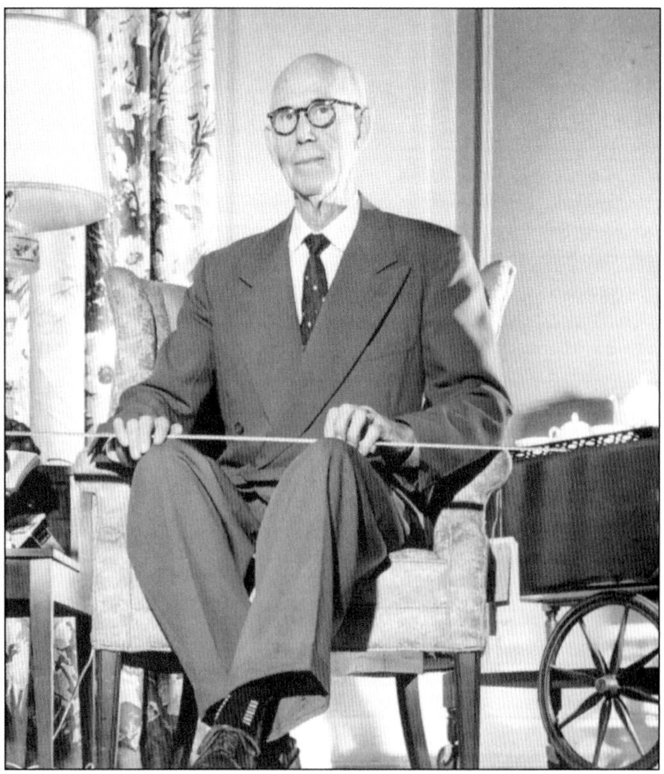

Davis-Early Vault. Robert Lee Davis (1863–1949) and his wife, Mary Ella Matheson Davis (1864–1935), operated Davis White Sulphur Springs, a summer resort. Robert also operated Davis Mills and pastored several rural churches. Daughter Annie Pearl Davis (1894–1982) married John Harold Early (1883–1963) in 1913. John (pictured) worked for B.F. Huntley Furniture until he and J. Frank Morris established Morris-Early Furniture, which John operated until he retired in 1957.

Four

Flowers in the Garden

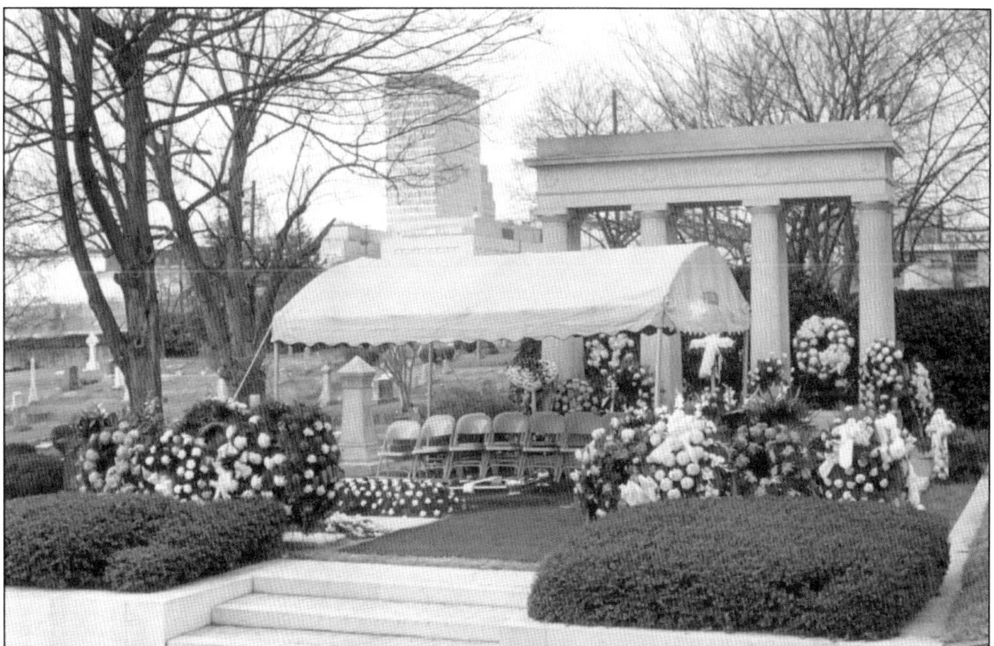

Flowers and Monuments. Located within sight and hearing of Winston-Salem's downtown, Salem Cemetery is a quiet contrast to a busy and noisy city. In this photograph, the scene is set, with flowers, tent, and chairs, for a funeral that will take place shortly. In the shadow of the Wachovia Building and the nearly hidden Reynolds Building, Charles Henry Babcock (see page 49), son-in-law of Richard Joshua Reynolds, will rest in the Reynolds family plot.

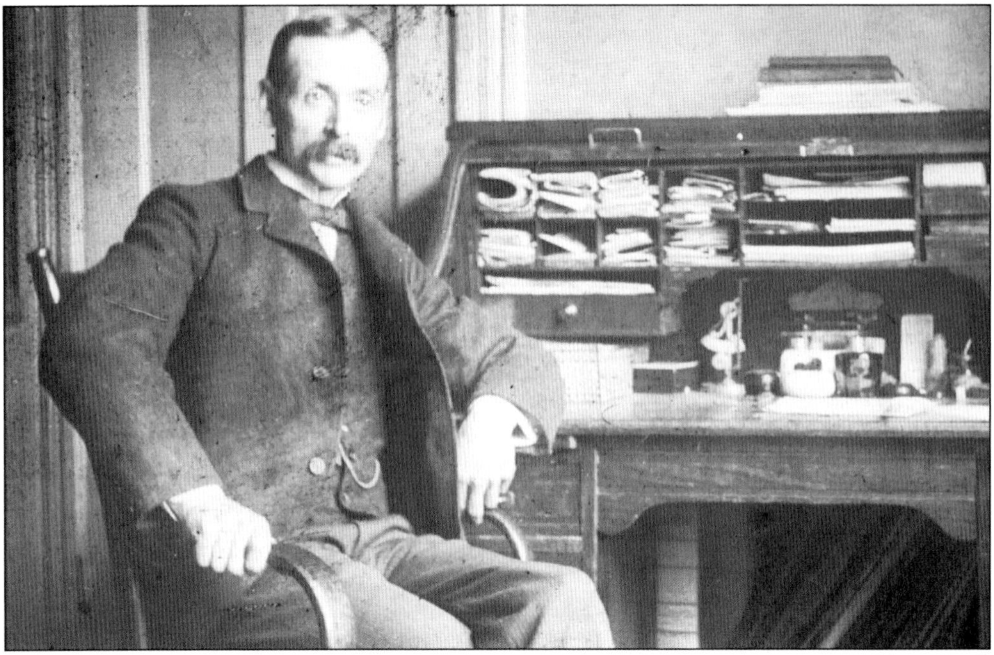

Robert Emory "Bob" Carmichael (1861–1944). Readers of the *Twin City Sentinel* knew Bob Carmichael as "Uncle Bob," the veteran newspaperman who wrote a daily column called "Town Topics." Born in Winston-Salem, Bob moved to Indiana and then Missouri with his parents, where he learned to set type during school vacations. He returned to the city in 1880 and began his 63-year newspaper career when he was hired by the *Western Sentinel.*

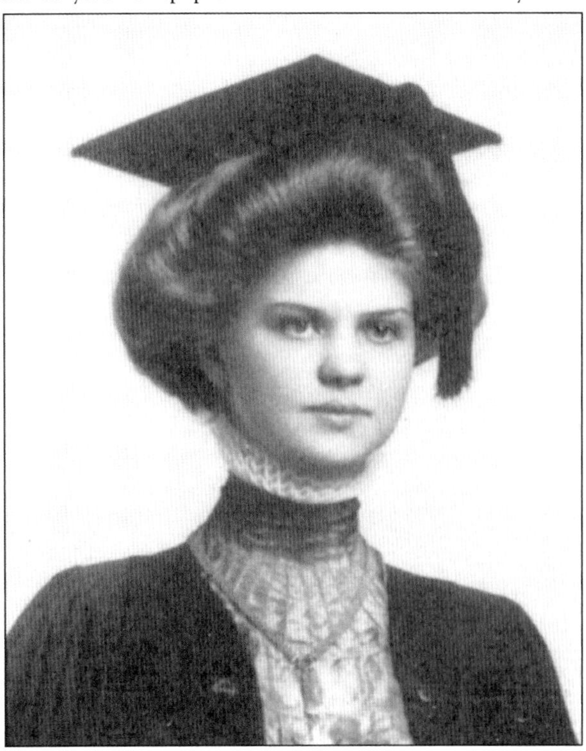

Maude Esther Carmichael Williamson (1890–1992). Maude Carmichael was born in Winston-Salem to Robert Emory and Alice Miller Carmichael (1865–1942). Maude graduated from Salem College in 1909 and married Rev. Elgin Williamson three weeks later. Reverend Williamson was formerly the minister at Burkhead Methodist Church and was pastor at Calvary Methodist in Charlotte at the time of their marriage. They lived in several towns in western North Carolina. After Elgin's death in 1937, Maude and their daughter, Alice Carmichael Williamson (1916–2011), returned to Winston-Salem. Maude worked for Draft Board No. 3 during World War II and later worked for Western Electric, Montaldo's, and McPhail's.

William Madison Nissen (1856–1934). Born in Waughtown to John Phillip and Sallie Vawter Nissen, William worked for the family business, Nissen Wagon Works, for more than 50 years before retiring in 1924. He married Ida Wade Wray (1874–1954) in 1898. He purchased the site of the old YMCA at Fourth and Cherry Streets, constructing the 18-story Nissen Building (pictured), which was completed in 1927. Over the years, it housed a bank, clothing store, barbershop, and many other small businesses. When William died in 1934, his funeral service was held in his apartment on the 18th floor.

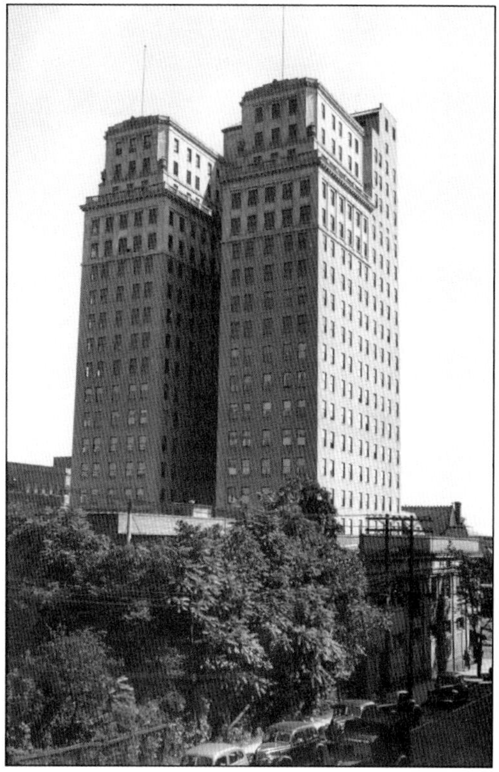

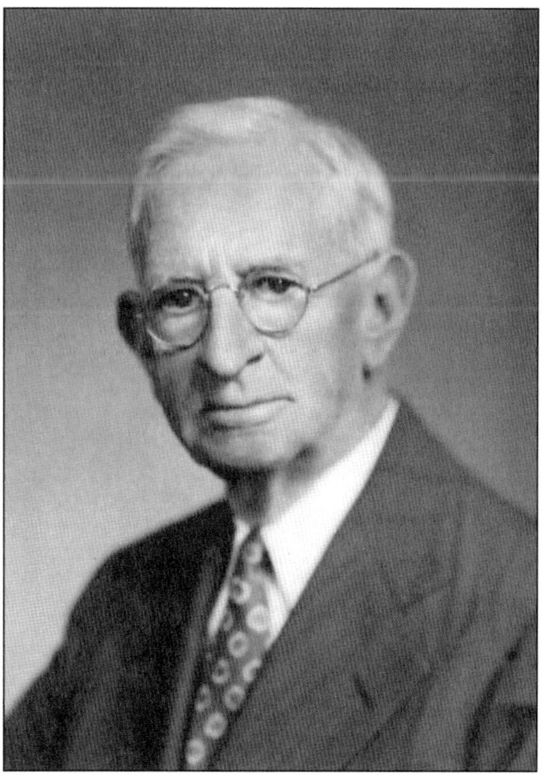

Edward W. O'Hanlon (1870–1958). Born in Fayetteville, Edward came to Winston in 1894 after earning his pharmacy degree. He bought the L.E. Steere Drug Company and established E.W. O'Hanlon Inc. on the corner of Fourth and Liberty Streets. He operated his drug business from the three-story S.A. Ogburn Building. A fire in 1913 damaged his business, but a second fire in 1914 forced his move across the street during construction of his new eight-story building in the previous location. The popular drugstore closed in 1961, and today, this early skyscraper houses a restaurant and business offices. Edward married Nancy Critz (1881–1967) in 1904.

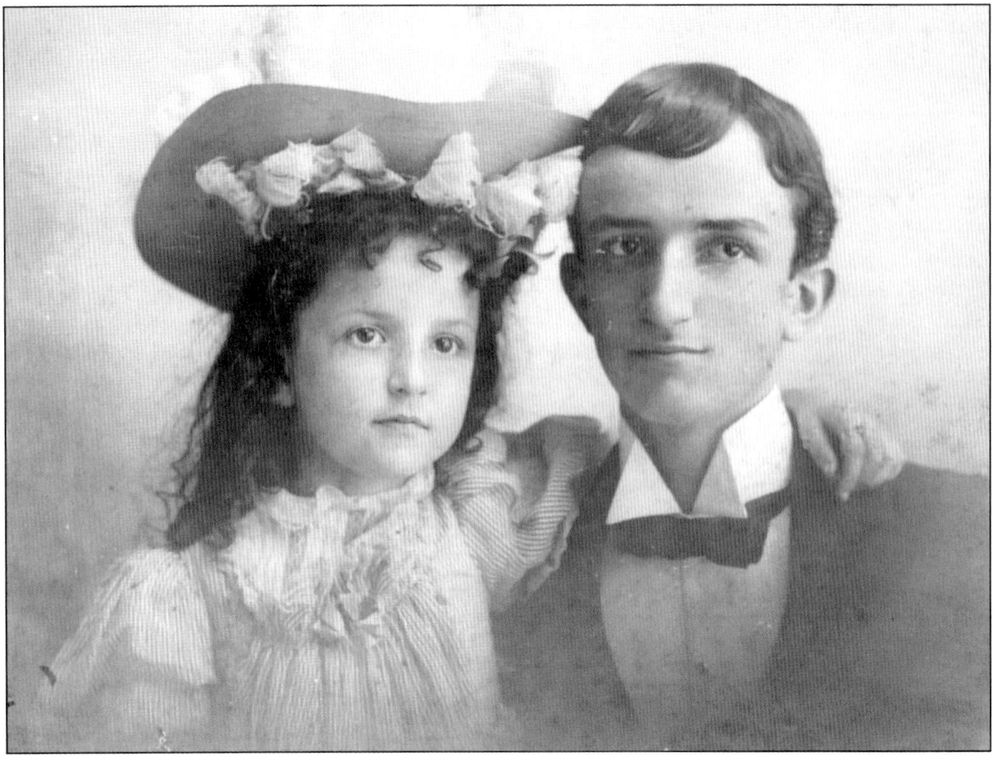

Edwina Lockett Abele (1890–1972) and Dr. Everett A. Lockett (1880–1934). Edwina and Everett were the children of Edward Lafayette Lockett (1845–1914) and Mary Everett Lockett (1853–1923). Edwina and Everett were raised in a home on West Fifth Street. Edwina married Carl Abele and lived in Ohio after working as a reporter for the *Winston-Salem Journal*. Everett married Annie Lindsay (1881–1955) and was a renowned doctor and surgeon who served his city and his country.

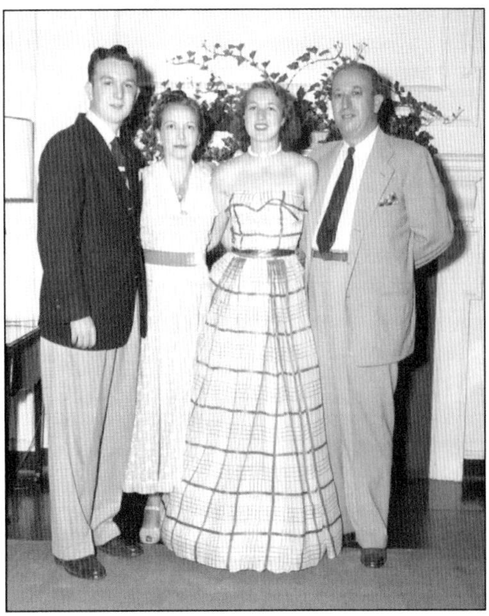

Mary Pfohl Lassiter (1904–1992) and Dr. Vernon Clark Lassiter Sr. (1901–1965). Mary was born in Winston-Salem to Bishop J. Kenneth and Bessie Whittington Pfohl. She graduated from Salem Academy and Salem College and worked as a registered nurse. Mary married Dr. Vernon Clark Lassiter in 1928 in Home Moravian Church. Vernon practiced medicine in Winston-Salem and was on the staff at City Memorial Hospital as a physician and a surgeon. From left to right in this 1951 photograph are Vernon C. Lassiter Jr. (1933–1977), Mary Pfohl Lassiter, Elizabeth Estelle Lassiter, and Dr. Vernon C. Lassiter Sr.

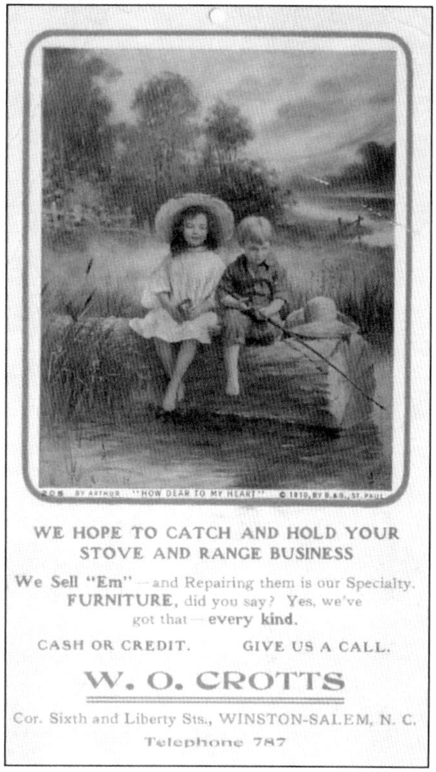

WILLIAM OSCAR "W.O." CROTTS SR. (1875–1926). Advertised as the "home of lowest prices," the W.O. Crotts furniture store on the corner of Liberty and Sixth Streets carried "everything from kitchen to parlor." The advertisement pictured was printed in the form of a postcard. W.O. was a native of Randolph County and came to Winston-Salem about 1906. He first worked for Huntley-Hill-Stockton Furniture before establishing his own business. He later operated the Auto Top, Paint, and Repair Company on Trade Street. He was married to Ella Ray Crotts (1880–1928). (WLB.)

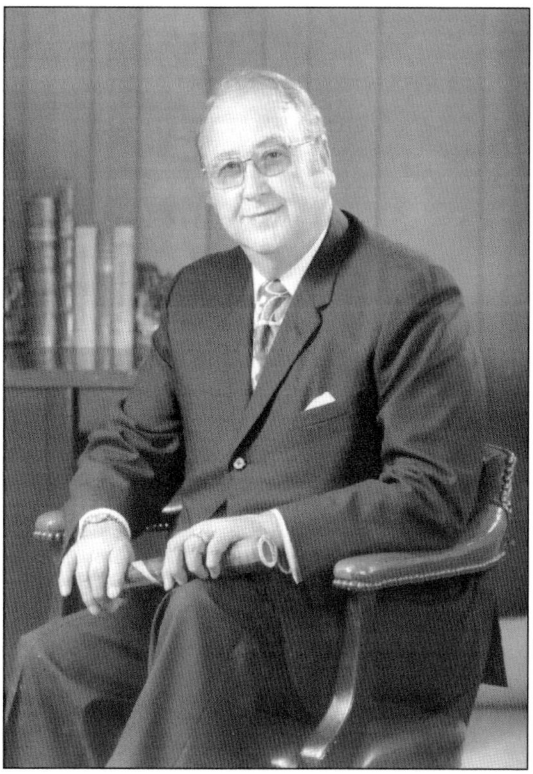

DR. HYLTON KENNETH CROTTS (1908–1981). Born in Winston-Salem to W.O. and Ella Ray Crotts, Hylton graduated from R.J. Reynolds High School, the University of North Carolina, and the School of Dental Medicine at the University of Pennsylvania. Hylton was a member of the glee club at the University of Pennsylvania. When he was a freshman, the well-known club's Thanksgiving concert was broadcast on the radio and could be heard locally. As the first oral surgeon in Winston-Salem, Dr. Crotts was a member of several dental and oral surgeon societies. He married Elva Grace Lockard (1911–1978) in 1936.

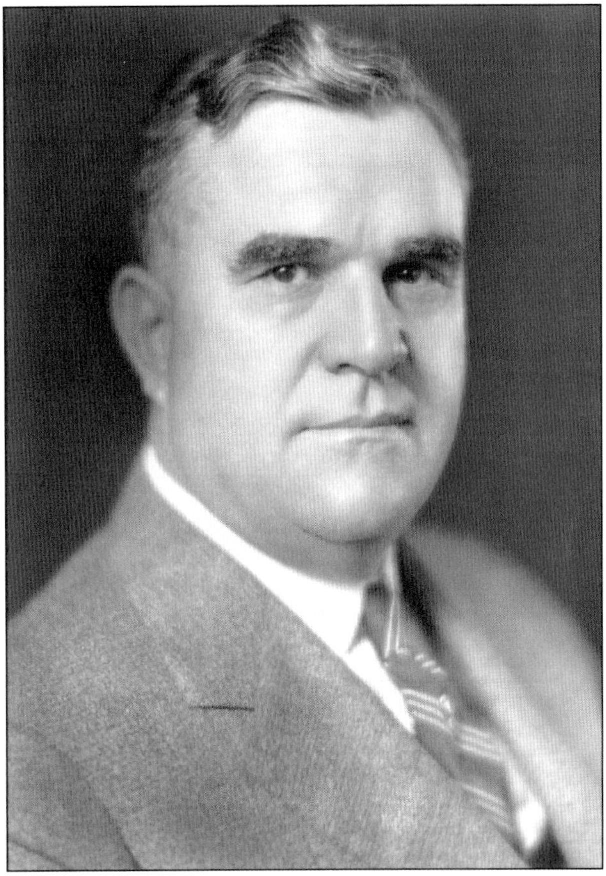

Dr. Charles Solomon Lawrence (1878–1930). A native of Stokes County, Charles attended Siloam Academy and then enlisted in the US Army in 1897, serving for six years. He graduated from George Washington University in medicine in 1908, married Alice Ruth George (1876–1959) in 1909, and began a private medical practice in Winston-Salem, where he specialized in surgery. Along with Dr. John Wesley Long of Greensboro, he organized a hospital unit during World War I. Then, after the war, he established the Lawrence Hospital with Dr. Grady Carlyle Cooke (1894–1957). The hospital closed about 1933, shortly after Charles died.

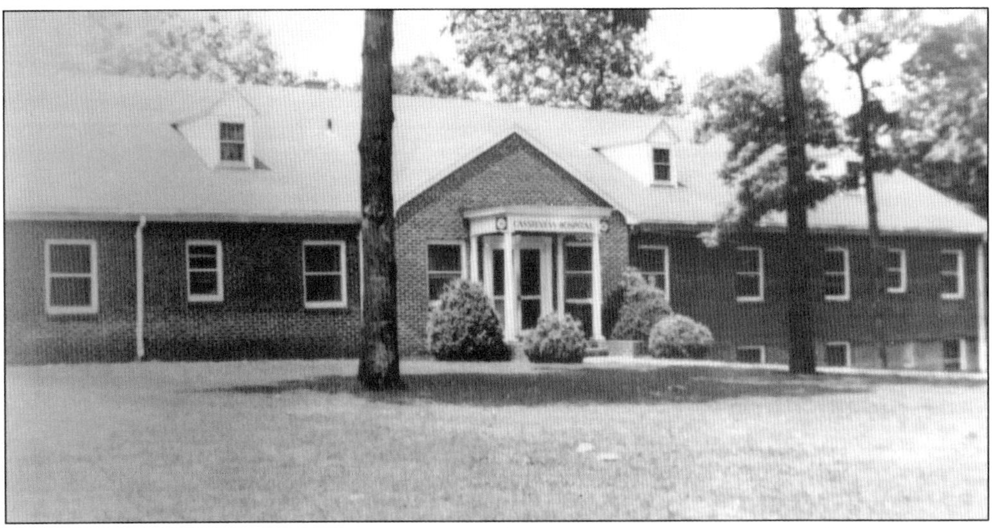

Dr. John Claude Casstevens Sr. (1900–1970). John Claude was born in Iredell County and graduated from Wake Forest College and the Medical College of Virginia. He founded the Casstevens Hospital (pictured) in 1945 and served as a physician and surgeon until he retired around 1960. Casstevens Hospital was located on South Stratford Road near Knollwood Street. He married Julia Esther Owen (1897–1987), a registered nurse whom he met during medical school.

William Joseph Conrad Jr. (1893–1971). Born in Winston-Salem to Dr. William Joseph Conrad (1856–1941) and Mary Elizabeth "Mollie" Watkins Conrad (1865–1949), William worked as a messenger boy at R.J. Reynolds Tobacco Company in 1904. He graduated from Wake Forest College, rejoined R.J. Reynolds in 1913, and was elected an officer in 1923. He was elected secretary of the company in 1940 and also served as director and vice president until he retired in 1960. He was a trustee for Wake Forest College and Appalachian State Teachers College. The Appalachian football stadium and athletic field were named for him in 1962.

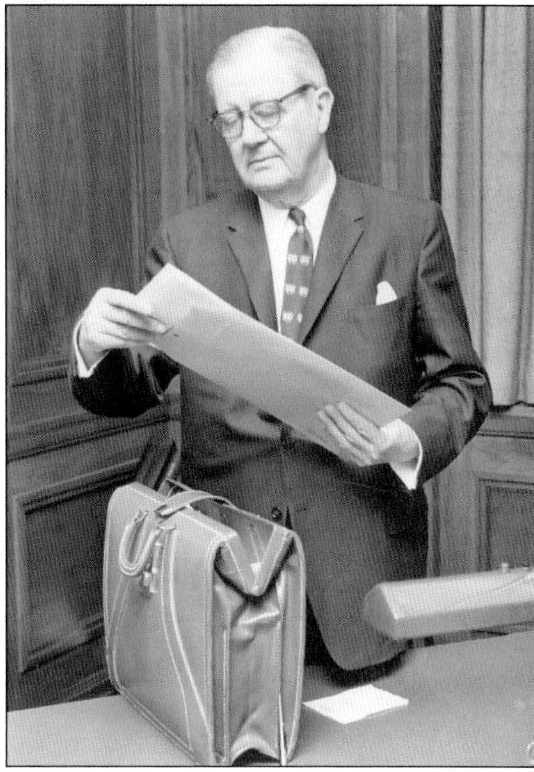

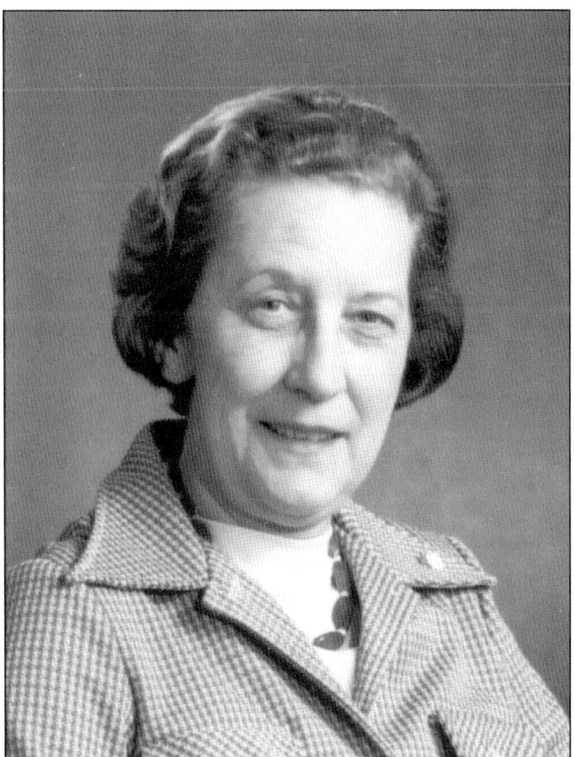

Dr. Elizabeth Conrad (1920–2013). Elizabeth was born in Indiana to Dr. Henry Brown Conrad (1891–1920) and Hally Hester Conrad (1892–1986). Her father was a Winston-Salem native and a World War I veteran. He practiced medicine in South Bend, Indiana, specializing in childhood diseases. He died of pneumonia in 1920 when Elizabeth was three weeks old. Elizabeth attended Johns Hopkins for her medical training, as did her father. One of the first three female physicians in North Carolina, she worked as a pediatrician for many years in Winston-Salem. Elizabeth trained tracking dogs and grew beautiful roses at her Hilltop Farm home.

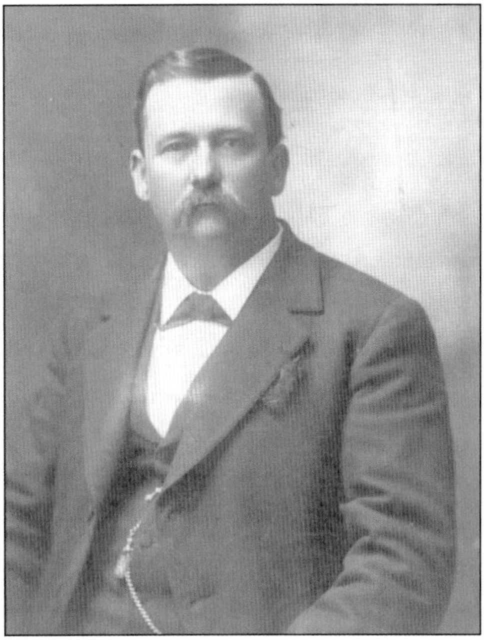

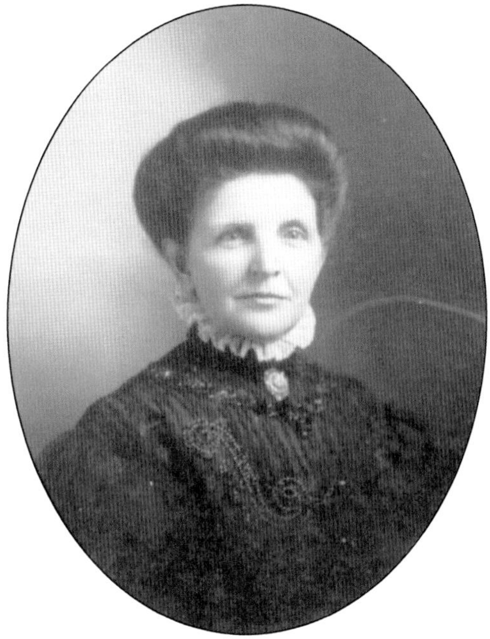

RUFUS ISAAC DALTON (1855–1937) AND CORA ALICE MCCANLESS DALTON (1860–1948). Rufus was one of seven children born in Stokes County to David N. and Melissa Rives Dalton. He manufactured tobacco and boxes and was connected to a large furniture and wholesale grocery concern. He was a member of the board of aldermen and served one term as mayor. Born in Danbury, Cora attended St. Mary's School in Raleigh and married Rufus in 1880.

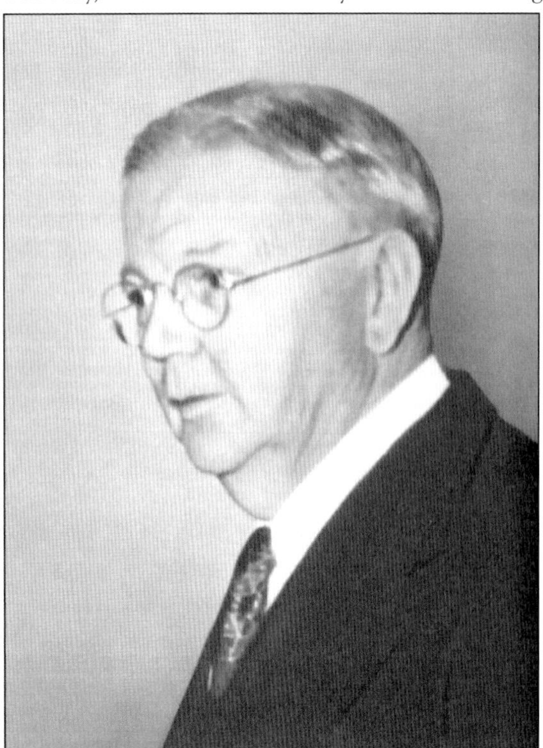

DR. WILLIAM NICHOLAS DALTON (1881–1953). Born in Danbury, William was the son of Rufus and Cora Dalton. He prepared for a career in the textile industry but changed to medicine and took professional courses at several colleges. He enjoyed playing sports and played football for each of the four colleges he attended. He played baseball for one of the schools. Dr. Dalton began his medical practice in Winston-Salem in 1904 and was elected to the office of coroner in 1908. He served as coroner for 45 years while also conducting a private practice. William married Lillian Spach (1892–1995) in 1913.

Dr. David Nicholas Dalton (1860–1928). Dr. Dalton was born at Dalton, an unincorporated community in Stokes County, on his father's estate. His father, David N. Dalton, had extensive landholdings with livestock, and he owned and operated flour and lumber mills. Younger David worked with his father before he left to study medicine at the University of North Carolina and New York University. He began his medical practice in Walnut Cove, but moved to Winston-Salem two years later, where he had a long and successful medical practice. He married Louisa Wilson Bitting (1864–1947), daughter of Joseph and Louisa Wilson Bitting, in 1887.

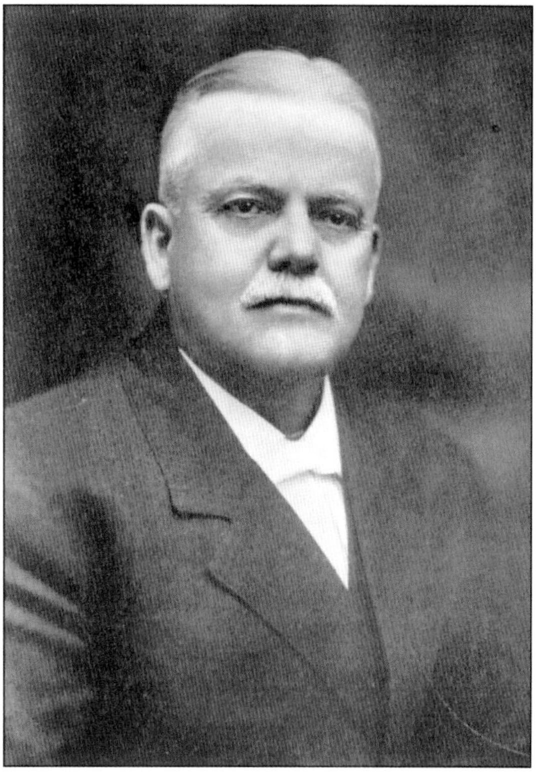

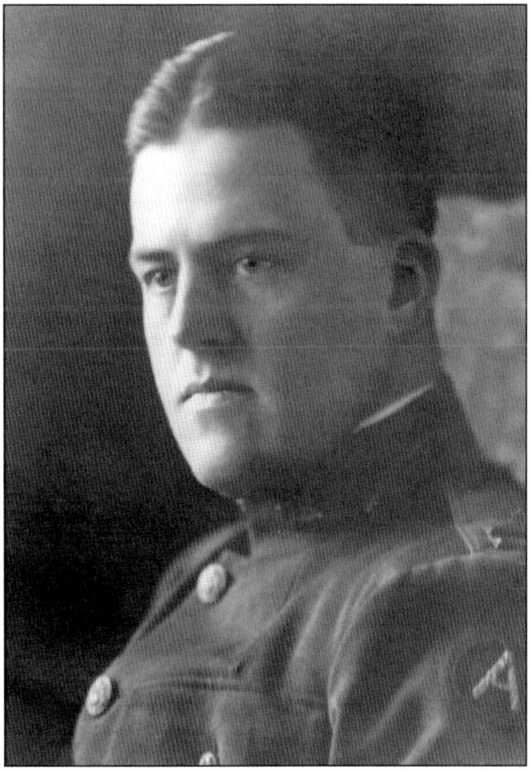

Maj. Gen. Joseph Nicholas "Joe" Dalton (1892–1961). Joe was born in Winston-Salem to Dr. David Nicholas and Louisa Dalton. He graduated from West End School and the Virginia Military Institute and was commissioned a second lieutenant in the Army in 1916. He rose through the ranks and was promoted to major general in 1943. He saw field service in Europe in World War I and held many staff and command positions in later years. Joe received decorations and awards during his career, including the Distinguished Service Medal (1945) and the Legion of Merit (1946). He retired in 1946.

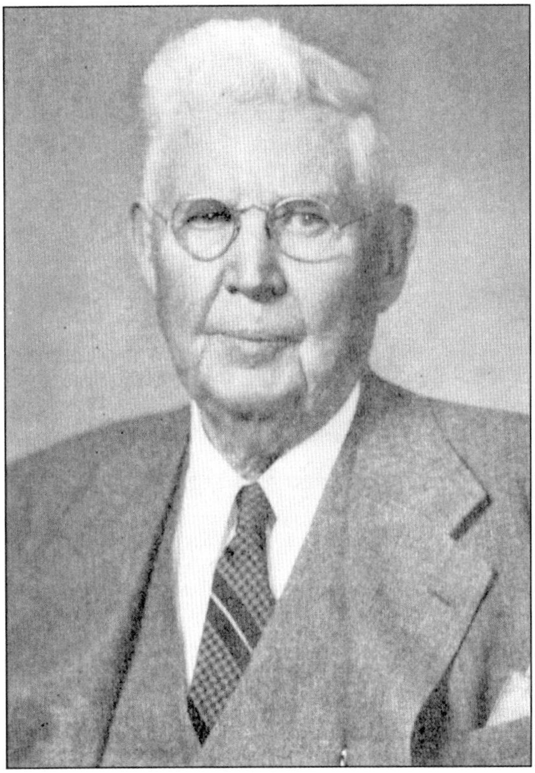

William Neal Reynolds (1863–1951). "Mr. Will" was born in Virginia, one of five sons born to Hardin Williams Reynolds (1810–1882) and Nancy Jane Cox Reynolds (1825–1903). He joined older brother, Richard Joshua, in Winston-Salem, became his tobacco buyer, and was later made a partner in R.J. Reynolds Tobacco Company. When Richard died in 1918, Mr. Will became president and rose to chairman of the executive committee. He retired in 1942. He and his wife, Kate Bitting Reynolds, lived their later years at Tanglewood, where he established stables for racehorses. Tanglewood became a public park after his death.

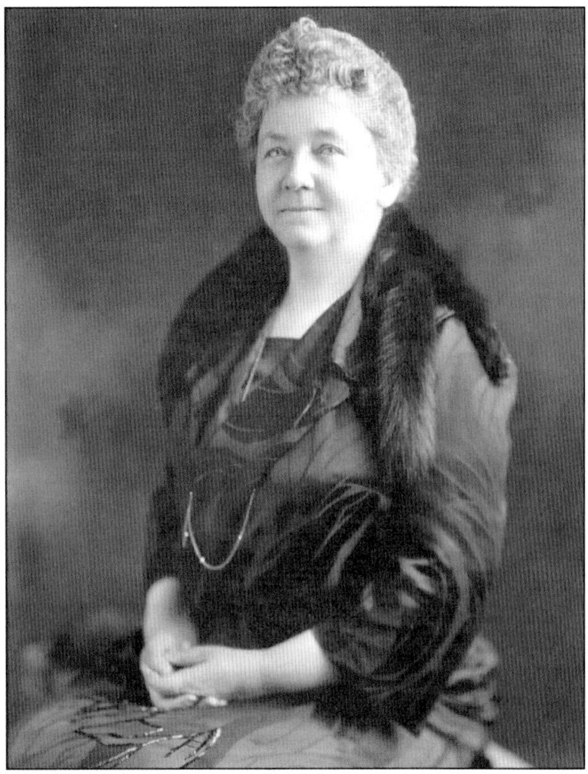

Kate Gertrude Bitting Reynolds (1867–1946). Kate was born in Yadkin County to Joseph and Louisa Wilson Bitting. She came to Winston-Salem as a child with her family and attended Salem College. She married William Neal Reynolds in 1889, and they established a home on West Fifth Street, near her parents and her married sisters. Kate was one of the ladies who founded the first hospital in Winston-Salem, which resulted in the building of City Hospital. William Neal Reynolds financed a hospital for African Americans in East Winston. It was named the Kate Bitting Reynolds Memorial Hospital in honor of his wife.

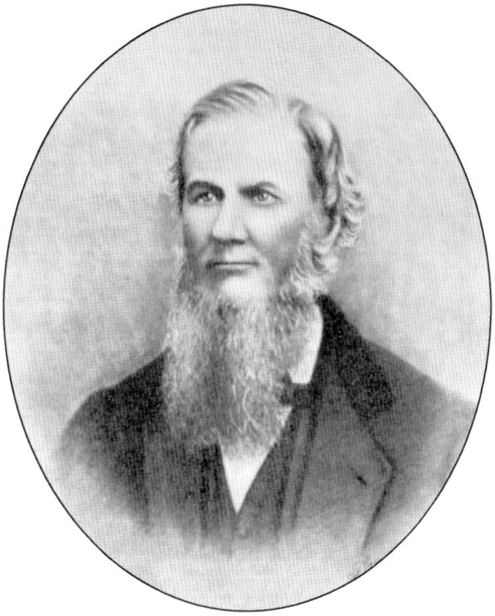
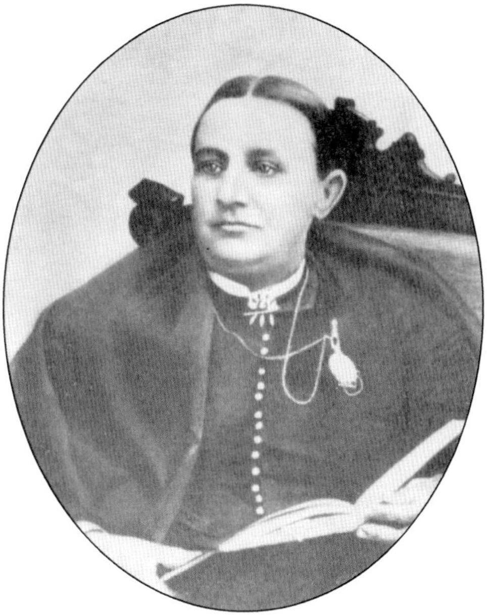

JOSEPH ANTHONY BITTING (1820–1901) AND LOUISA WILSON BITTING (1837–1919). Joseph was born on his father's farm in Stokes County. He bought a plantation in Yadkin County where he farmed and manufactured tobacco. In Winston, he operated as Bitting & Whitaker and then as Bitting & Hay. Joseph married Louisa Wilson in 1858. Louisa was born in Bethania. She and Joseph had 13 children and lived on West Fifth Street.

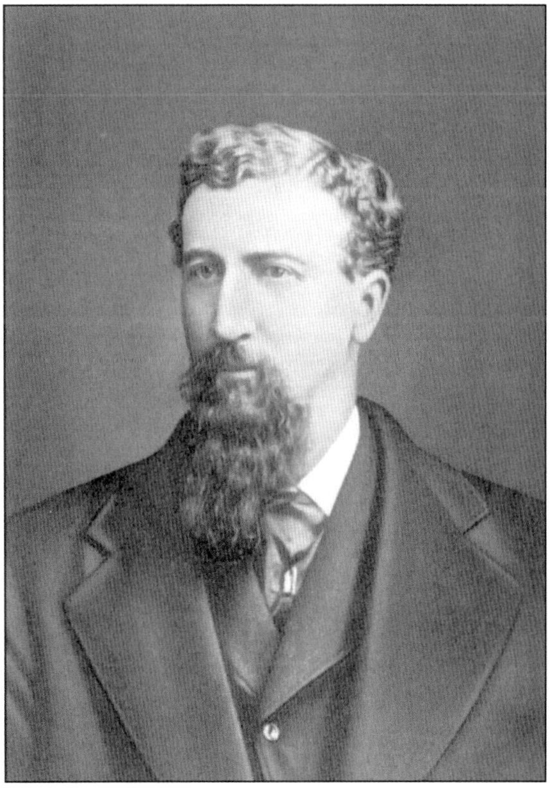

WILLIAM ASBURY WHITAKER (1843–1912). William was born in Yadkin County and served in the Civil War. In the early 1870s, he worked in Georgia as a representative of Joseph A. Bitting, a Yadkin County tobacco manufacturer. He came to Winston-Salem to become a member of the Bitting & Whitaker partnership and later formed the business of Whitaker-Harvey, with Thomas Rucker and William L. Harvey. William A. Whitaker worked to establish the town's first graded school, named West End Graded School. The new school in Buena Vista was named after him in 1953. He married Anna Henrietta Grace Bitting (1859–1934), daughter of his early employer.

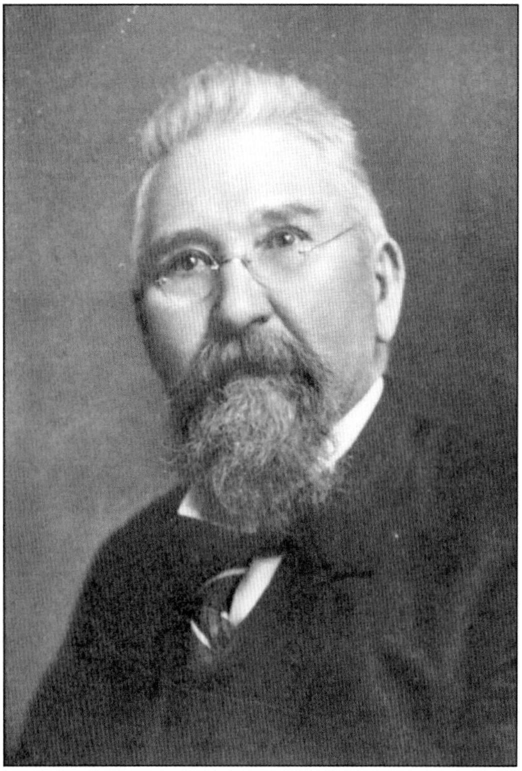

Richard Joshua "R.J." Reynolds Sr. (1850–1918). A native of Patrick County, Virginia, R.J. worked on his father's farm and in his tobacco factory before he attended college and business school. He came to Winston in 1875 and began to manufacture tobacco. He added his brother William Neal Reynolds and bookkeeper Henry Roan (1856–1925) to the partnership, establishing the R.J. Reynolds Tobacco Company. The company began in a "little red factory," and gradually grew to over 100 buildings. It was a major employer in the Winston-Salem area, offering exceptional wages and benefits. R.J. married his cousin Mary Katharine Smith in 1905. He managed the company until his death in 1918.

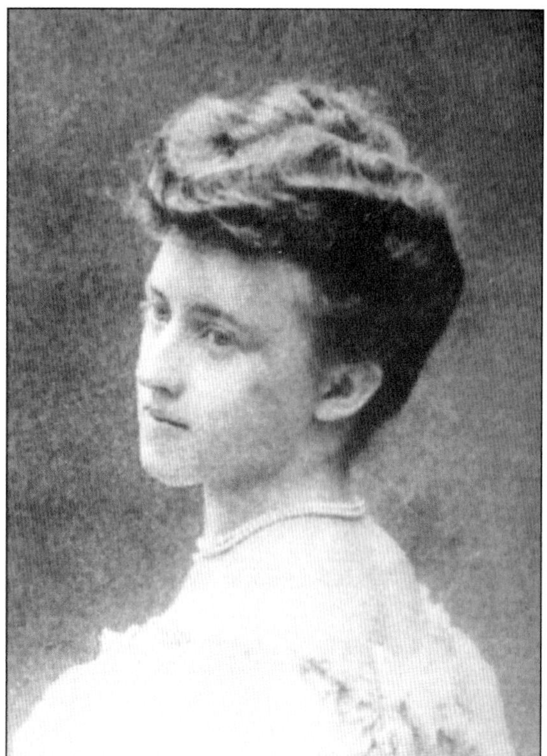

Mary Katharine Smith Reynolds Johnston (1880–1924). Katharine was born in Mount Airy. She married Richard Joshua Reynolds and they lived on West Fifth Street, where they raised four children. Katharine, with R.J.'s encouragement, planned a working country estate that came to fruition when the family moved there in 1917. Reynolda Estate included a house with a lake, cottages for estate workers, an extensive garden, a dairy, and other buildings. After R.J.'s death in 1918, Katharine married schoolmaster John Edward Johnston. She commissioned a high school and auditorium named for her first husband, among her many accomplishments.

CHILDREN OF RICHARD AND KATHARINE SMITH REYNOLDS. The R.J. Reynolds family lived at 666 West Fifth Street before they moved to Reynolda in 1917. This photograph shows the family gathered outside of their Fifth Street home, some of them seated on a blanket, with snow in the yard. Katharine is standing, holding the youngest child, Zachary Smith Reynolds (1911–1932). Mary Reynolds (1908–1953) is seated at left, next to Nancy Susan Reynolds (1910–1985). Next is their cousin James Stamper Dunn Jr. (1909–1922). R.J. Reynolds Jr. (1906–1964) is seated at far right, with his father, R.J. Reynolds Sr., behind him.

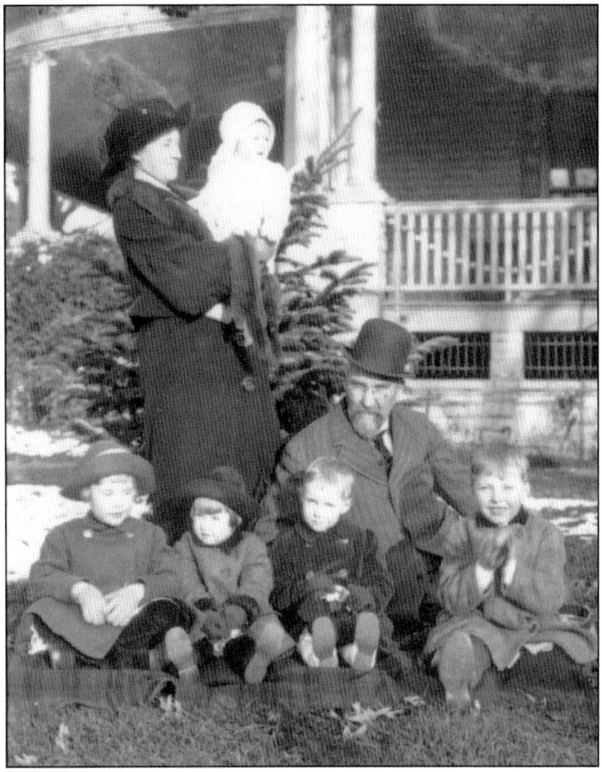

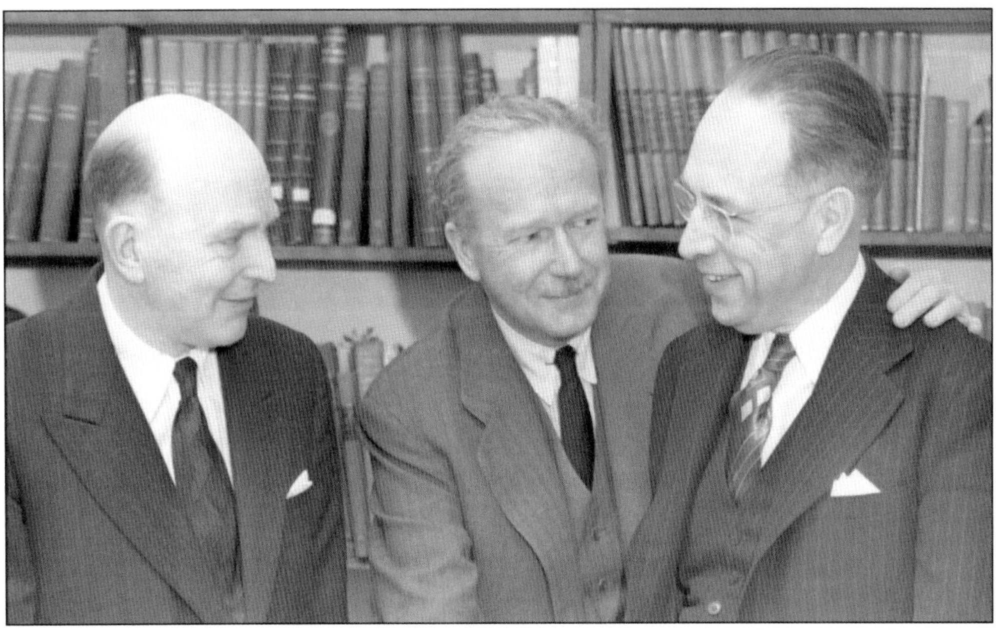

CHARLES HENRY BABCOCK (1899–1967). Charles, son of Charles Henry and Ella Park Babcock, was born in Indiana and married Mary Katherine Reynolds in 1929. Charles was an investment banker and philanthropist and was active in many community and business activities in Winston-Salem. He is pictured left with Wake Forest College architect Jens Larson (center) and school president Harold Tribble (right). Charles was instrumental in bringing Wake Forest to Winston-Salem.

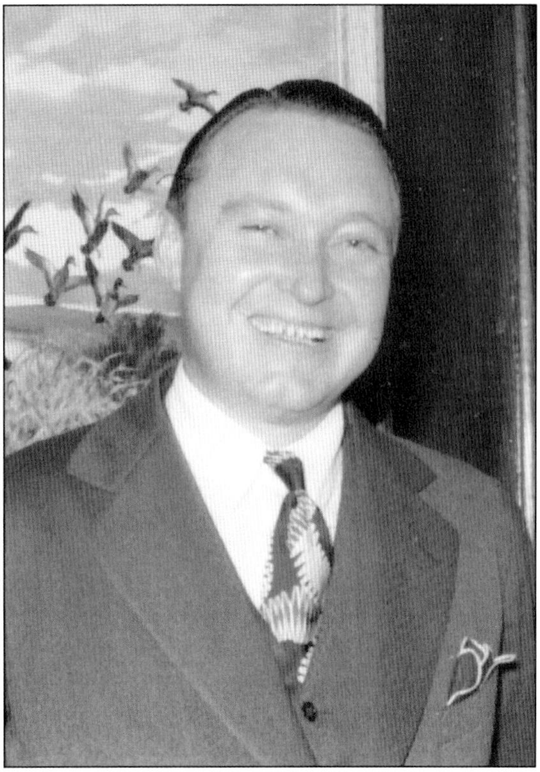

Richard Joshua "Dick" Reynolds Jr. (1906–1964). Born in Winston-Salem as the oldest child of Richard Joshua Sr. and Katharine Smith Reynolds, Dick was raised in town and at Reynolda Estate. He worked two summers in one of his father's cigarette factories and then worked as a seaman, nicknamed "Kid Carolina." Dick had many adventures, including winning the transpacific yacht race in 1939 and holding an aviation pilot's license. He was elected mayor of Winston-Salem in 1941 and served for a year. Dick was buried in Switzerland, and his sister Susan was buried in Virginia; both have markers in Salem Cemetery.

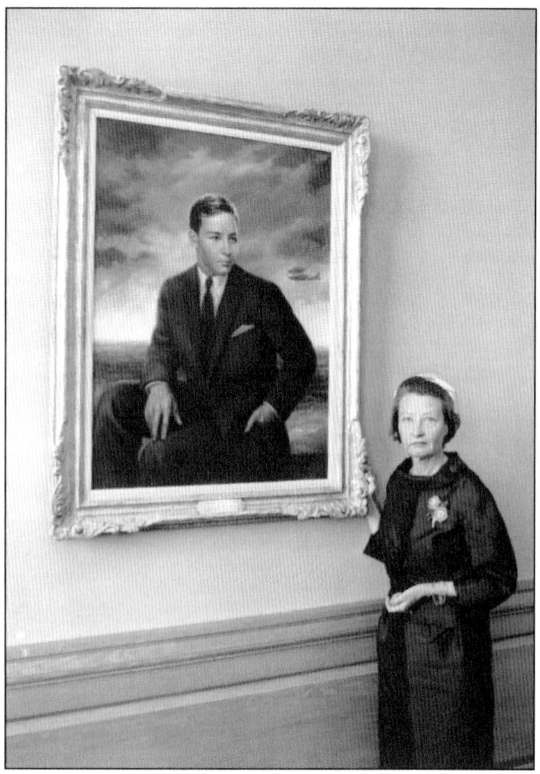

Zachary Smith Reynolds (1911–1932). As the youngest child of Richard Joshua Sr. and Katharine Smith Reynolds, Smith shared older brother Dick's interest in aviation and bought an airplane, which he planned to fly around the world. He was married twice and died under mysterious circumstances at Reynolda when he was 21 years old. The Z. Smith Reynolds Foundation was established with funds that he inherited from his parents. The Z. Smith Reynolds Airport and terminal building bear his name, as does the Wake Forest University Library. Smith's sister Nancy Susan Reynolds unveiled Joe King's portrait of Smith at the library in 1964.

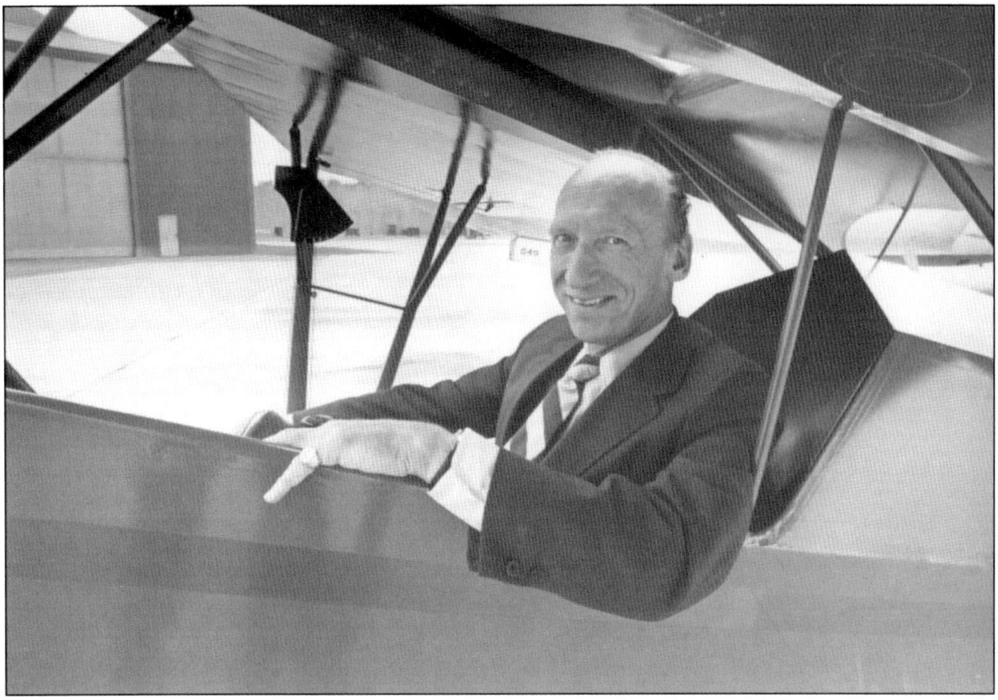

THOMAS HENRY "TOM" DAVIS (1918–1999). Tom Davis loved airplanes and flying as a young man. He developed his early passion into the respected and profitable Piedmont Airlines, established as Piedmont Aviation in 1940 in Winston-Salem. The company grew as more flights and airplanes were added to the business. Piedmont Airlines' maiden voyage was in 1948. The company was purchased by USAir Group in 1987. Tom was married to Nancy Teague Davis (1921–1985).

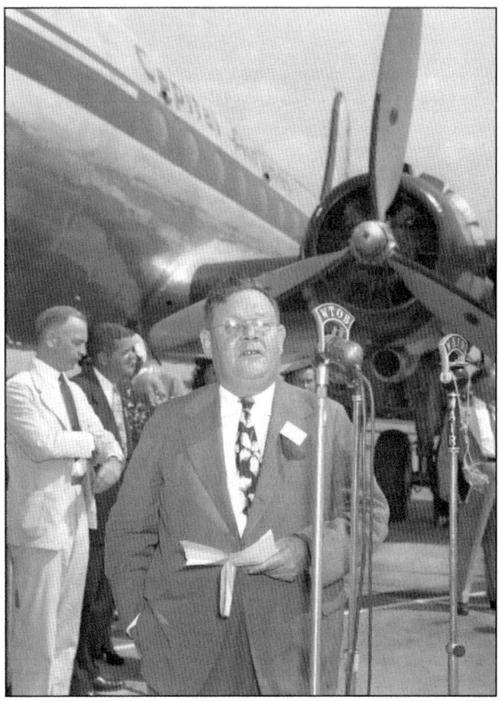

CHARLES EDWARD "CHARLIE" NORFLEET (1902–1973). Charlie (pictured at the microphone) was born in Winston-Salem to James Kirkpatrick Norfleet (1870–1930) and Nannie Walker Norfleet (1871–1930). He worked for Wachovia Bank and Trust Company, retiring as vice president. Charlie served as secretary of the Winston-Salem Foundation for almost 20 years, and he was instrumental in developing the fairgrounds and the Memorial Coliseum. He was credited with building Smith Reynolds Airport and championing aviation in Winston-Salem. Charlie served on the Airport Commission for 26 years, resigning in 1955. Norfleet Drive at the airport was named in his honor. Charlie married Katy Norwood (1905–1976) in 1933.

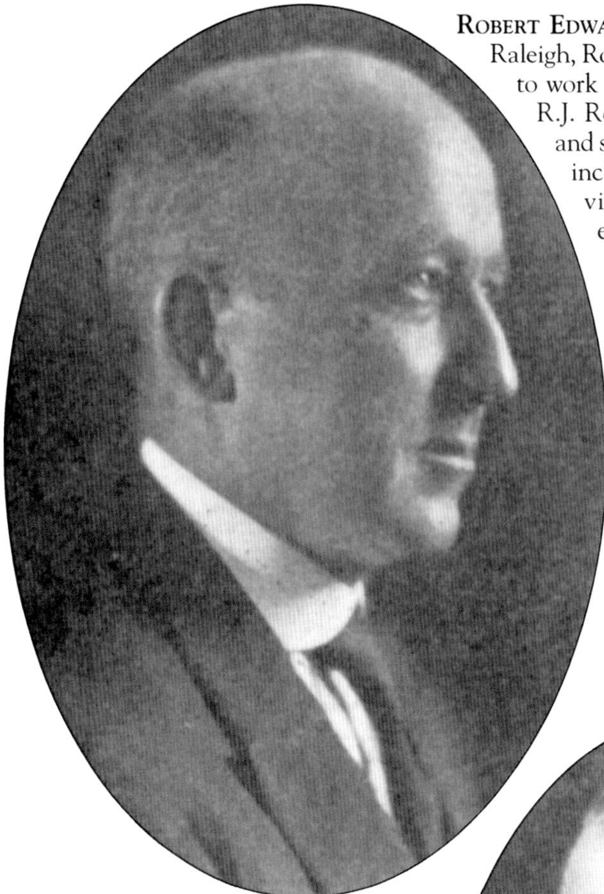

ROBERT EDWARD LASATER (1867–1954). Born in Raleigh, Robert came to Winston-Salem in 1889 to work for P.H. Hanes Company. He joined R.J. Reynolds Tobacco Company in 1891 and served the company in many positions, including director, factory superintendent, vice president, and as a member of the executive committee. Robert married Nancy Lybrook (1877–1952) in 1901. He financed the transformation of Miller Field into an airport. Camp Lasater was named for him when he gave land for a Boy Scout camp. His Forest Hills Farm on the Yadkin River featured a waterwheel at the mill, where cornmeal was ground.

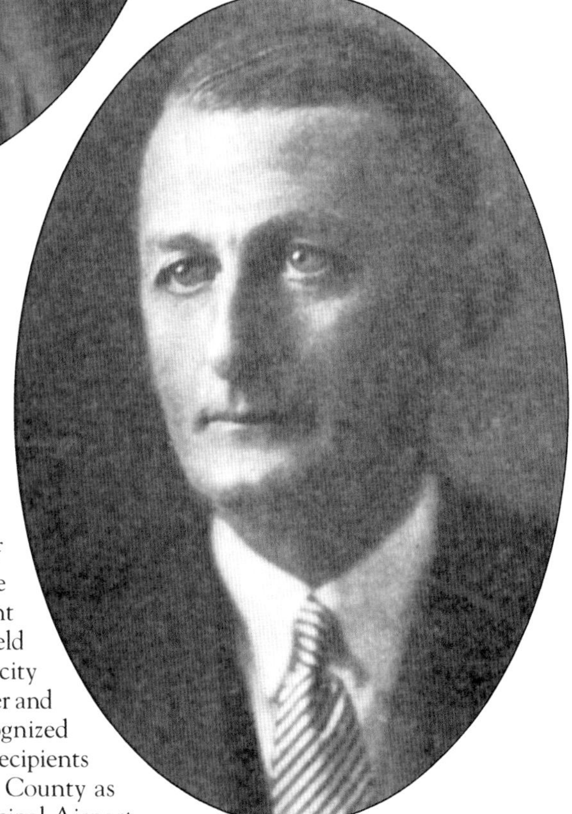

ALEXANDER CLINTON "CLINT" MILLER (1879–1948). Born in Oklahoma to Frank Miller (1836–1919) and Ida Wharton Miller (1850–1908), Clint came to Winston-Salem as a child. He was a banker, a businessman, and one of the city's most generous benefactors. He contributed funds to purchase equipment for the landing field that became Miller Field in 1927. He gave land in Ardmore for a city park, named Miller Park in his honor. Miller and Robert Lasater (profiled above) were recognized in 1928 as Distinguished Service Award recipients for their outstanding service to Forsyth County as promoters and financiers of Miller Municipal Airport.

Armon Burne Banner Jr. (1921–1944). Aviation cadet and Tennessee native Armon Banner was the son of Armon B. Banner Sr. (1895–1985) and Peggy Cora Collis Banner Huber (1897–1993). He graduated from Gray High School, attended Draughon's Business School, and worked for Motor Transit Company. He married Anna Rea McDonald in 1941, entered military service in 1942, and received preliminary flight training at Chickasha, Oklahoma. During his last basic training flight in 1944, he crashed and was killed at Coffeyville, Kansas. His 44-F US Army Air Forces classmates honored Armon with a monument, inscribed with the words, "The Soul immortal lifts its wings—to never ending day." (MGR.)

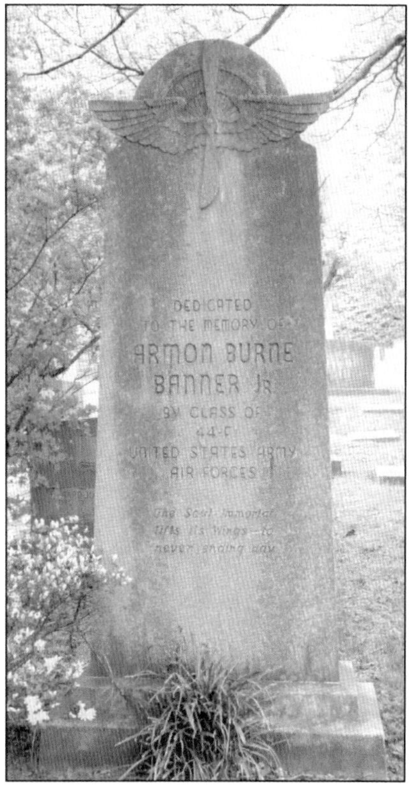

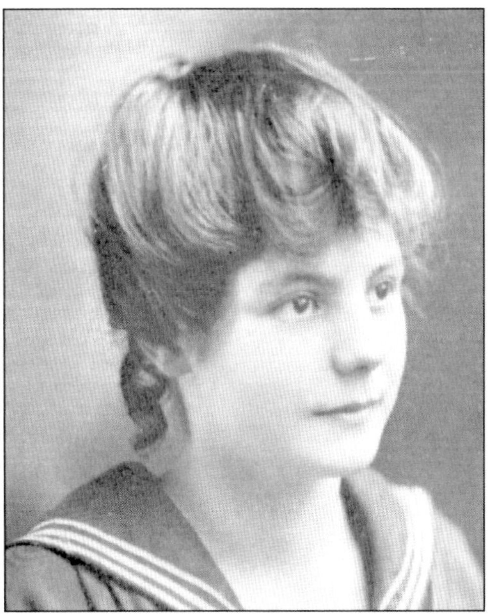

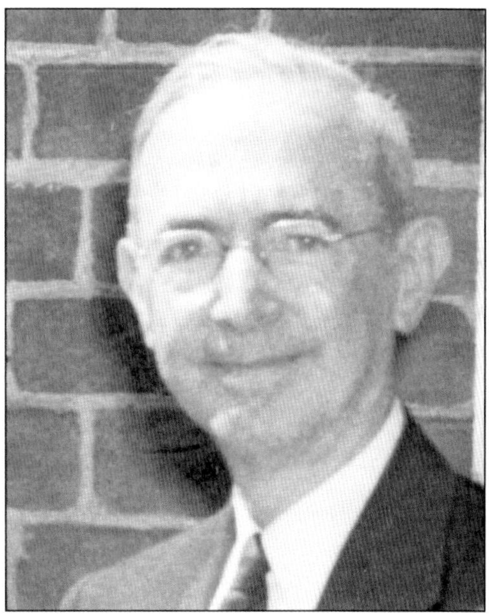

Louise Henley Vogler (1900–1993) and Herbert Augustus Vogler (1888–1980). Louise, photographed as a schoolgirl in 1917, was the first Winston-Salem girl to take a ride in an airplane. She flew with Lieutenant Merrill in 1919 from Maynard Field for a joy ride. In 1923, Louise married Herbert Vogler, who worked for Wachovia Bank and Trust Company for 44 years. Louise and Herbert were active members of Home Moravian Church.

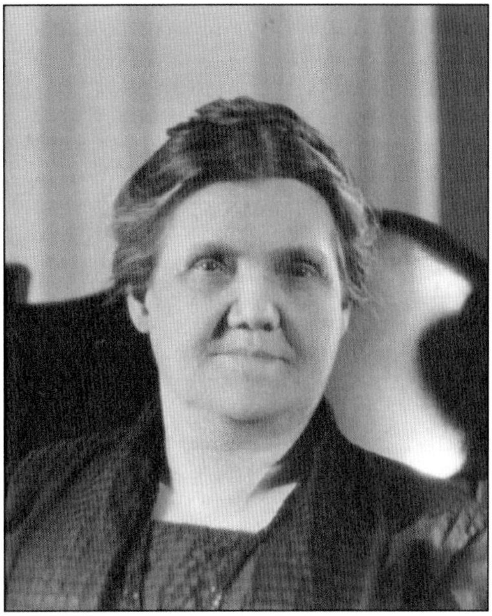 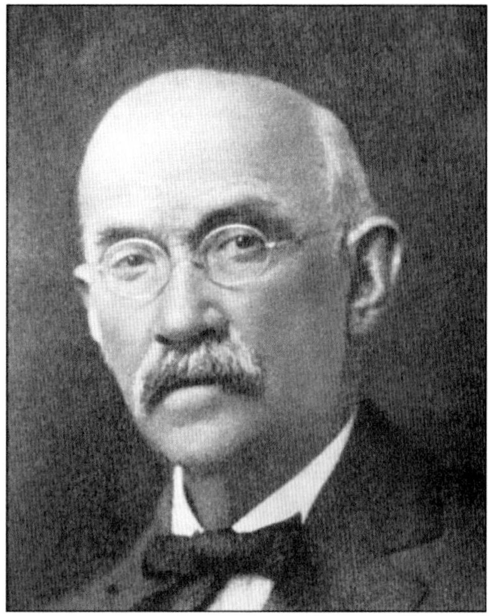

Augusta Miller Poindexter (1850–1930) and Henry Dalton Poindexter (1849–1922) and Family. Originally from Yadkin County, Henry opened a mercantile store shortly after he came to Forsyth County. He and Augusta moved into a small house on Spruce Street in 1874. Henry later built a 19-room home for his growing family (nine children in all) next door, on the corner of Spruce and Fifth Streets. In 1893, his new home was surrounded by forests, but gradually, other homes and businesses were built, and First Baptist Church was constructed across the street. His mercantile store, located on Trade Street, carried a variety of goods and operated until 1910. Three of their daughters are pictured below: Ruth (1889–1977), Catherine "Kate" (1880–1967), and Polly (1898–1977) Poindexter. The house was later moved to a lot on West End Boulevard.

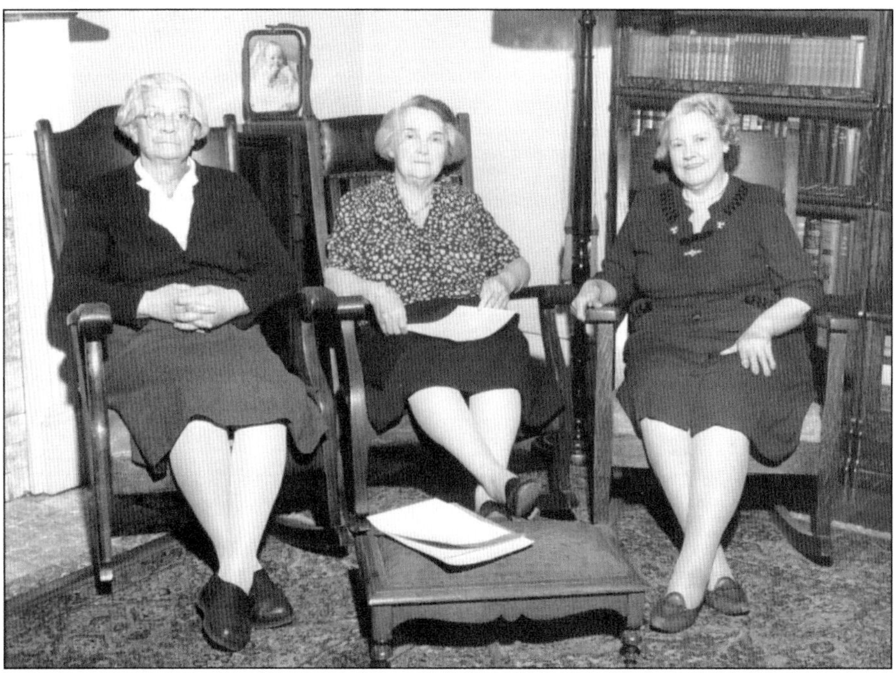

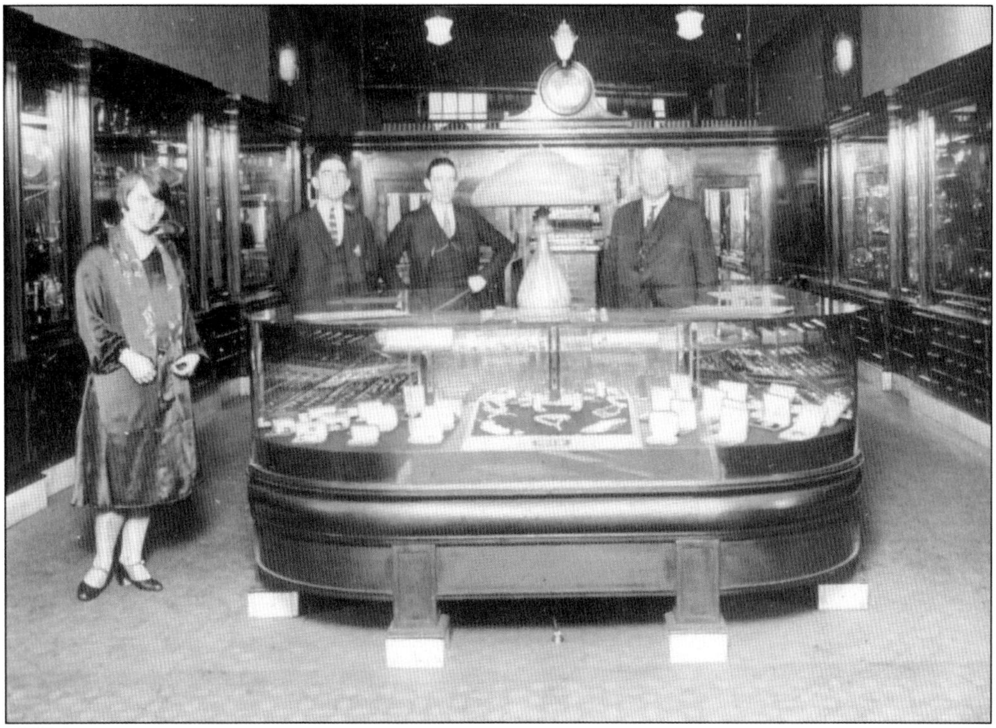

Rev. Frederick Newton "Fred" Day (1864–1949). Fred was born in Berea and started his jewelry business in Winston-Salem in 1893. His jewelry store, located at 428 North Trade Street, is pictured, with Fred at far right. He was known as the "jeweler-evangelist," for his career and evangelistic work as an ordained Baptist minister. Fred was married first to Mary Isabella Hunt (1871–1934) and secondly to Stella Banister Day (1889–1966).

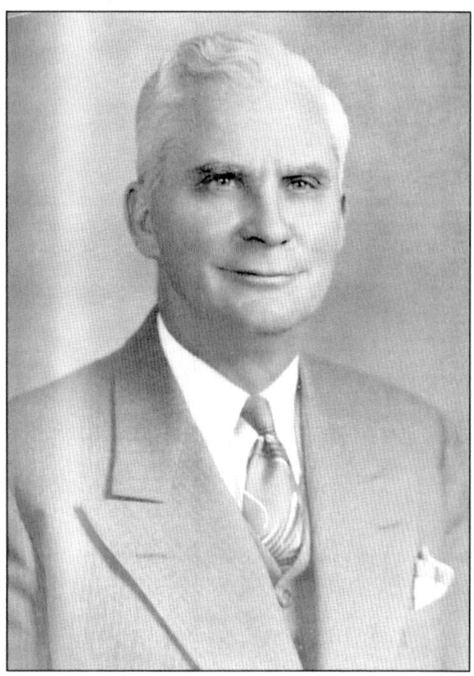

Alvis Thad Lewallen Sr. (1888–1945). A native of Asheboro, Thad came to Winston-Salem in 1919, after serving with the Pioneer Infantry during World War I. He and Paul Bennett organized the Bennett-Lewallen Company. Around 1935, he organized Goody's Limited to manufacture a headache powder known as Goody's. Thad was active in the American Legion and was commander of the Clyde Bolling Post No. 55. Thad married Nellie Shippey Lewallen (1897–1979), and they were the parents of Alvis Thad Lewallen Jr. (1924–1964), husband of Mary Louise Westbrook Lewallen (1928–1964).

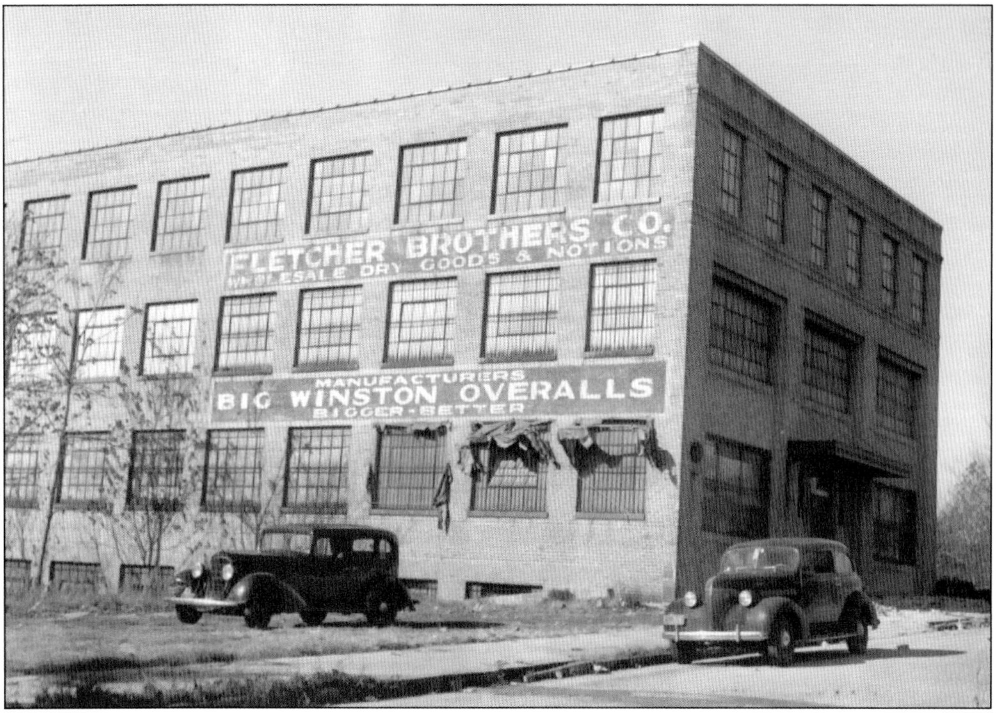

JOSEPH REID FLETCHER SR. (1866–1935). Joseph, son of John F. Fletcher (1842–1907) and Nancy Brann Fletcher (1841–1934), was born in Yadkin County. He worked for P.H. Hanes Tobacco Company before he organized Fletcher Brothers, a retail clothing store that eventually became a wholesale dry goods business (pictured). His partners were his brothers Newton Gwyn (1867–1925), John Henry (1872–1932), and Thomas L. Fletcher (1874–1905). Joseph married Katherine Broughton (1877–1978).

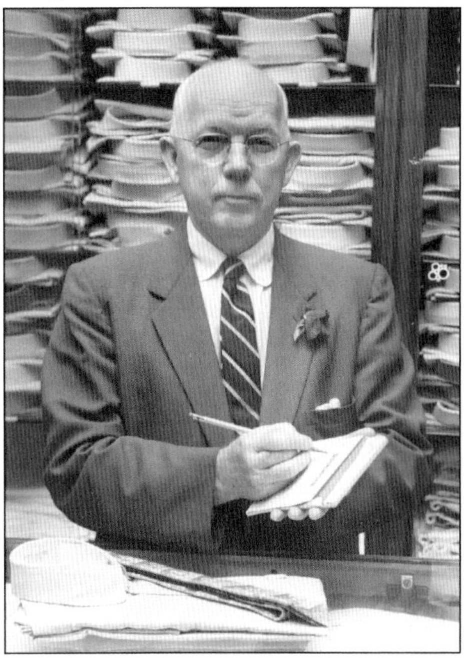

FRANK ADNA STITH SR. (1884–1964). The son of Julius B. Stith (1851–1925) and Octavia Wilson Stith (1855–1896), Frank first worked in the tobacco business and then changed his focus to the clothing industry. He worked for several merchants before establishing his own clothing business, Frank A. Stith Company, around 1900. He constructed a store in the Chatham Building at Fourth and Cherry Streets in 1931. Frank was married to Viola Doub Stith (1885–1964).

Ella Eugenia Griffin (1864–1889). Ella was born to Robert Dalton Griffin (1841–1926) and Martha Jane Hennis Griffin (1833–1911). Robert served in the Civil War and was a member of the 22nd Regiment of the North Carolina Troops Company H. He was captured near the end of the war and imprisoned in New York. Robert moved to Forsyth County from Stokes County in 1882 and worked in the leaf tobacco business. Ella worked as a dressmaker, and she and her family were active in the Broad Street Baptist Church. Ella contracted typhoid fever and passed away just one day short of her 25th birthday.

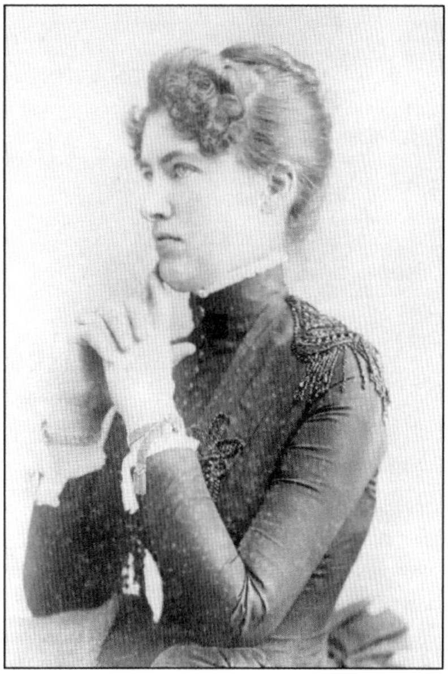

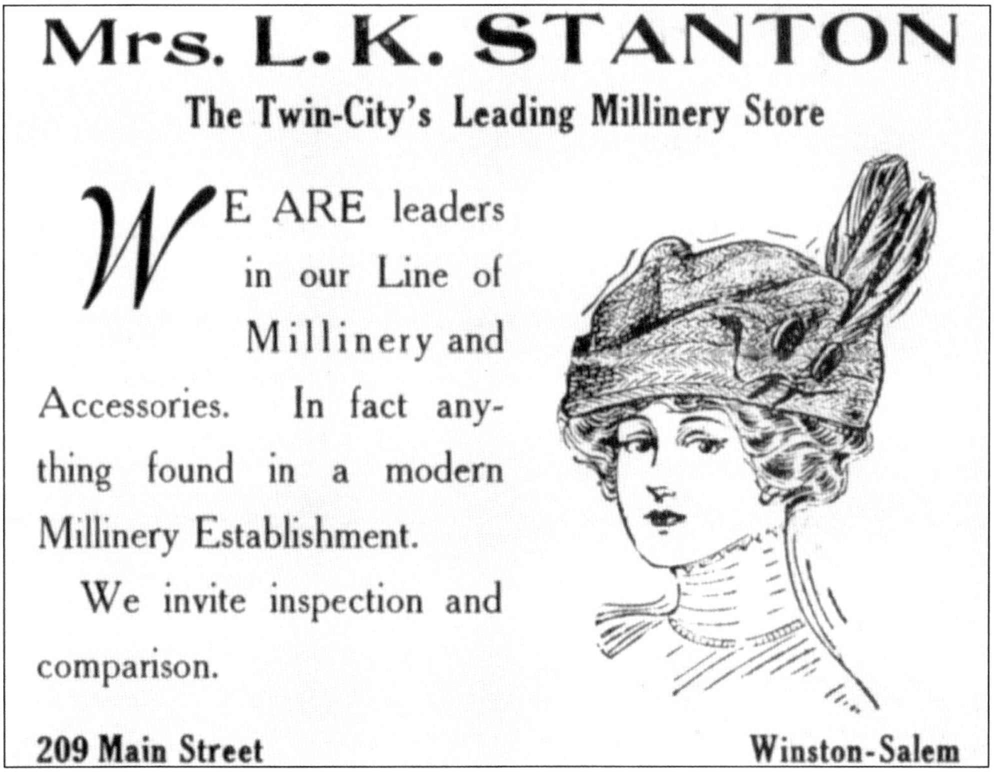

Louisa Kirkman Stanton (1853–1947). Louisa, born in Guilford County, was married in 1884 to Julius Porgan Stanton (1853–1944). She operated a millinery business at 209 North Main Street, which she inherited from her sister Mattie Kirkman Reed (1849–1880), wife of John W. Reed (1842–1914). Louisa's shop featured the very latest styles and accessories, including feathers, ribbons, and mourning veils, which she purchased in New York City during her semiannual shopping excursions.

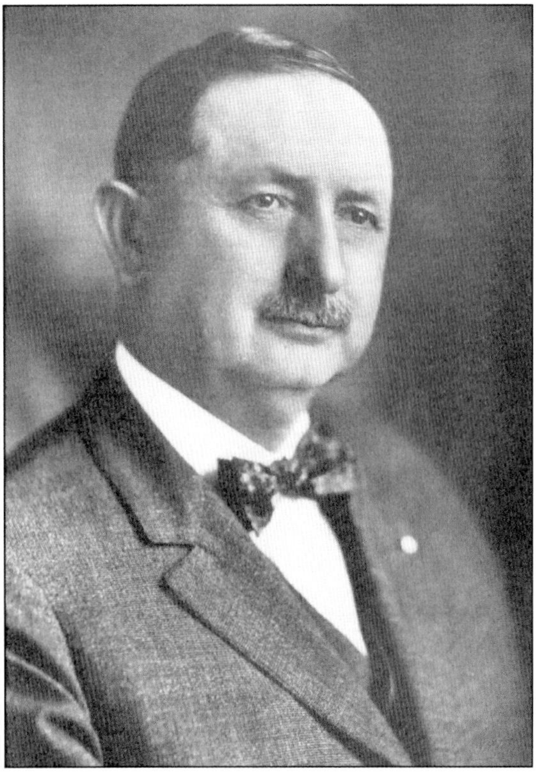

Benjamin Franklin Huntley (1862–1925). Benjamin was born in Union County, where he grew up during the Reconstruction period. He came to Winston-Salem, worked as a traveling salesman for High Point Furniture Company, and then he organized this furniture company in Winston-Salem. In 1900, he founded the Huntley-Hill-Stockton Furniture Company and expanded the business into Greensboro in 1904. He formed the Oakland Furniture Manufacturing Company in 1906, which later became B.F. Huntley Furniture Company. Benjamin was an alderman and the first president of the local Kiwanis Club. He married first Eliza F. (1867–1892) and secondly Josephine Leona "Josie" Myers (1876–1947).

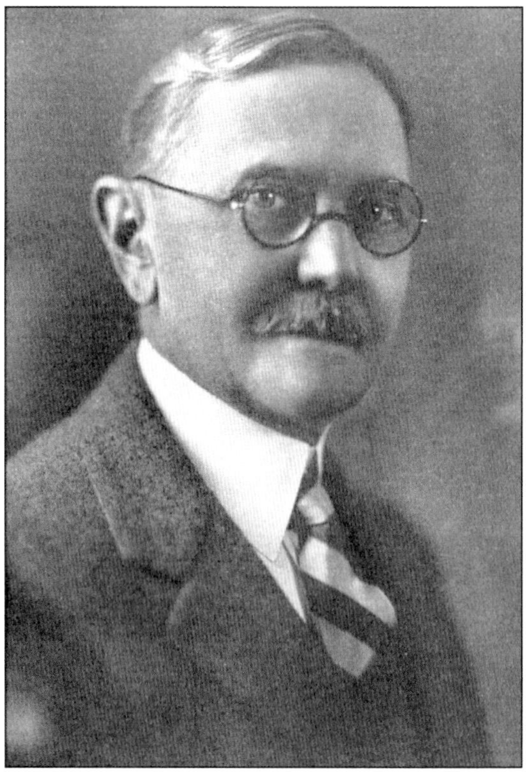

Madison Doughty Stockton (1861–1944). Madison was born in Kernersville to John Branch Stockton (1819–1884) and Martha Madison McGehee Stockton (1825–1891). He moved to Winston-Salem in 1869 and attended school at Winston Academy. He worked as a bookkeeper in the register of deeds office and then he worked in the office of P.H. Hanes Tobacco Company. He became president and treasurer of the Huntley-Hill-Stockton Furniture Company and then helped organize the B.F. Huntley Company, where he served as secretary and treasurer. Madison married Martha Vaughn (1865–1942), daughter of Jerome B. Vaughn (c. 1815–1889) and Nancy Leake Vaughn (c. 1823–1881).

Norman Vaughn Stockton (1889–1972). Norman was born in Winston-Salem to Madison D. and Martha Stockton. He graduated from Winston High School and the University of North Carolina. He purchased an interest in a clothing store that was renamed the Mock-Bagby-Stockton Company. Mock dropped out of the business, and Norman purchased Bagby's interest, so the store became Norman Stockton Inc. It was located on Trade Street until it moved to Cherry Street. A branch location opened in the Thruway Shopping Center and another at Hanes Mall. The business relocated to a new building on Stratford Road in 1985, closed in 2010, and reopened in 2015. Norman married Emorie Barber (1890–1972), daughter of Thomas Barber and Maybelle Gray Barber.

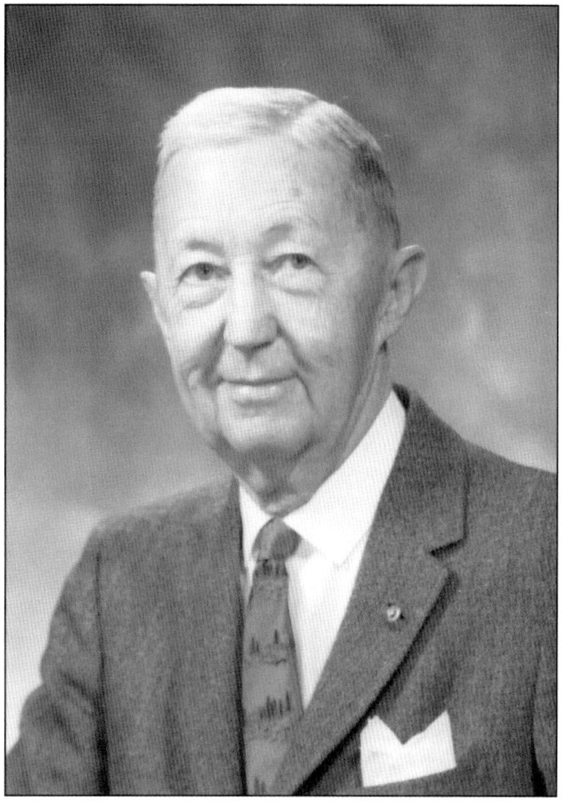

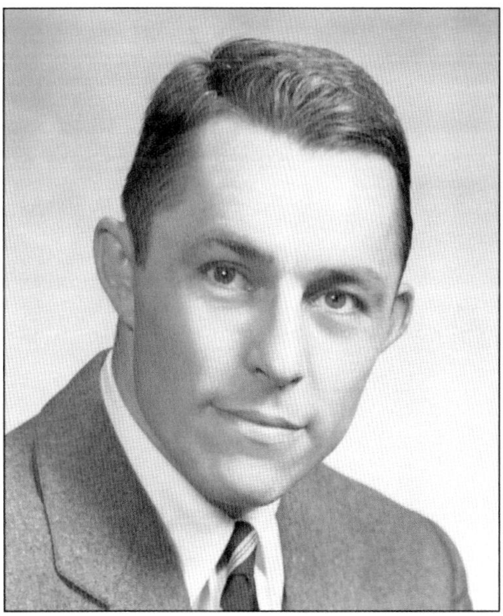

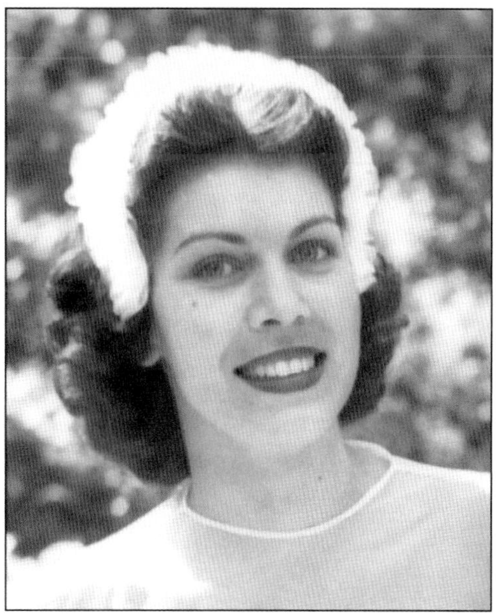

Robert Gray Stockton Sr. (1923–2006) and Edmonia "Monie" Rowland Stockton (1930–2002). Monie Rowland was a graduate of Salem College, where she was May Queen in 1952 (pictured). She married Robert Stockton, son of Norman and Emorie Stockton. Robert was honored with the Air Medal in 1945 for distinguished service in World War II. He was a partner in the Kilpatrick & Stockton law firm and was active in the American Red Cross.

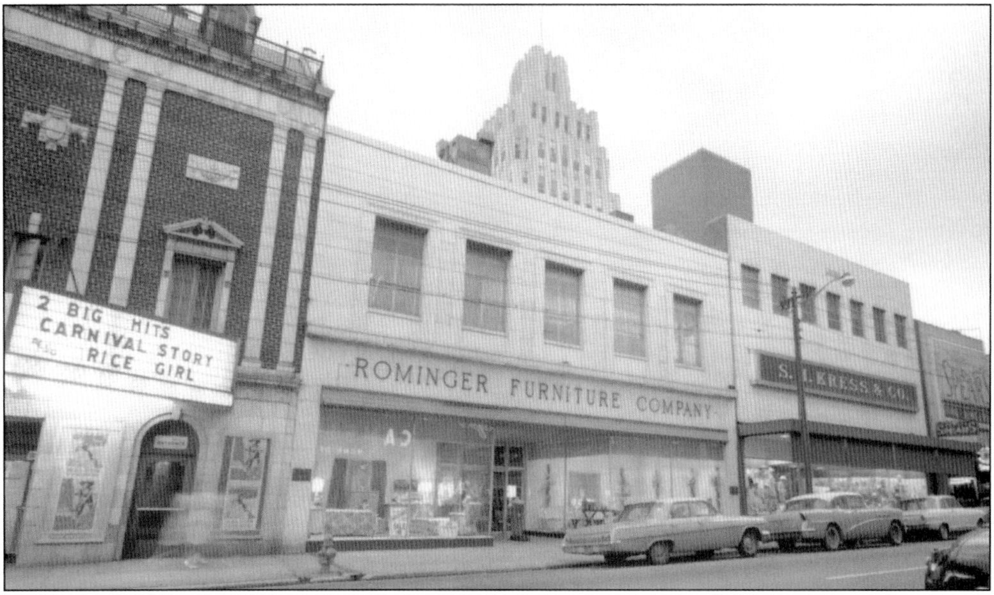

ROMINGER-CUNNINGHAM FAMILIES. Charles Danforth Rominger (1860–1949) was born in the young town of Winston and founded the Rominger Furniture Company in 1900. The business had several early locations before it moved to 423 North Liberty Street (pictured in 1963). Charles married Sallie Wiles (1872–1949) in 1906. Their second store, Southern Furniture Company, opened in 1927 at North Liberty and Twelfth Streets. John Wilson Cunningham (1904–1996) married Elizabeth Rominger (1907–1986), daughter of Charles and Sallie, in 1930. Wilson and Elizabeth are pictured below. Wilson became president of the business in 1946, and Elizabeth was chairman after her father's death. The downtown store closed in 1986, and the operations were consolidated at the renamed store, Rominger Southern Furniture Company. Sally Bet Cunningham Nevius, granddaughter of the founder, is at the helm of the oldest family-owned furniture company in Winston-Salem.

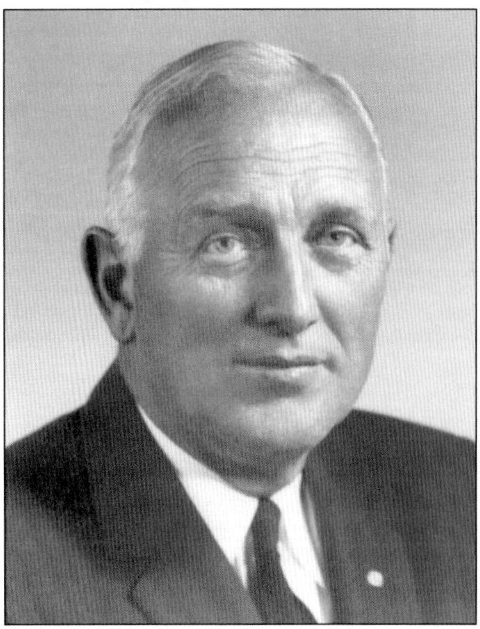

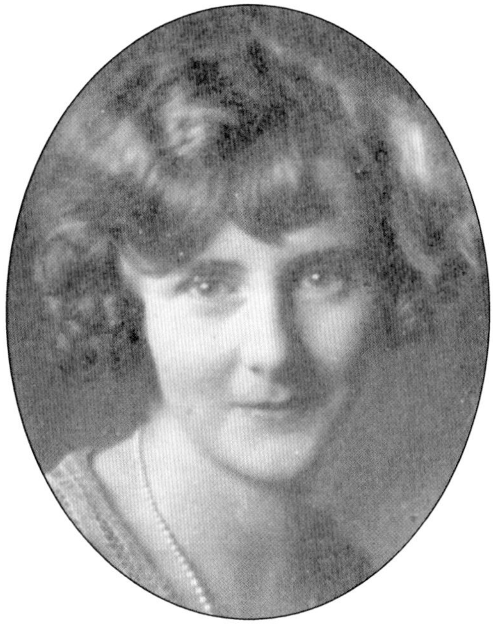

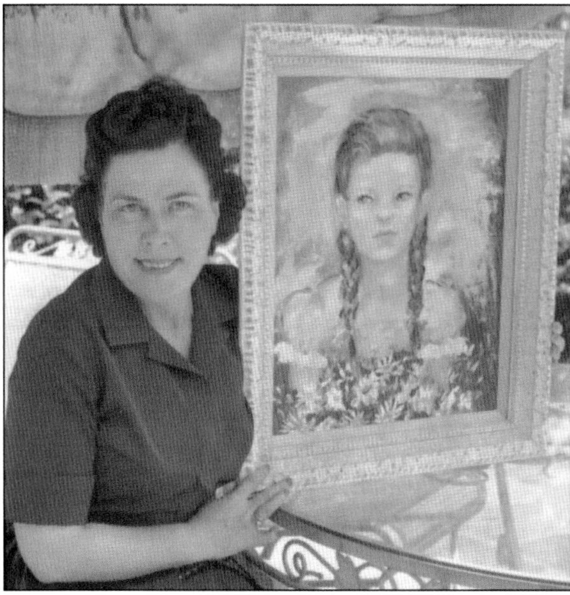

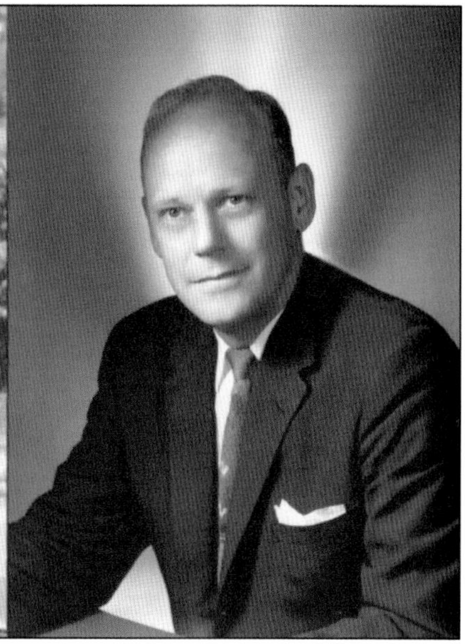

ELEANOR LAYFIELD DAVIS (1911–1985) AND EGBERT LAWRENCE DAVIS JR. (1911–2006). Virginia-native Eleanor was a scenic painter and founder of the Associated Artists of Winston-Salem. Born in Yadkin County, Egbert worked for family-held Atlas Supply Company, serving as president for 37 years. He established scholarships at Wake Forest and Meredith Colleges, helped fund the Davis Memorial Chapel at Baptist Hospital in honor of his parents, and began the Davis family reunion.

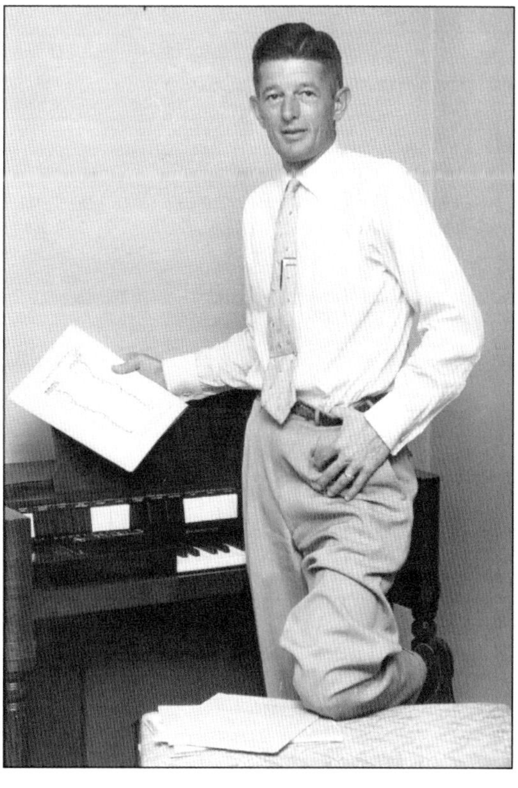

CLIFFORD WEBSTER "CLIFF" PERRY SR. (1915–1983). Cliff was born in Winston-Salem to Frank Wilson Perry (1887–1973) and Elizabeth Fetter Perry (1889–1955). He graduated from R.J. Reynolds High School and Duke University and spent his entire working career with the Hanes textile organization. His area of expertise was finance, and he became secretary, director, treasurer, and senior vice president at Hanes Hosiery. Cliff served on the school board and helped with the merger of the county and city schools. He married Annie Pauline "Pinkie" Davis (1916–2011) in 1941. Cliff played the chord organ, and they both enjoyed traveling and playing golf.

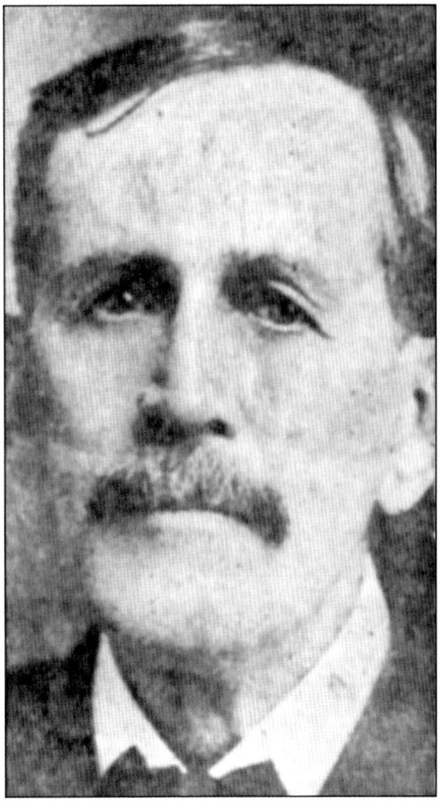

Capt. John Eli Gilmer (1842–1916). A native of Guilford County, John Eli lived on his family farm until he left to serve in the Civil War as an officer with the 21st Regiment of the North Carolina Troops. He was wounded at Fredericksburg, which sidelined him for a year, but he returned to serve until 1864. John Eli resided in Greensboro after the war and established a mercantile business, which he relocated to Winston-Salem. He was one of the first men to engage in retail merchandising in the young town of Winston. He married Laura Lash (1842–1893).

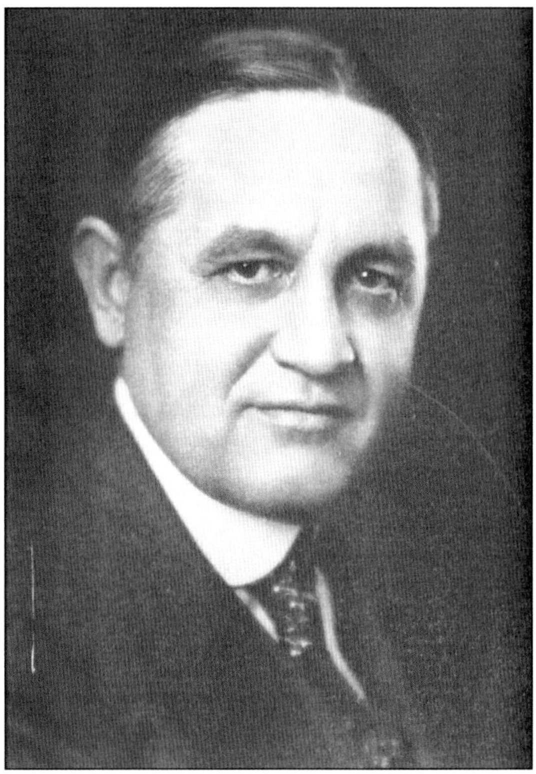

John Lash Gilmer (1872–1947). John Lash, son of John Eli and Laura Lash Gilmer, was born in Walnut Cove. His father turned over his retail business to his sons John Lash and Powell Gilmer (1874–1945) when he retired in 1893. The brothers switched from retail to a wholesale dry goods and notion company called Gilmer Brothers. John opened the first Buick agency in 1907, and the brothers established the Motor Sales Company, a distributor for Chrysler and Plymouth automobiles. In 1926, John organized Camel City Lines, a bus company that later merged with Atlantic Greyhound. He married Emma Rison Jones (1877–1959).

King Solomon Fulk (1878–1958). Fulk was born in Surry County and came to Winston-Salem in 1901. He married Elizabeth Ann "Eliza" Ashburn (1873–1946) in 1897. In 1913, he was the proprietor of Fulk's Bowling Parlor, located at 501 North Liberty Street, across from the post office. Fulk's advertisement touts the bowling parlor as "the best equipped and most modern parlor south of Washington. Bowling [is] the only athletic game exercising every muscle in the body, at the same time." Fulk was reported to have founded the city bus line around 1923, which he later sold. He was also an independent realtor.

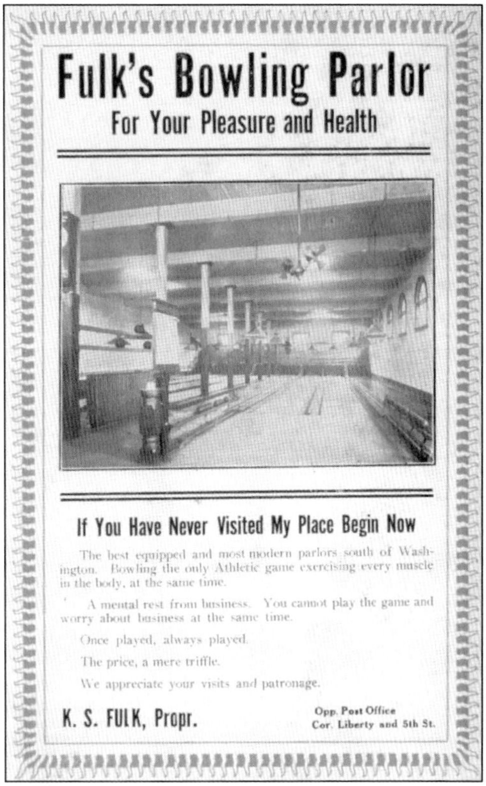

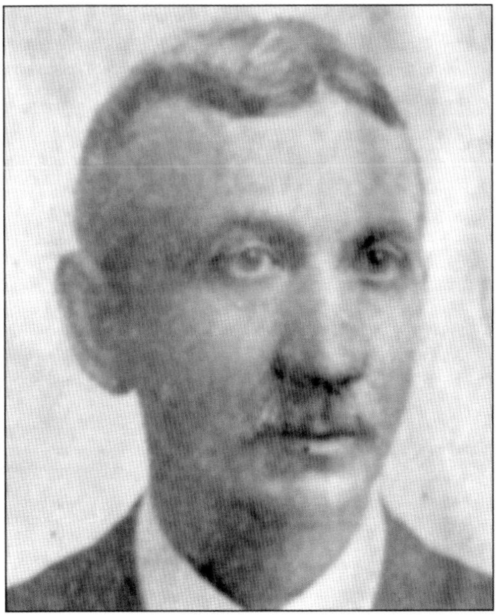

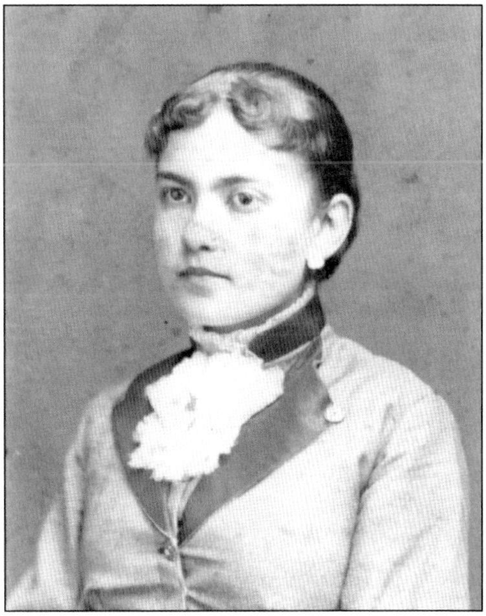

Capt. William L. Stagg (1858–1927) and Sallie Hay Stagg (1862–1948). William was born in Durham and came to Winston-Salem in 1881. He worked for the Danville & Southern Railway and the Southern Railway for 50 years as a conductor. Sallie was the daughter of Dr. Randall Duke Hay (1827–1885) and Sarah Ruth Penn Hay (1829–1890). William and Sallie were the parents of Frank Asbury Stagg (1886–1963), husband of Lena Brewer Stagg (1889–1977).

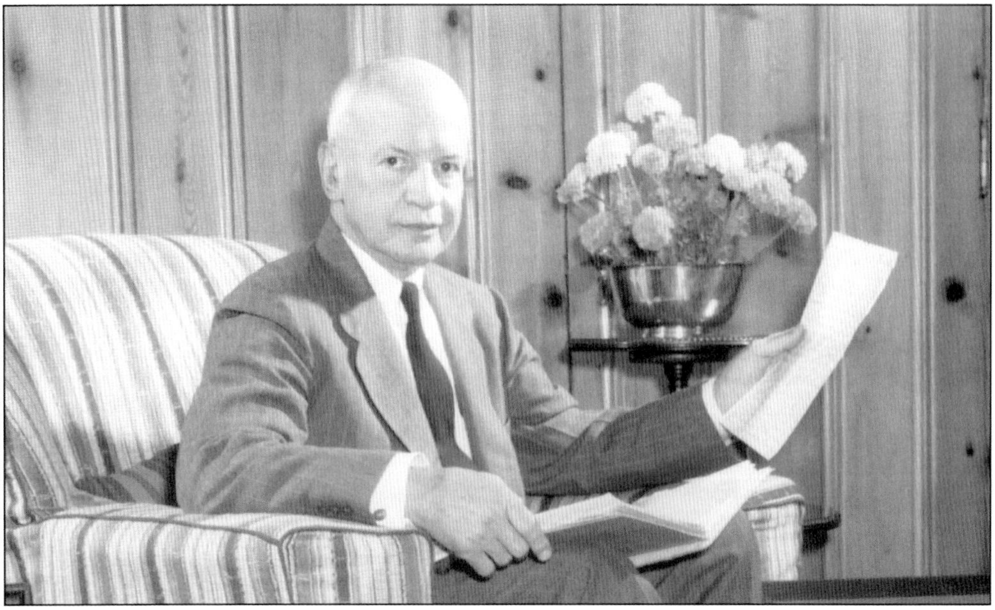

HIRAM SEDGWICK CODY SR. (1888–1971). Hiram, born in Chicago, was the third cousin, twice removed, of the famous William F. (Buffalo Bill) Cody. Hiram opened Cody Realty and Mortgage Company in Winston-Salem in 1933 and was president of the company until he retired in 1962. He was active in real estate, appraisal, and civic organizations. Hiram was first married to Harriet Mary Collins (1887–1944) and secondly to Ann Van Dorsten.

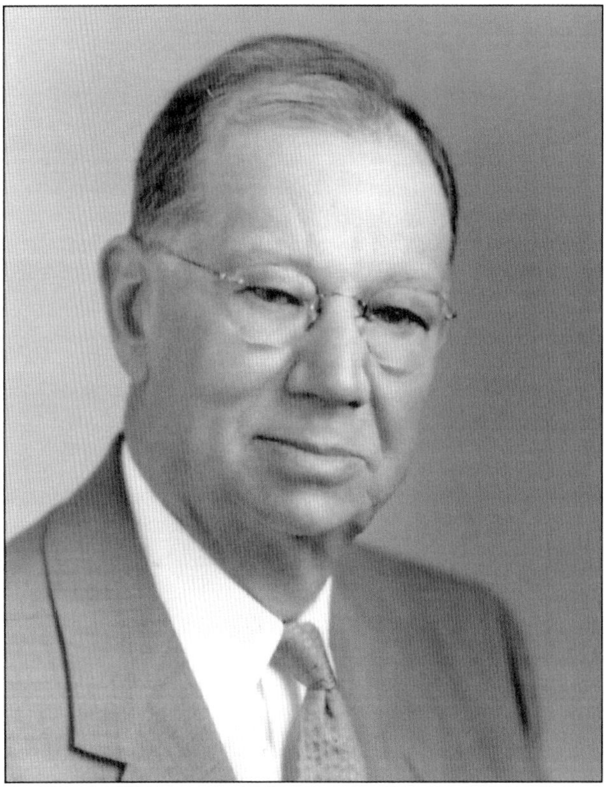

WALTER GRAY JEROME SR. (1887–1967). Born in Bladen County, Walter taught mathematics and was a high school coach in Winston-Salem. He entered the real estate business in 1911 and helped develop the Ardmore and West End neighborhoods and Roaring Gap. Walter served two terms as president of the Winston-Salem Board of Realtors, was president of the North Carolina Board of Realtors, and was an alderman. He joined the Federal Housing Administration and was made chief underwriter in 1957. He was married to Elizabeth Pollard (1892–1996). Their daughter Elizabeth Jerome Holder (1914–2009) was the first baby born in Ardmore, and Elizabeth Avenue was named for her.

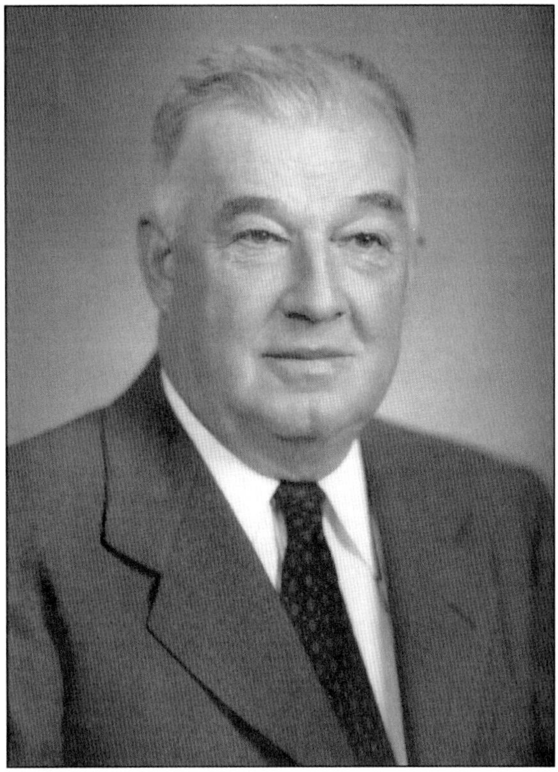

Frank L. Blum (1891–1954). Frank was born in Winston-Salem to Dr. James Alfred Blum (1846–1917) and Sarah Elizabeth "Lizzie" Wilson Blum (1851–1909). Frank held several engineering jobs as a teenager and during the World War I period. He returned to Winston-Salem in 1922 to help build R.J. Reynolds High School and established Frank L. Blum & Company in 1923. The list of structures erected by his company (renamed Frank L. Blum Construction Company), both past and present, is extensive and includes many businesses, public buildings, and houses, plus restoration work in Old Salem. Frank was married to Helen Woolley (1899–1983).

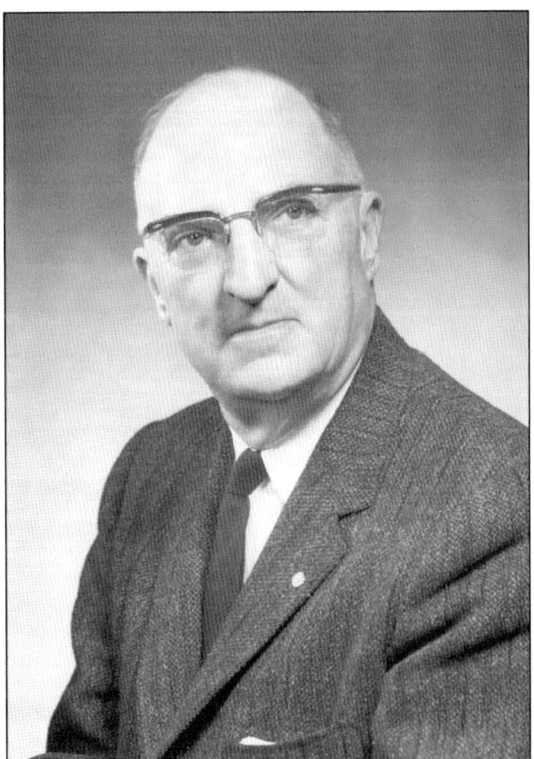

Lawrence Gordon Pfefferkorn (1904–1980). Lawrence was born in Georgia and came to Winston-Salem in 1929 to manage Winston-Salem Bond and Mortgage Company. He became president of the company in 1937 and chairman of the board in 1962. The name of the company was changed to Pfefferkorn Company in 1968. Lawrence was a past president of the Winston-Salem Board of Realtors and held memberships in civic and professional organizations. He was active in the High Rock Lake Association. Lawrence married Eleanor Holmes Franklin (1907–1983) in 1930, the daughter of William Edward Franklin (1865–1933) and Annie Barham Franklin (1869–1939).

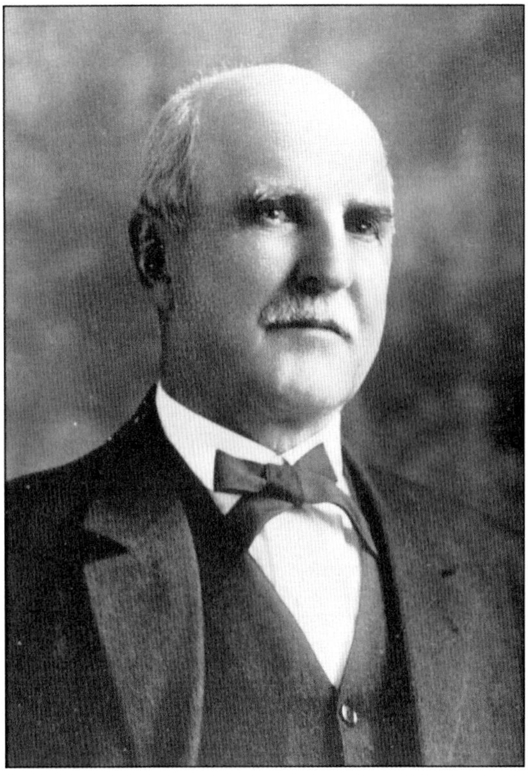

Pleasant Henderson Hanes Sr. (1845–1925). Born in Davie County, Pleasant served in the Civil War before returning to his family farm and becoming a tobacco farmer and salesman. With his brother John Wesley Hanes and Maj. Thomas Jethro Brown, he established P.H. Hanes Tobacco Company, which he sold in 1900. He organized the P.H. Hanes Knitting Mills for the manufacture of two-piece heavyweight underwear, which grew and exists today as Hanesbrands Inc. Pleasant operated a model stock, grain, and tobacco farm, and he donated 50 acres to establish Hanes Park. He married Mary Lizora Fortune (1855–1915) in 1873.

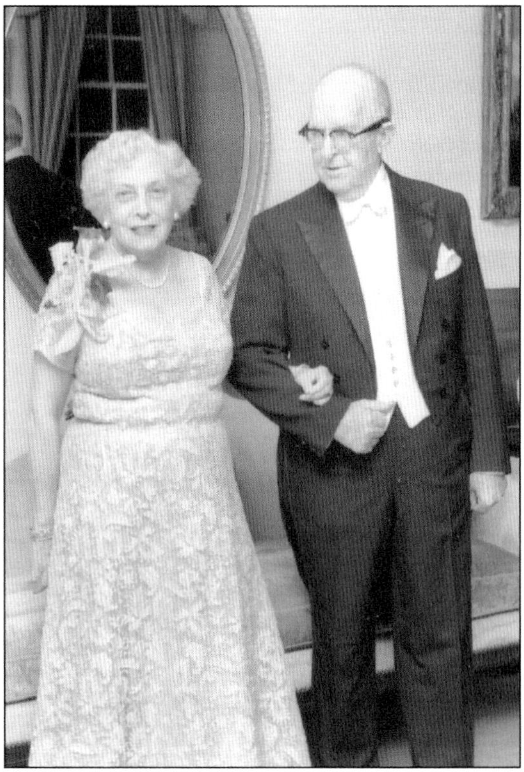

Evelyn Hazen Hanes (1885–1975) and Pleasant Huber Hanes Sr. (1880–1967). Pleasant Huber, son of Pleasant Henderson and Mary Lizora Hanes, attended local public schools and graduated from Trinity College (Duke University) and Eastman Business School. He began work as a cotton mill hand in Fries and Mayodan. He was one of the original partners, with his father and brother, in the P.H. Hanes Knitting Company, where he served as chief executive officer until his retirement in 1956. Pleasant Huber and his wife, Evelyn, are photographed at their 50th wedding anniversary celebration in 1959.

Pleasant Huber Hanes Jr. (1915–1974) and Jane Knox Hopkins Hanes (1917–2009). Pleasant Huber Jr. was the son of Pleasant Huber and Evelyn Hanes. Following in his father's footsteps, he attended Duke University and headed the P.H. Hanes Knitting Company. He was part of the 1965 merger with Hanes Hosiery Mills, which established Hanes Corporation, of which he became president. Health problems necessitated that he reduce his business workload, so he redirected his energies to local government and raising cattle. Land development was his passion, and Hanes Mall is named in his honor. He married Jane Knox Hopkins in 1941.

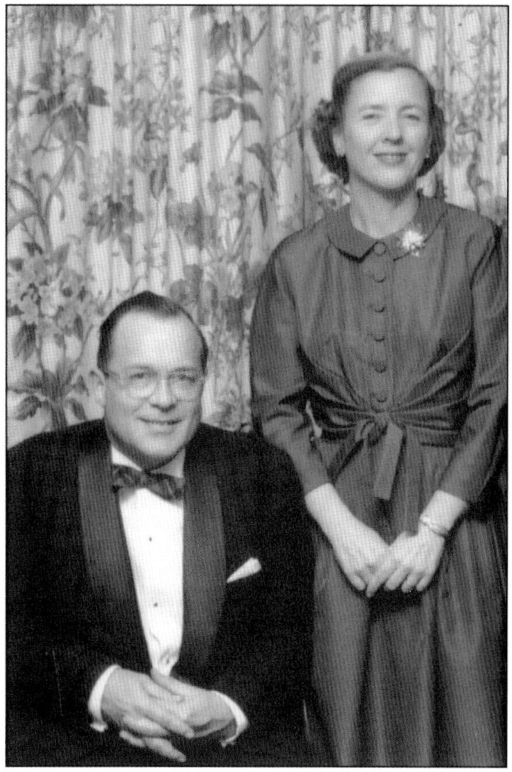

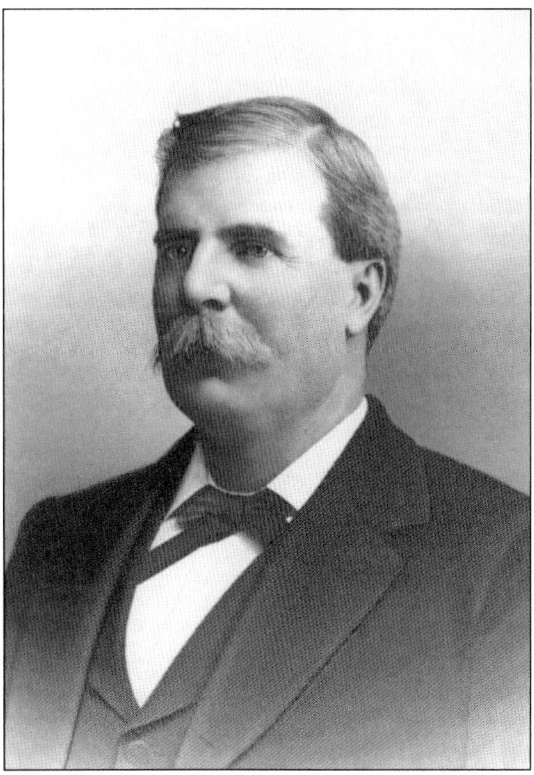

John Wesley Hanes Sr. (1850–1903). John Wesley was the ninth of eleven children born to Alexander Martin and Jane March Hanes in Davie County. He and his brother, Pleasant Henderson Hanes, founded P.H. Hanes Tobacco Company, which they sold in 1900. Having married in 1879 to Anna Jannette Hodgin (1857–1947), daughter of Stephen Henley Hodgin (1827–1904) and Lucy Parthena Moir Hodgin (1832–1879), John Wesley purchased the old Hodgin tobacco plant. He established Shamrock Knitting Mills (later P.H. Hanes Hosiery Mills), producing infants' hose and men's socks. North High School was renamed John Wesley Hanes High School in his honor.

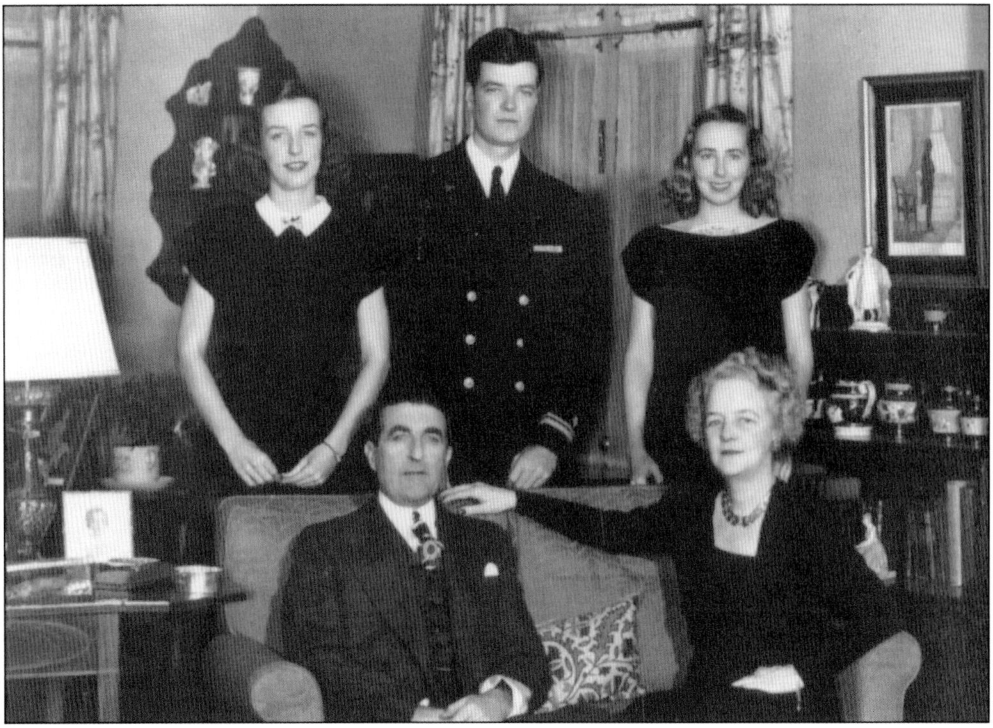

Robert March Hanes (1890–1959) and Family. Born in Winston-Salem to John Wesley and Anna Hanes, Robert joined Wachovia Bank and Trust Company after he served in World War I. During his 25 years as president, Wachovia became the largest bank in the Southeast. In the 1940s photograph above, Robert is seated next to his wife, Mildred Borden Hanes (1891–1971), whom he married in 1917. Standing behind them, from left to right, are daughter Sarah Anne Hanes, who married Meade Willis (see page 86); son Frank Borden Hanes Sr. (1920–2013); and Frank's wife, Barbara Lasater Hanes (1920–1990). The photograph below shows the family in 1958. Frank Borden Hanes worked as a reporter and columnist for local newspapers, published several books, and championed local history. Barbara, known as "Bob-Ed," was a trustee of Old Salem and the first woman director of First Wachovia Corporation.

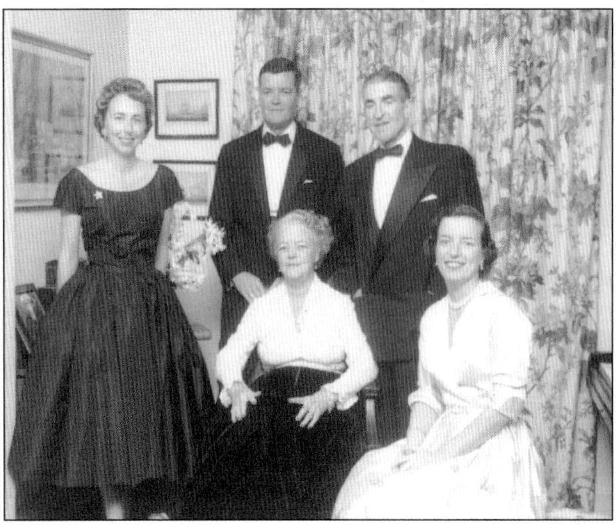

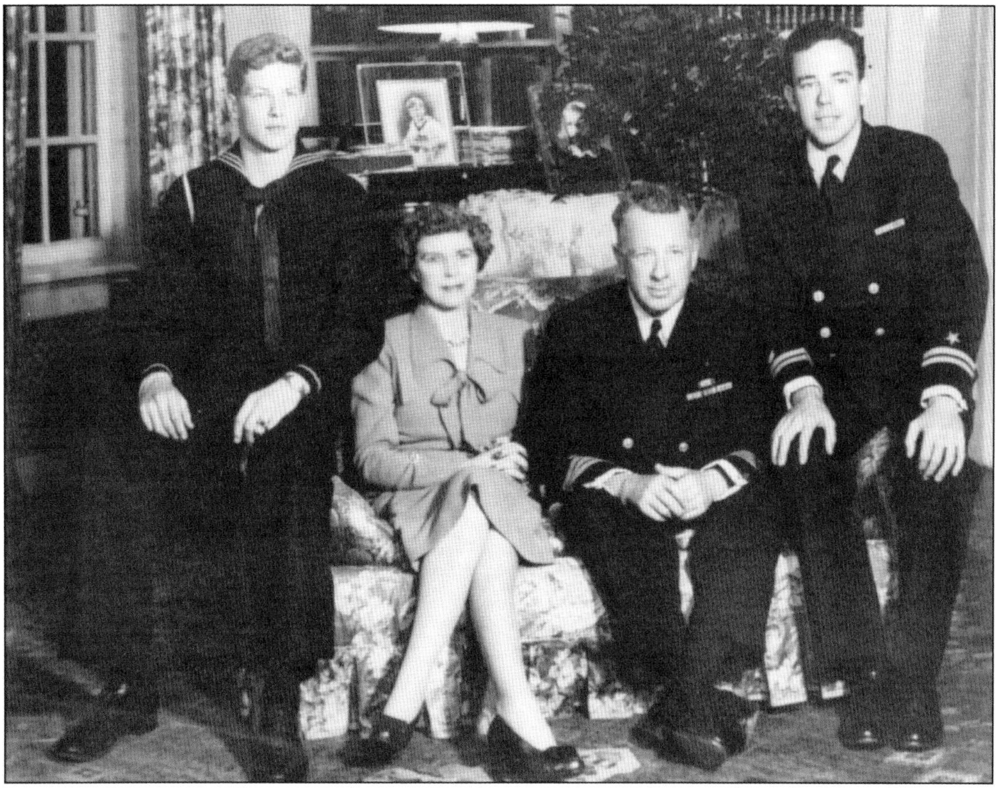

RICHARD THURMOND CHATHAM (1896–1957) AND FAMILY. Thurmond was born in Elkin as the son of Hugh Gwyn and Martha Lenoir Chatham and grandson of Alexander Chatham, founder of Chatham Manufacturing Company. After completing his service in the Navy during World War I, he began his lifelong career with Chatham Manufacturing Company. Thurmond also served with distinction in the Navy during World War II and in the US Congress for four terms (1949–1957). Thurmond first married Lucy Hodgin Hanes (1895–1949), daughter of John Wesley and Anna Hanes, in 1919. The 1940s photograph above shows sons Richard Thurmond Chatham Jr. and Hugh Gwyn Chatham seated on either side of their parents. Thurmond secondly married Patricia Firestone Coyner (1915–1971). The photograph below shows the naval honor guard firing three volleys at Thurmond's gravesite, followed by a Marine Corps bugler playing "Taps."

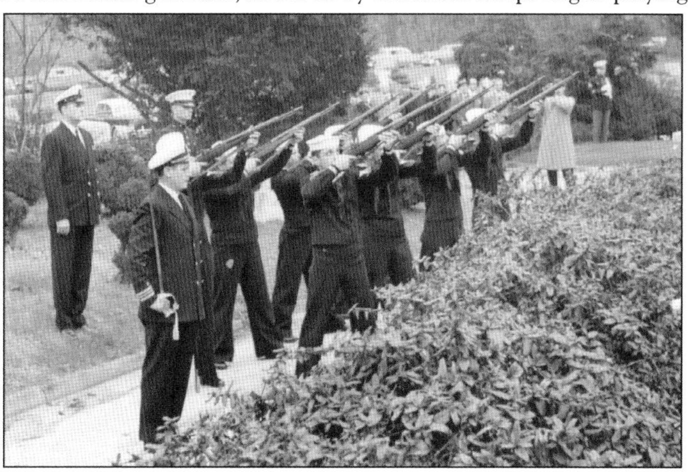

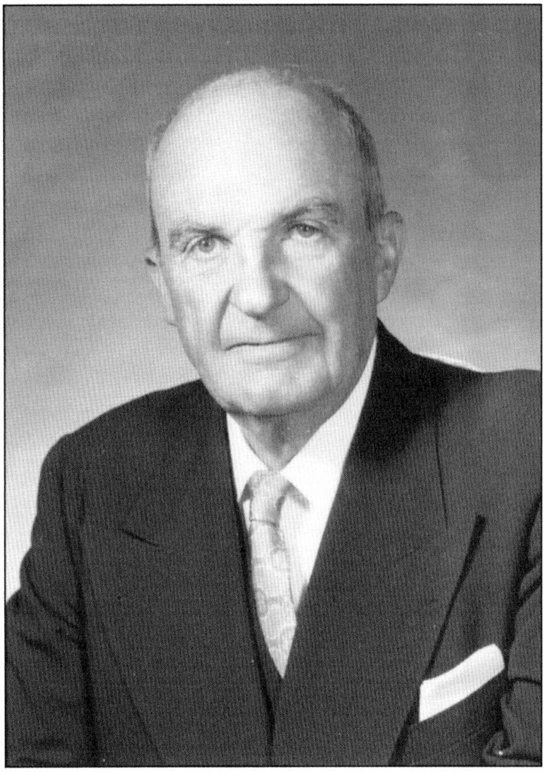

JAMES GORDON HANES SR. (1886–1972). Jim, son of John Wesley and Anna Hanes, began working for his father's business, Shamrock Hosiery Mills, after college. He became president of the renamed Hanes Hosiery Mills and then was elected board chairman in 1938, retiring as chairman emeritus in 1954. Jim was elected an alderman (1917), mayor (1921–1925), and county commissioner (chairman for 22 years). Hanes Community Center was named in his honor. Jim was first married to Emmie Louise Drewry (1889–1916) and secondly to Mary Walton "Mollie" Ruffin (1898–1957). Jim and his five brothers and two brothers-in-law once formed an illustrious and formidable polo team.

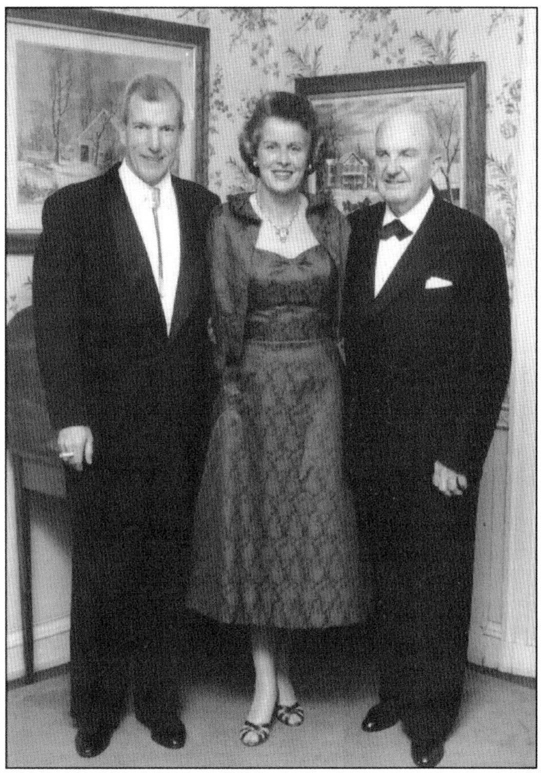

JAMES GORDON HANES JR. (1916–1995) AND FAMILY. Gordon was the son of James Gordon and Emmie Hanes. He joined the family business, Hanes Hosiery Mills, in 1939. After 40 years of service, he retired as chairman and chief executive officer of the Hanes Corporation. He married Helen "Copey" Greever Copenhaver (1917–2013) in 1941. Born in Virginia, Copey came to Winston-Salem to teach voice and drama at Salem Academy and College. Copey was active in the arts community, and both she and Gordon were instrumental in helping establish the University of North Carolina School of the Arts. In this 1958 photograph, from left to right, are Gordon, Copey, and Jim Hanes.

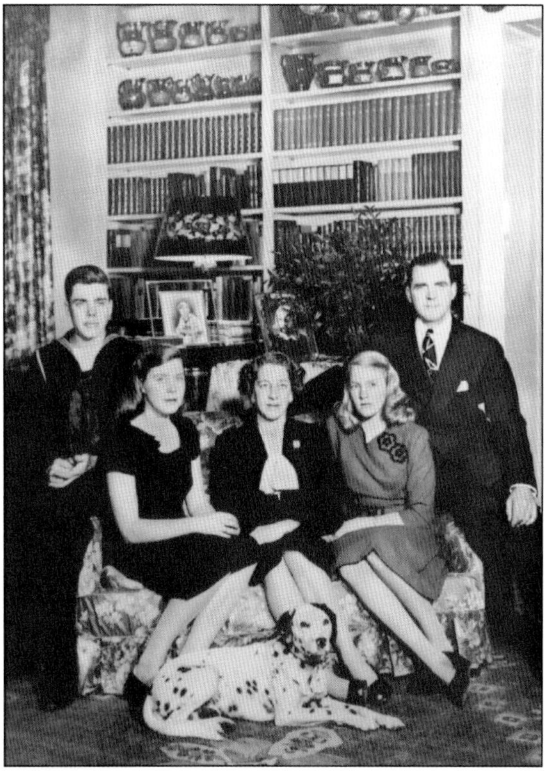

Ralph Philip Hanes Sr. (1898–1973) and Family. Ralph, son of John Wesley and Anna Hanes, married DeWitt Chatham (1899–1990) in 1923. In this 1940s photograph, from left to right, are son Ralph Philip Hanes Jr.; daughter Martha Lenoir, who married Calder Womble; DeWitt; daughter Anna Hodgin (1931–1997), who married Thomas Lenoir Chatham (1927–1997); and Ralph Sr. In 1924, Ralph began his lengthy employment with a new Hanes venture, Hanes Dye and Finishing Company, and served as president and chairman of the board. His many interests included architecture, decorating, historic preservation, and the arts. He single-handedly raised funds for a new public library, built in 1953.

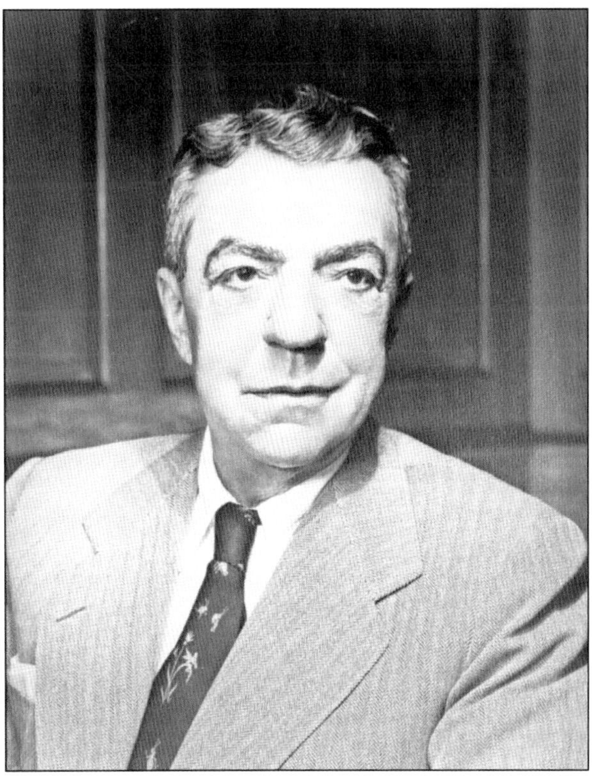

James Nelson "Jim" Weeks (1892–1962). Born in New York, Jim brought his bride, Beulah Lathers Weeks (1893–1976), to Winston-Salem in 1915. He came to work for Hanes Hosiery as an accountant and first worked in an annex to the Hanes Shamrock Mill on Marshall Street. Jim played baseball as a boy and organized the sports teams at Hanes Hosiery. He played on the first basketball team and was a supporter for the firm's national championship semiprofessional girls' basketball team. He served in several positions at Hanes and was president and chairman of the board. The Hanes Weeks plant, north of Winston-Salem, was named for him.

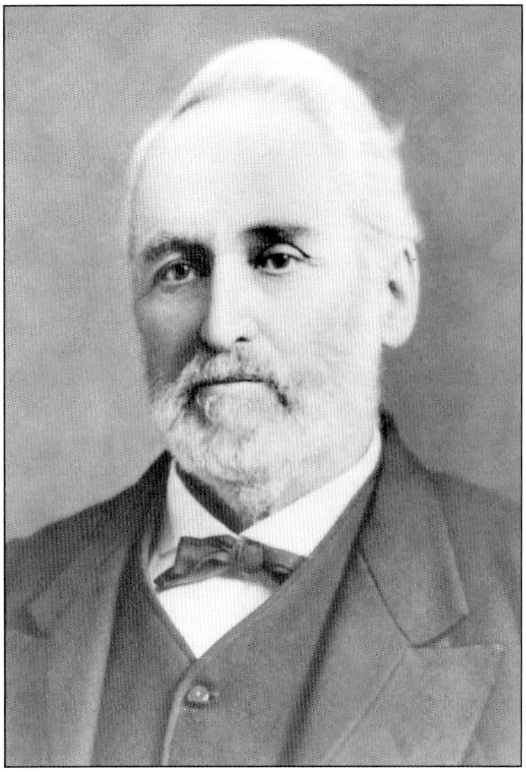

THOMAS JOHNSTON WILSON JR. (1815–1900). Judge Wilson was born in Stokes County, in the area now included in Forsyth County. He attended local schools and Clemmonsville Academy. He taught school for a few months before he studied law and was granted a license to practice law in 1840. He was elected county solicitor for Stokes, Davidson and Forsyth Counties, a delegate from Forsyth County to the Secession Convention, mayor of Winston for several years, and judge of the Eighth North Carolina Judicial District. He helped found First Presbyterian Church and gave land for the church building. He married Julia Lindsay (1823–1892) in 1847.

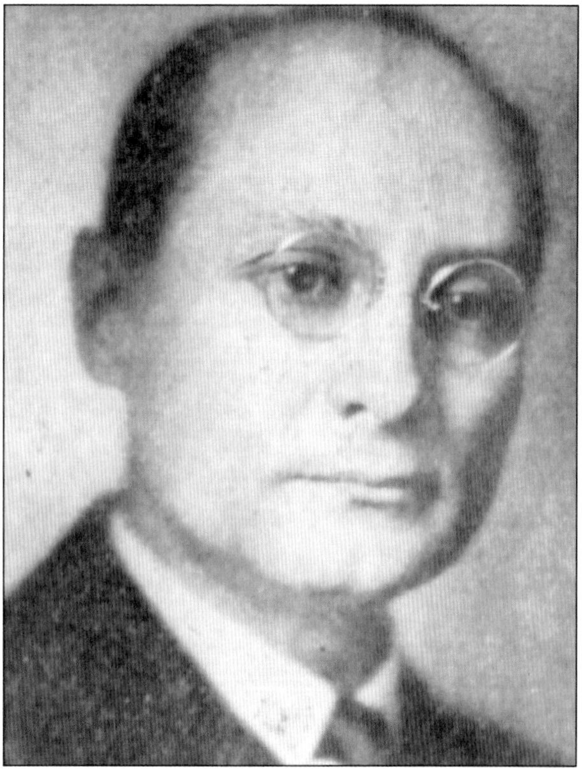

WILLIAM THOMAS WILSON (1884–1963). William was born to Edgar Henry Wilson (1860–1916) and Lula Champion Wilson (1861–1948). His father, Edgar, was a businessman who worked for Bell Telephone Company. William was the grandson of Judge Thomas J. Wilson Jr. and followed in his footsteps, as he studied law and was admitted to the bar. He practiced law for several years, served as municipal court judge, and was elected mayor of Winston-Salem in 1935. He received the largest vote count in the city's history, quadrupling the number of ballots cast for his two Democrat opponents. Wilson married Alice Franklin (1888–1953) in 1909.

George William Coan Sr. (1867–1939) and Oscar Benjamin Eaton (1858–1945). George (left) and Ben were members of the first draft board for Winston-Salem, established in 1918. George was from Virginia and received business training before entering the tobacco business. He married Loula Brown (1868–1939), daughter of Col. William A. Brown. Ben was born in Davie County and came to Winston in 1885. He was employed as treasurer by the B.F. Hanes Tobacco Company. He served as mayor of Winston from 1900 to 1911 and mayor of Winston-Salem from 1913 to 1917, for a total of 15 years as mayor. Ben was married to Mary Gaston Hough (1875–1933).

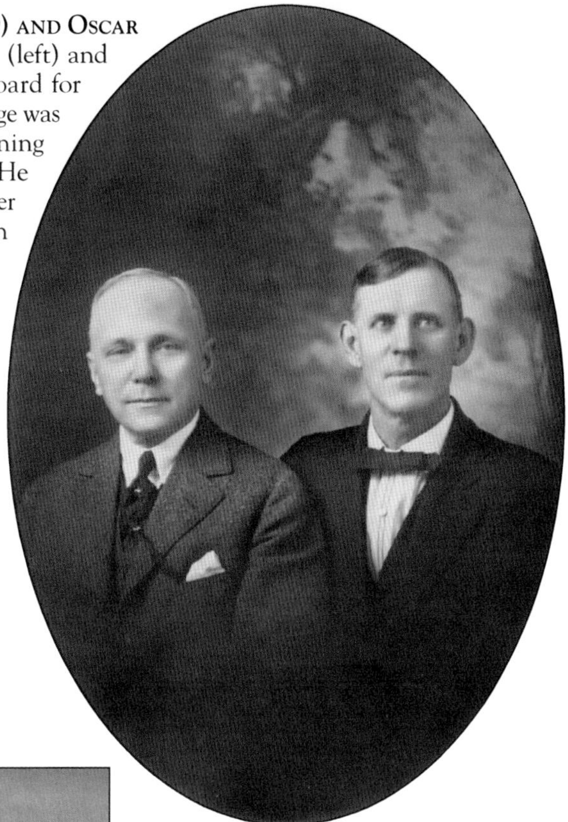

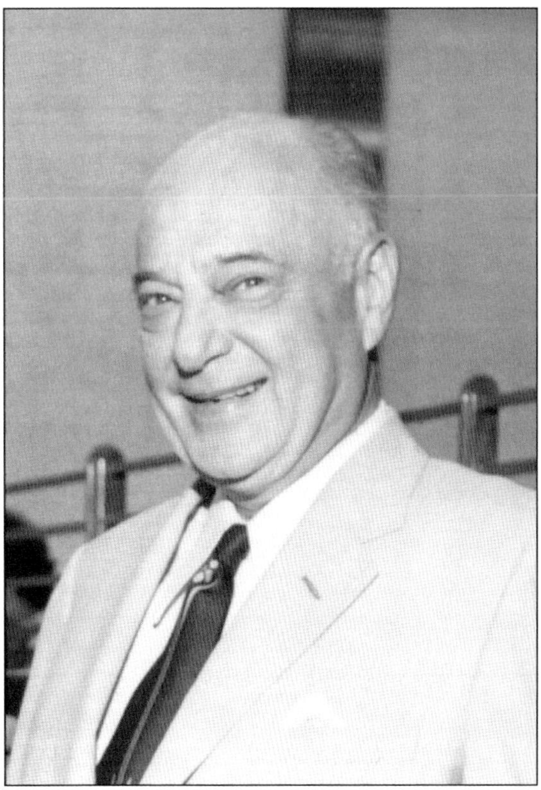

George William Coan Jr. (1892–1975). George Jr. was born in Virginia to George William Coan Sr. and Loula Brown Coan and moved to Winston-Salem in 1899. After college, he worked for R.J. Reynolds Tobacco Company. In 1917, he and his father organized the Morris Plan Bank (later City National Bank), which merged with First Union National Bank. George Jr. served several terms as mayor and was named the Works Progress Administrator for North Carolina. He built Bowman Gray Stadium, Reynolds Park, and Smith Reynolds Airport. He was married first to Mary Wiggins Coan (1890–1958) and secondly to Dorothy Lindsey Coan (1912–1990).

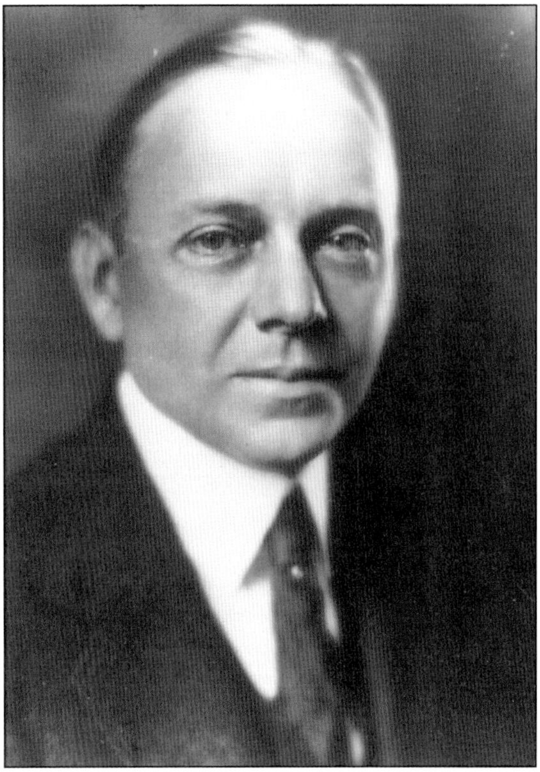

Thomas Barber (1878–1967). Thomas was born in Winston-Salem at the Gray homestead on Third Street to Thomas Barber (1840–1907) and Maybelle Gray Barber (1850–1922). He attended local schools and Davis Military School. He learned the insurance business from his uncle Eugene Early Gray Sr. (1855–1940). Thomas worked as an insurance agent before he joined Wachovia Bank and Trust Company as manager of the insurance department. He was also a director and vice president at Wachovia. Thomas served as mayor of Winston-Salem from 1925 to 1929. He married Louise Horton (1892–1992), daughter of Hamilton V. and Annie Laurie Cowles Horton.

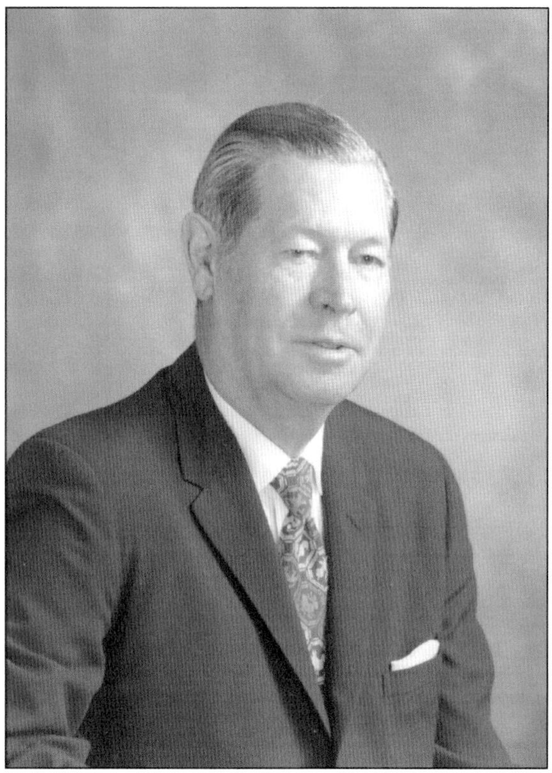

George Dallas Lentz Sr. (1906–1988). George was born in Rowan County and came to Winston-Salem as a child. He graduated from R.J. Reynolds High School, where he played a variety of sports. After graduation, he worked for Lentz Transfer and Storage Company for 44 years and served 30 years as president. George was active in local politics, serving as mayor from 1945 to 1949 and as an alderman for 10 years. He served on the Winston-Salem Board of Education and the Winston-Salem Finance Committee and was president of the Winston-Salem and North Carolina Jaycees. George was married to Rozelind Landquist (1906–1984).

ROBERT WILSON GORRELL SR. (1871–1931). Robert was born in Winston-Salem to Albert Burrow Gorrell (1840–1898) and Frances Lenora Wilson Gorrell (1849–1908). His father established the Farmers Warehouse, and Robert worked at the warehouse, beginning as a young boy. When his father died, Robert and his brother Peter Albert Gorrell (1878–1924) shared management duties until Peter's death. Robert and his father served terms as mayors and were on the school board. Robert's first term as mayor began in 1917 and was consumed with war-related activities on the home front. Robert was married to Margaret Bell Bailey (1880–1968).

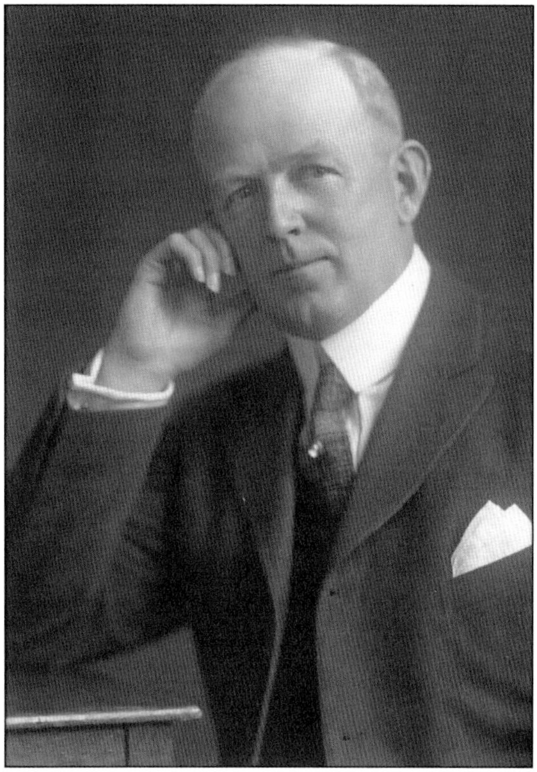

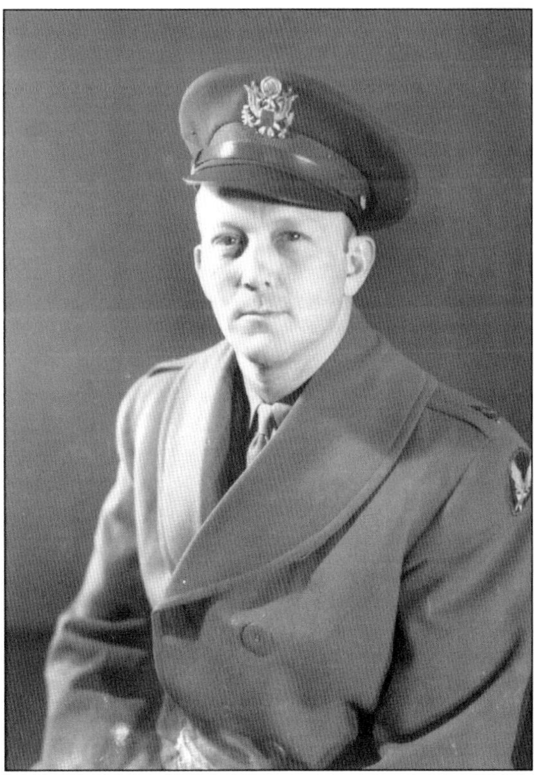

ROBERT WILSON "BOB" GORRELL JR. (1910–1964). Bob was born in Winston-Salem to Robert Wilson and Margaret Bailey Gorrell. Following his graduation from Davidson College, Bob worked for Security Life and Trust Company. He became an associate general agent in 1946 and was in partnership with Charles N. Siewers for the Gorrell and Siewers General Agency of Security. Bob served in the Air Corps during World War II and was the city's first civil defense director. He married Marguerite Willingham (1918–2006) in 1941. Marguerite was the daughter of Richard Furman Willingham (1885–1939) and Rosa Eleanor Fries Willingham (1887–1954).

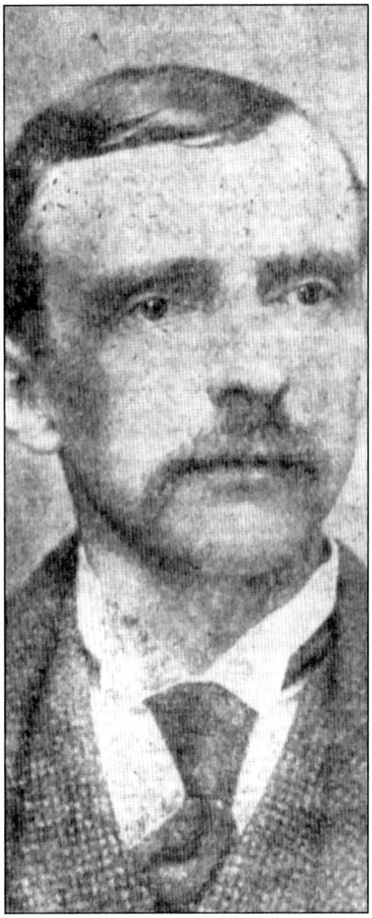

George Hanes Rights (1858–1922). George was born in Winston-Salem to Constantine Lazarus and Lizzie Hanes Rights. He attended the Salem Boys' School, where his father was a teacher. He worked more than 50 years in the printing business, starting as an apprentice in Blum's printing office, the home of the *People's Press* and *Blum's Farmer's and Planter's Almanac*. He worked in the offices of the *Western Sentinel* and then moved to the *Union Republican*, where he became local manager and then managing editor, for a total of 37 years. George was first married to Emma Jones (1859–1897) and secondly to Jessie M. Shore.

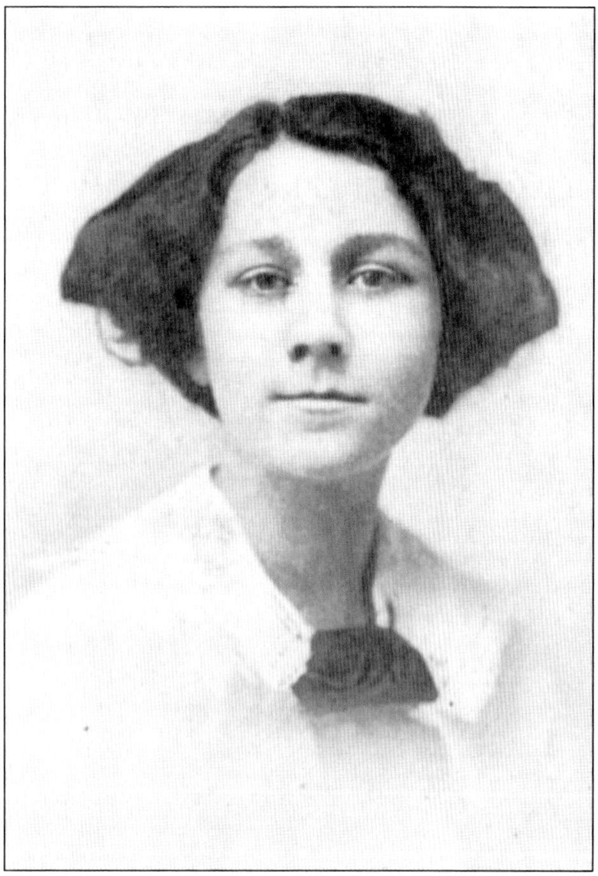

Irene Belle Morris (1894–1994). Irene was the fifth of nine children born to Charles Wilson Morris (1867–1949) and Susan Mitchell Morris (1861–1936). She graduated in 1911 from City High School on Cherry Street, where she learned shorthand and typing. Irene first worked as a legal secretary and then took a job with Piedmont Publishing Company in 1941. She worked as secretary for the newspaper publishers/general managers for the next 23 years, retiring in 1964. The front page of the *Twin City Sentinel* was devoted to Irene when she retired, filled with personal reminiscences from newspaper staff members.

William King Hoyt (1889–1982). Originally from New York, William became general manager of the *Winston-Salem Journal* in 1925. He later became general manager of the *Twin City Sentinel* as well, when the newspapers came under joint ownership. He was president of Triangle Broadcasting Company, which ran WSJS radio, and later helped establish WSJS television in 1953. He was president of Piedmont Publishing Company, retiring in 1959. William and his wife, Miriam, lived in the restored 1793 Ebert-Reich House in Old Salem, the first house restored for personal occupancy. He was one of the 17 incorporators of Old Salem Inc.

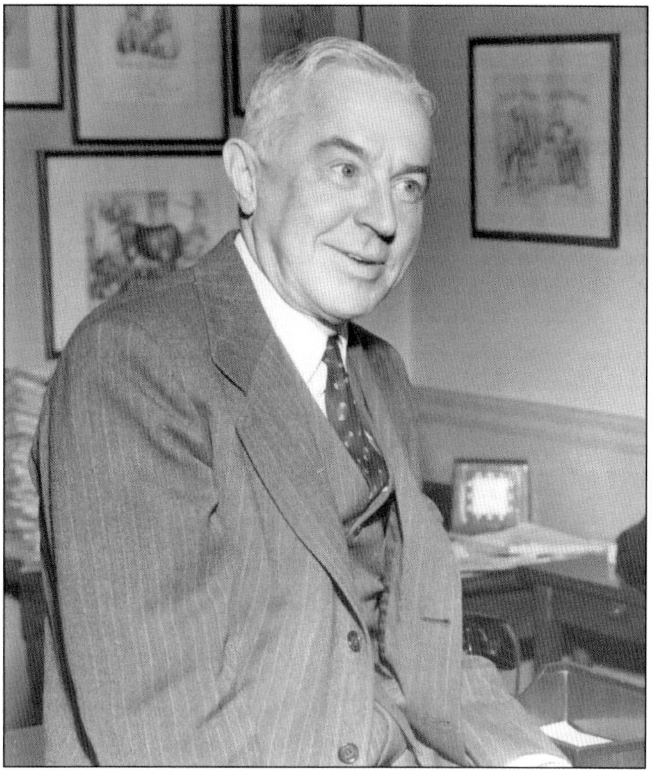

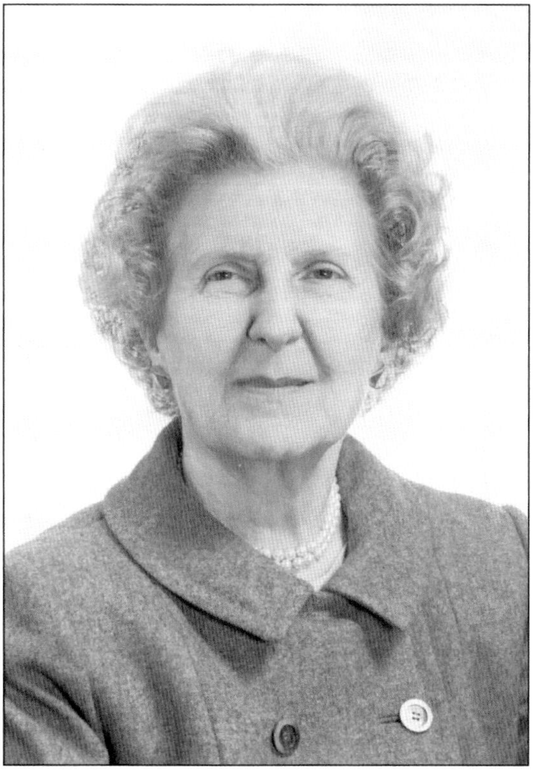

Miriam Katharine Efird Hoyt (1901–1998). Miriam was born in Winston-Salem to Jason Adam Efird (1860–1909) and Mary Salome Stafford Efird (1872–1953). Miriam's father managed the Phoenix Hotel, located on the corner of West Fourth and North Liberty Streets. Miriam was born in the hotel, where the family lived. She graduated from Salem College and taught English and biology at Salem Academy. She traveled abroad extensively prior to her marriage to William K. Hoyt in 1935. Miriam volunteered with many local organizations and Salem College and was most passionate about conserving and promoting the planting of trees in public places.

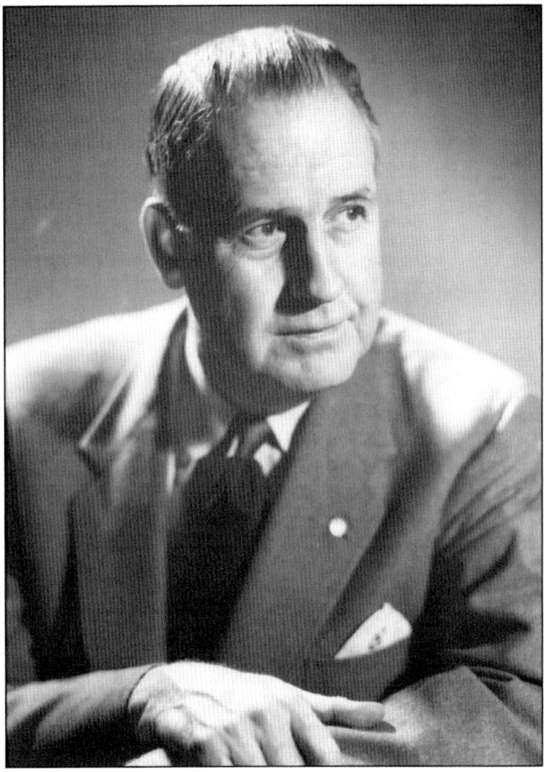

Joseph Worth Bacon Sr. (1900–1960). Born in Albemarle, Worth worked for several North Carolina newspapers before he became city editor for the *Winston-Salem Journal* in 1926. He became managing editor for the *Journal* and the *Twin City Sentinel* in 1944. Health concerns prompted him to reduce his work duties, so he was named associate editor for community service in 1959. He was known as an excellent newspaper technician and taught the newspaper business to many cub reporters. He married Lucile Wilmoth Thomas (1900–1982). Worth and Lucile were parents to Joseph Worth Bacon Jr. (1933–1934) and Catherine Bacon Carter Ebert (1924–1998).

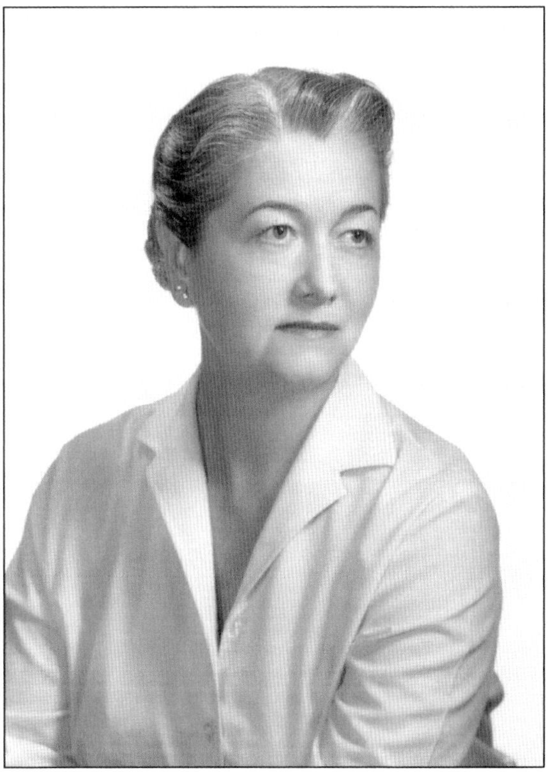

Annie Lee Singletary (1910–2002). Annie Lee was born in Whitakers to John Ivey Singletary (1880–1927) and Annie Mickey Singletary (1888–1978). As a nine-year-old child, Annie Lee's writing talent was recognized when she won a $10 gold piece for her paper on "What are the benefits of an enlistment in the United States Army?" Her winning essay was printed in the newspaper. This was the first of her many columns, stories, and features that graced the pages of the *Winston-Salem Journal and Sentinel*, where she worked for 37 years. She wrote a book column, covered women's news, fashion, and travel, and garnered more awards during her illustrious career.

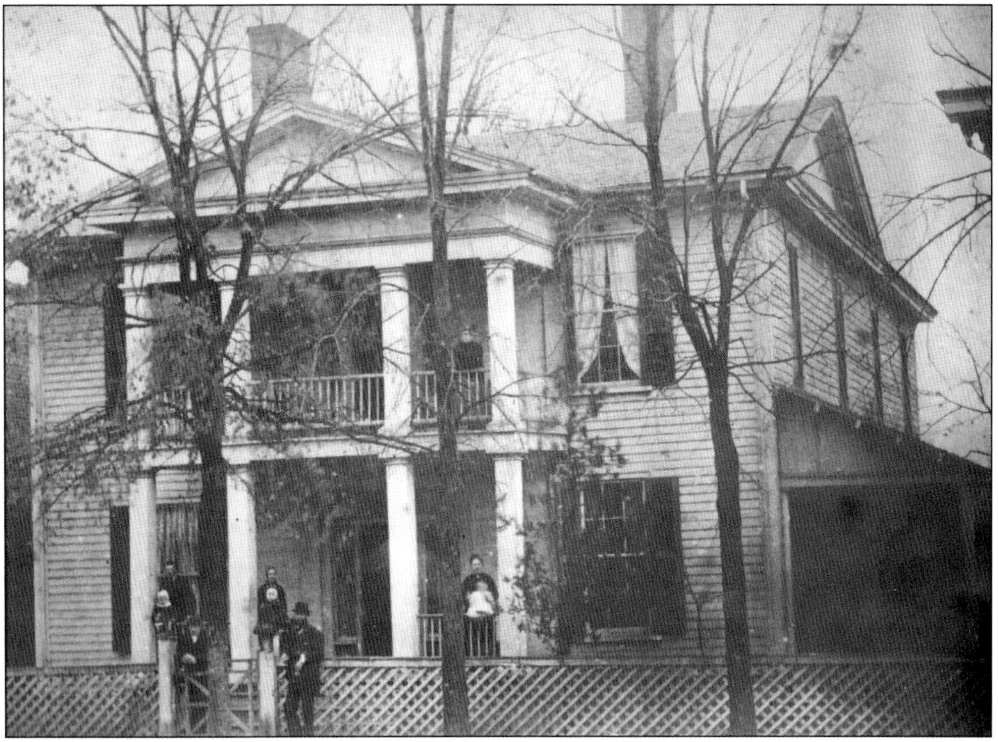

ROBERT GRAY (1814–1881), MARY MILLIS WILEY GRAY (1818–1904), AND FAMILY. Born in Randolph County, Robert bought a lot in the new Forsyth County in 1849. Located on West Third Street, it extended from Main Street to Liberty Street and nearly to Second Street on the south. The house, pictured above, faced the courthouse and burned in 1882. Robert manufactured cotton and paper and served as mayor (1861–1862). Robert and Mary had seven sons and two daughters. The oldest son, Samuel Wiley, was killed at Gettysburg. The surviving six sons are pictured below. From left to right are (first row) Robah Fidus (1852–1900), who married Lelia Wilson (1858–1924); James Alexander (1846–1918), who married Aurelia Bowman (1869–1914); and Robert Terelius (1848–1912), who married Carolina Lilly (1852–1946); (second row) Eugene Early (1855–1940), who married Elizabeth Huske (1861–1946); William Theodore (1860–1918), who married Ada Dodson (1865–1902); and Emory Shannon (1857–1934), who married Theodosia Fitzgerald (1868–1901).

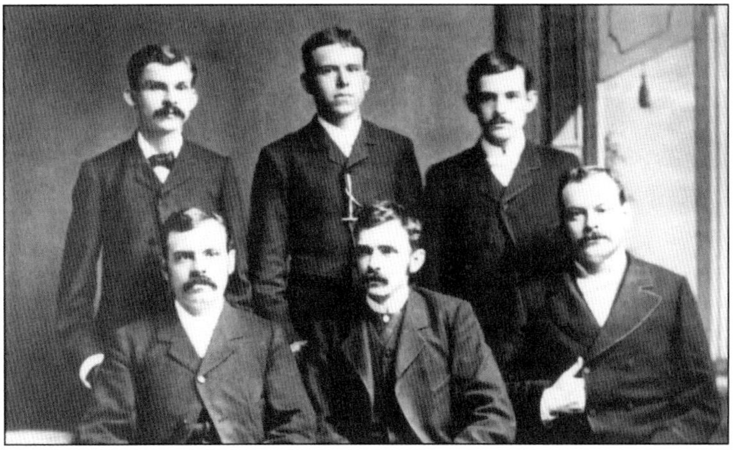

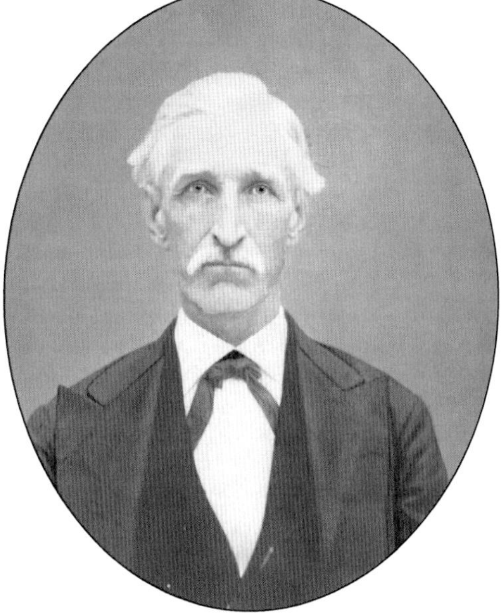
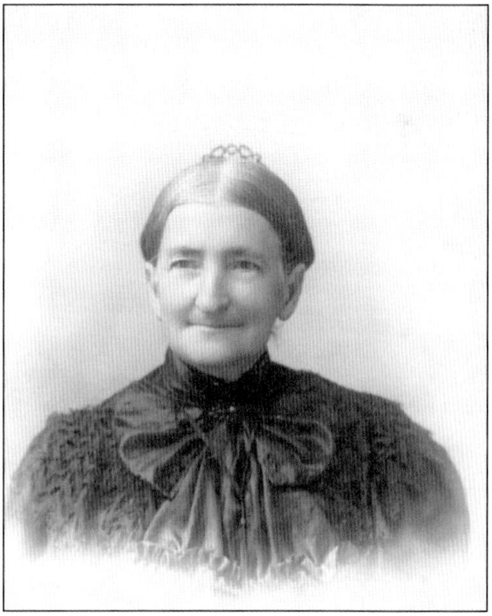

WYATT FLETCHER BOWMAN AND JAMES ALEXANDER GRAY FAMILIES. Wyatt Bowman (1820–1882) and his wife, Mary Eliza Lindsay Bowman (1822–1910), both pictured above, were born in Guilford County. They married in 1846, lived in High Point, and then moved to Winston-Salem in the 1870s to be near their daughter Aurelia Bowman Gray (1848–1914) and her husband, James Alexander Gray Sr. (1846–1918), both pictured below. Born in Randolph County, James came to Winston in 1852, attended local schools, fought in the Civil War, and was taken prisoner at Fort Fisher. James was instrumental in organizing Wachovia National Bank and served as the bank's first cashier and its president during his 39-year career. When Wachovia National Bank merged with Wachovia Loan and Trust Company, he was elected vice president. James A. Gray High School was named in his honor.

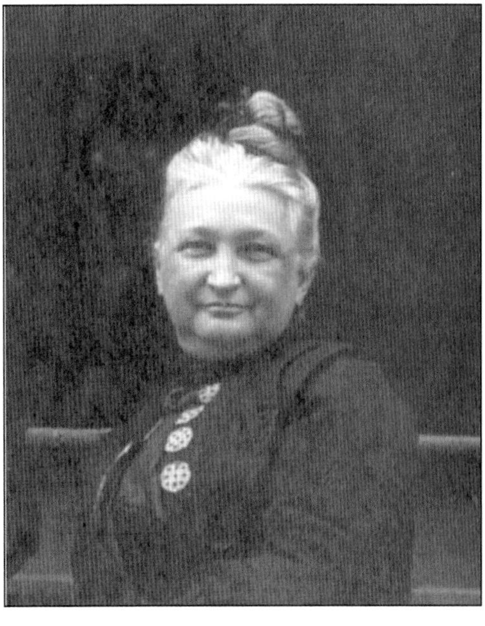
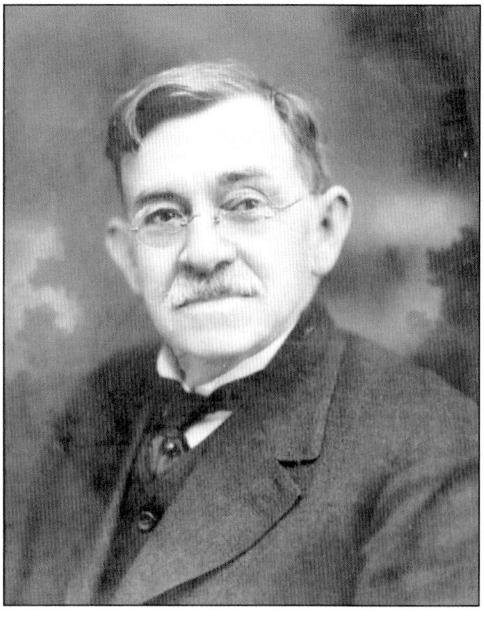

CHILDREN OF JAMES ALEXANDER AND AURELIA BOWMAN GRAY. James and Aurelia were parents to six children, four of whom reached adulthood. From left to right are Mary Eliza (Mamie) Gray (1876–1944), who married Alexander Henderson Galloway Jr. (1870–1935); Bowman Gray (1874–1935), who married Nathalie Fontaine Lyons (Bernard) (1884–1961); and Bessie Lindsay Gray (1879–1963), who married Charles Edwin Plumly (1874–1939). The youngest child, James Alexander Gray Jr., is not pictured (see page 83). Bowman was an executive at R.J. Reynolds Tobacco Company. He died and was buried at sea, but a granite obelisk stands at Salem Cemetery in his memory.

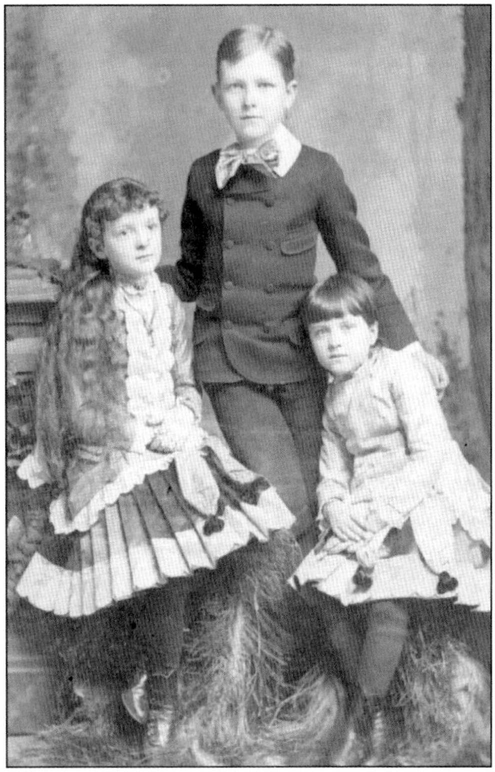

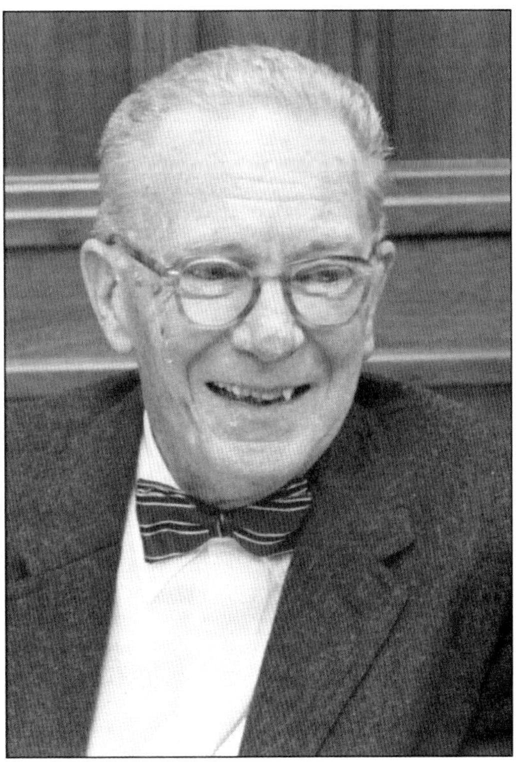

BOWMAN GRAY JR. (1907–1969). Bowman was born in Baltimore. He joined R.J. Reynolds Tobacco Company as a salesman after he graduated from the University of North Carolina. During his 39-year career at Reynolds, he rose to the position of chairman of the board of directors. He was featured on the cover of *Time* magazine in 1960, accompanying a report on the tobacco industry. Bowman worked with naval intelligence during World War II. Bowman married Elizabeth Palmer Christian (1915–1974) in 1936. They bought 800-acre Brookberry Farm, built a house, and raised cattle and agricultural products.

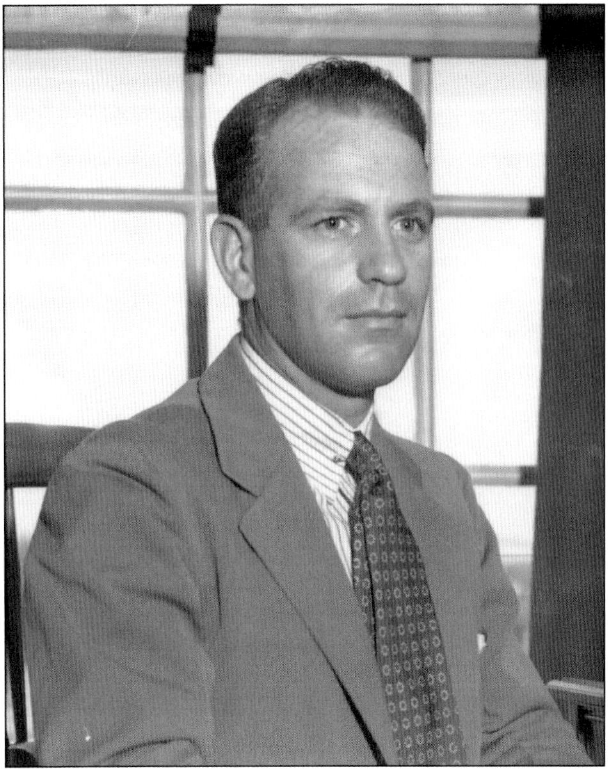

Gordon Gray (1909–1982). The younger son of Bowman and Nathalie Gray, Gordon was born in Baltimore and moved to Winston-Salem in 1911. He graduated from the University of North Carolina, received his law degree from Yale University, practiced law with firms in New York and in Winston-Salem, and then became president and publisher of Piedmont Publishing Company. Gordon served in World War II as a private and later became secretary of the Army. He was elected president of the University of North Carolina. Gordon was first married to Jane Boyden Henderson Craige (1914–1953) and secondly to Nancy Maguire Beebe.

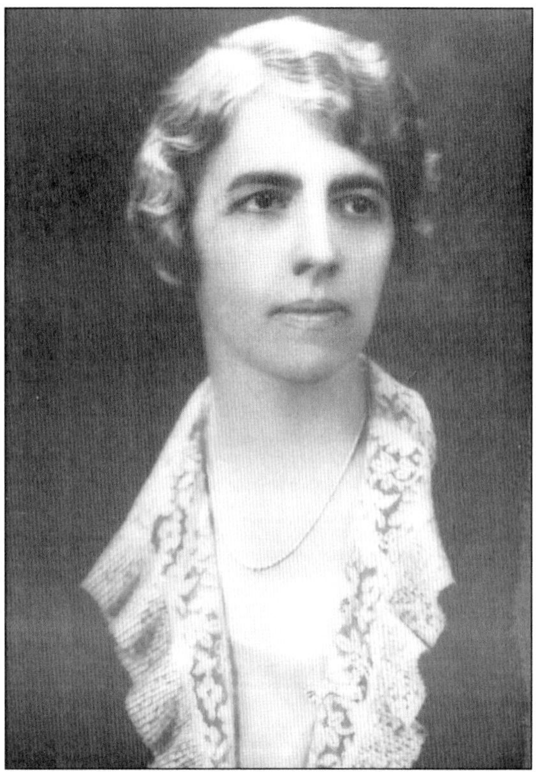

Alice Shelton "Polly" Gray (1886–1982). Polly was the daughter of Dr. Robah Fidus and Lelia Gray. She served as a World War I volunteer Red Cross nurse for the US Army Medical Corps in hospitals in France. She aided in the organization the American Legion, was the first woman to serve on its executive committee, and helped found the Clyde Bolling Post, the Winston-Salem Chapter of the American Legion. She helped found the Forsyth County Chapter of the American Red Cross, and she organized the groundbreaking medical and nursing service at R.J. Reynolds Tobacco Company in 1920.

James Alexander Gray Jr. (1889–1952). James was the youngest child of James A. and Aurelia Bowman Gray. He graduated from the University of North Carolina and joined Wachovia Bank and Trust Company as manager of the savings department. He later served as treasurer until he joined R.J. Reynolds Tobacco Company in 1920 as a director and vice president. He became president and chairman of the board for Reynolds and maintained ties with Wachovia by serving as a director and chairman of the board. He also represented Forsyth County in the North Carolina Senate. James married Pauline Lisette Bahnson (1891–1955).

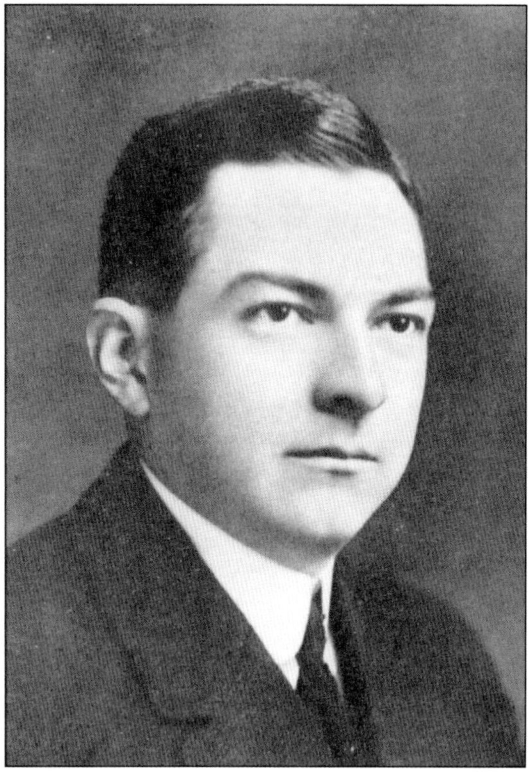

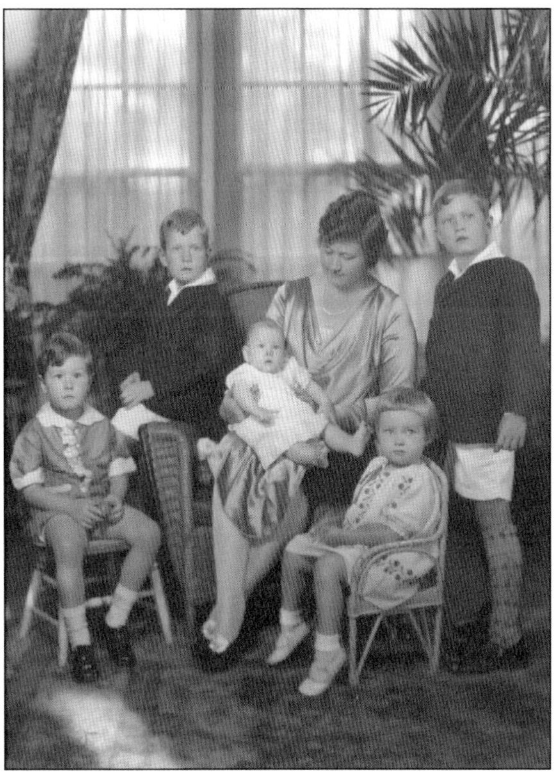

Family of James Alexander Gray Jr. James Jr. married Pauline Bahnson in 1918. Born in Winston-Salem, Pauline graduated from Salem College with a degree in art. She pursued painting as a hobby, and her paintings were exhibited in several galleries in North Carolina. She restored and gave the John Vogler House to Old Salem. She and James were parents to six children: James Alexander Gray III (1920–2003), Bahnson Gray (1922–1970), Howard Gray (1925–2009), Emma Christine Gallaher (1927–2006), Pauline Louise Robinson (1929–2007), and Aurelia Elizabeth Eller. The photograph shows Pauline with five of her children.

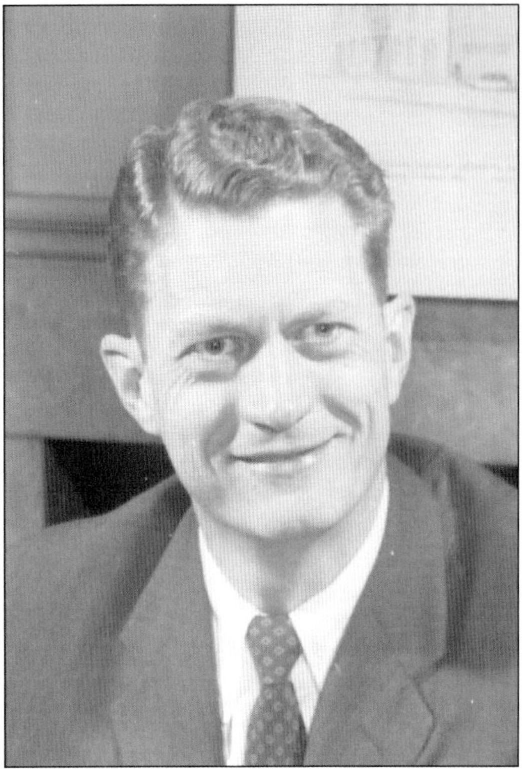

James Alexander "Jim" Gray (1920–2003). As the oldest son of James A. and Pauline Bahnson Gray, Jim was born in Winston-Salem and graduated from the University of North Carolina and Harvard University. He worked as personnel director for local newspapers and later became general manager and publisher. He served in the US Navy during World War II and was chairman of the Forsyth County Centennial Committee in 1949. Jim was interested in historic preservation and was president of Old Salem Inc. from 1962 to 1970. He was survived by wife Jane Frazier Gray.

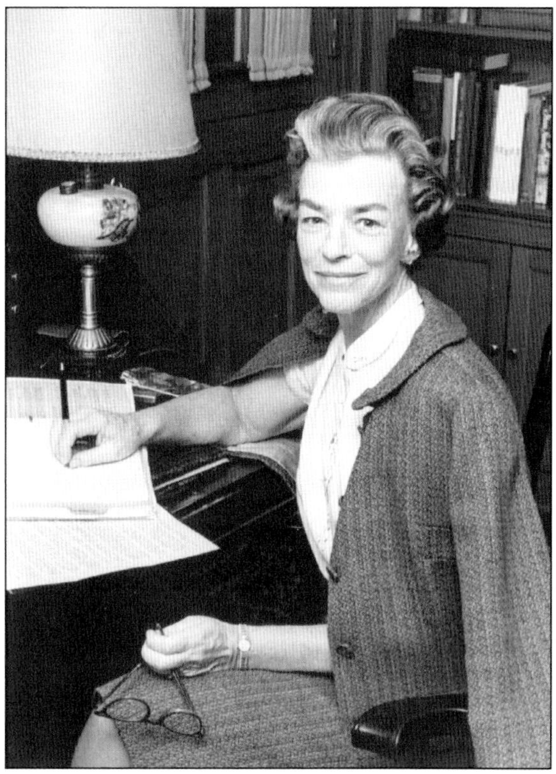

Aurelia Bowman Plumly Spaugh (1910–1991). Born to Charles Edwin and Bess Gray Plumly, Aurelia graduated from R.J. Reynolds High School and earned the Montague Medal for having the highest grade point average in her senior class. She graduated from Smith College and was a founder of Summit School, where she was business manager and taught English, physical education, and social studies. Aurelia served in World War II and was the first WAVE (Women Accepted for Volunteer Emergency Service) from Winston-Salem. She married Ralph Edward Spaugh (1902–1991), a Winston-Salem native and a vice president of Wachovia Bank and Trust Company who helped establish the Moravian Home.

Mary Louise Haywood Davis (1916–2010) and Archibald Kimbrough "Archie" Davis (1911–1998). Born in Winston-Salem to Dr. Thomas Whitmel Davis Jr. (1876–1952) and Frances Conrad Davis (1880–1956), Archie graduated from the University of North Carolina in 1932. He worked for Wachovia Bank and Trust Company and reentered his alma mater, after he retired as chairman of the board and senior vice president, to earn his master's degree in history. A newspaper article written about Archie described him as "a gentleman and a scholar." He married Mary Louise Haywood, daughter of Thomas Holt Haywood Sr. (1887–1964) and Mary Louise Bahnson Haywood (1889–1964).

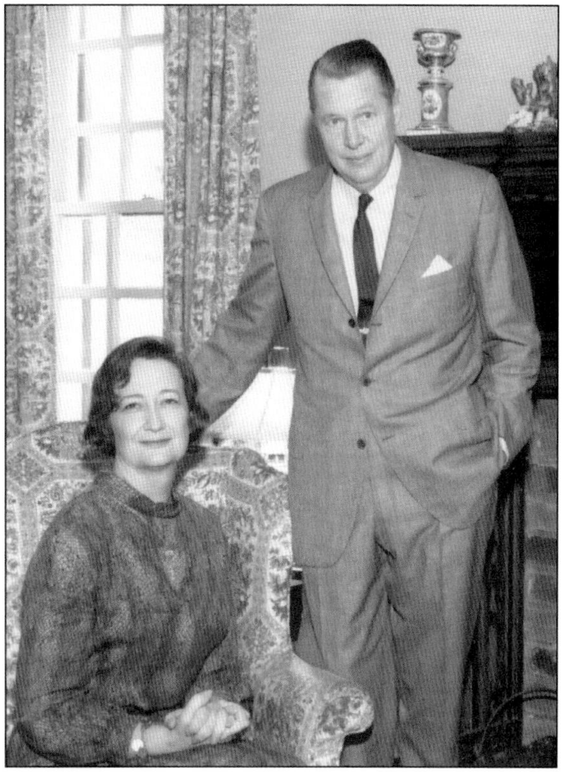

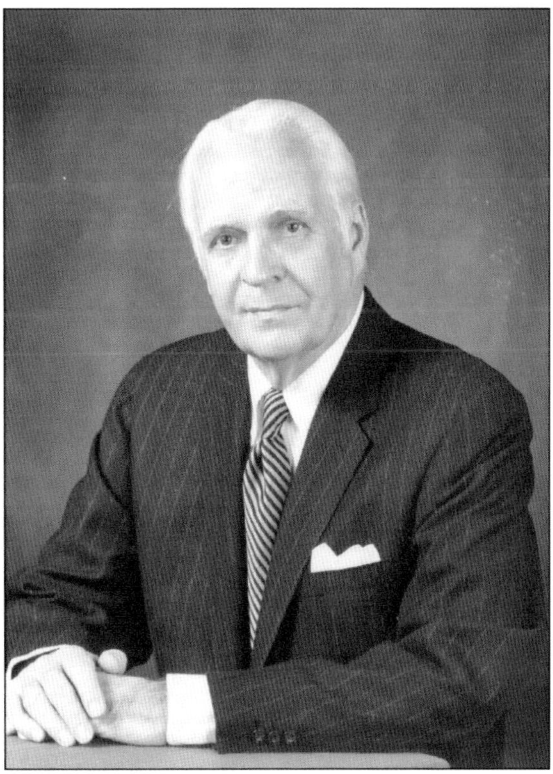

John Francis Watlington Jr. (1911–1999). John was born in Reidsville, where his father was president of the Bank of Reidsville. After graduating from Washington and Lee University in 1933, he joined Wachovia Bank and Trust Company, where he and Archie K. Davis were a working team for 40 years. John became chief executive of Wachovia Corporation in 1956, and he retired in 1976, when the bank's assets were $3.5 billion. John was married to Margaret Jones Watlington (1919–2011). Watlington served on the board of visitors for the Bowman Gray School of Medicine and helped raise money to fund the school.

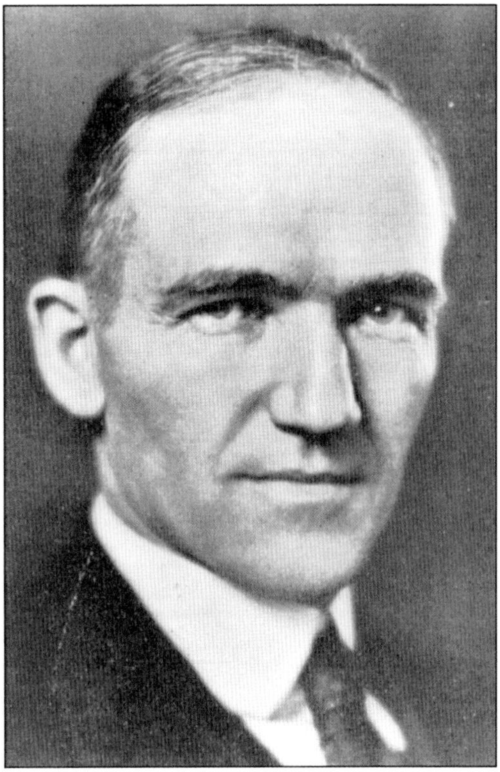

Meade Homer Willis Sr. (1878–1967). Born in South Carolina, Meade worked as a telegraph operator with the Southern Railway Company and attended Eastman's Business School in New York. He came to Winston-Salem to organize the high school commercial department. He was hired by Wachovia Bank and Trust Company and became vice president, a director of the bank, and head of the bond department. He was chairman of the first Liberty Loan drive in Forsyth County during World War I and championed the local library and the Red Cross. He was first married to Rosalind Rutherford Sheppard (1880–1962) and secondly to Marian Finley.

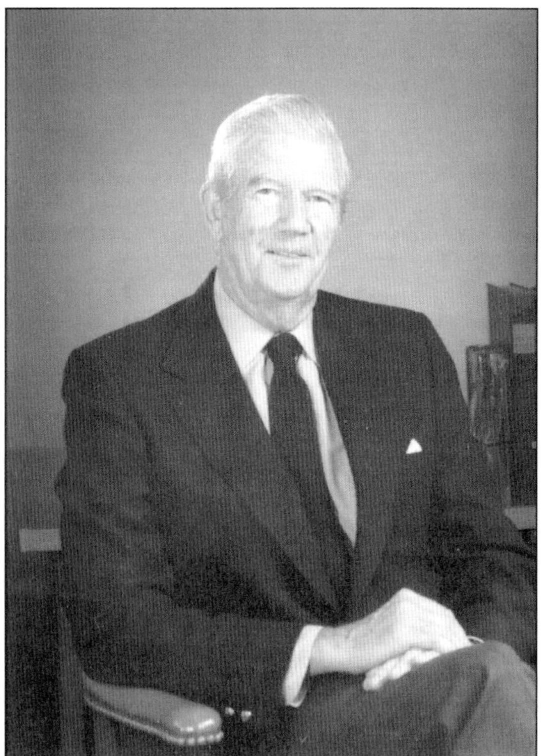

Meade Homer Willis Jr. (1909–1999). Meade Jr. was born in Winston-Salem to Meade Homer Sr. and Rosalind Willis. He began his long association with Wachovia Bank and Trust Company, where his father was employed, when he worked as a messenger during the summer as a child. He joined the bank full time in 1931 and retired in 1973 as senior vice president in charge of the Winston-Salem office. Meade Jr. served in World War II and was captured in the Philippines and taken to Japan. He spent more than three years in captivity. Meade Jr. was married to Sarah Anne Hanes (1922–1997).

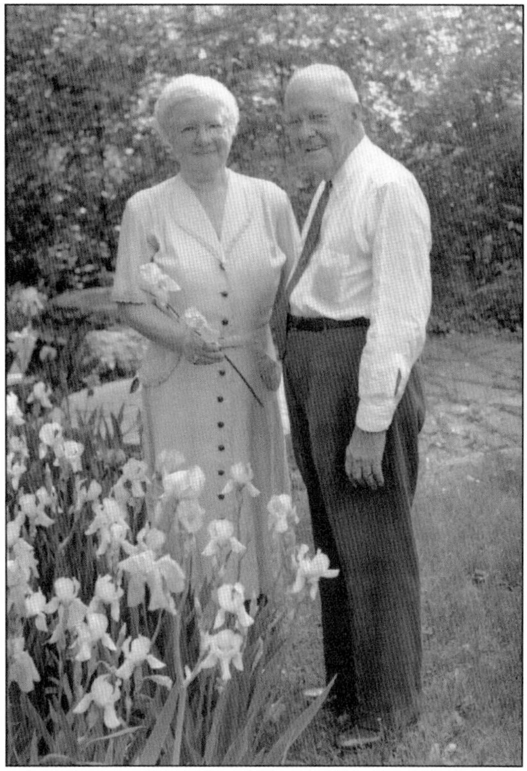

Corrine Price Baskin Norfleet (1885–1979) and Charles Milner Norfleet (1881–1957). Corrine was born in Mississippi. She came to Winston-Salem to attend Salem College and met her future husband, Charles. Active in Reynolda Presbyterian Church, Corrine also worked as a volunteer at Forsyth Memorial Hospital when it opened in 1964 until 1977. Born in Winston-Salem to Marmaduke and Ellen Kirkpatrick Norfleet, Charles worked in his father's tobacco warehouse and then became president of Norfleet Motors. When First National Bank was chartered in 1934, Charles was appointed president. He was elected chairman of the board in 1948.

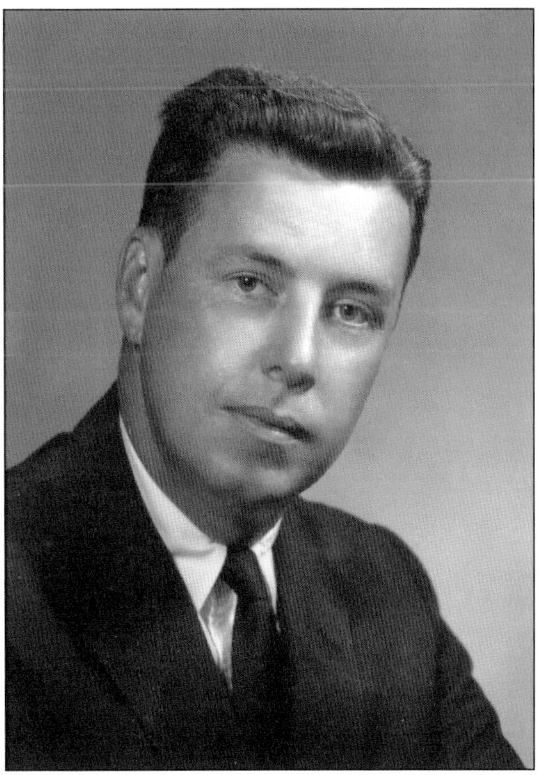

Robert Penick "Bob" Whaling (1923–2006). Born in Virginia to Charles Alexander Whaling (1886–1941) and Ruth Penick Whaling (1893–1991), Bob served in the Army during World War II. He worked for Pilot Insurance Agency and became the senior managing partner in 1980. The agency was sold to Aon Risk Services, and he was chairman of the board until he retired in 1991. Bob was active in many civic and professional organizations and was an avid golfer. He helped identify photographs for the Forsyth County Public Library and located historical photographs for displays in local organizations. He was married to Mary Lu Wright.

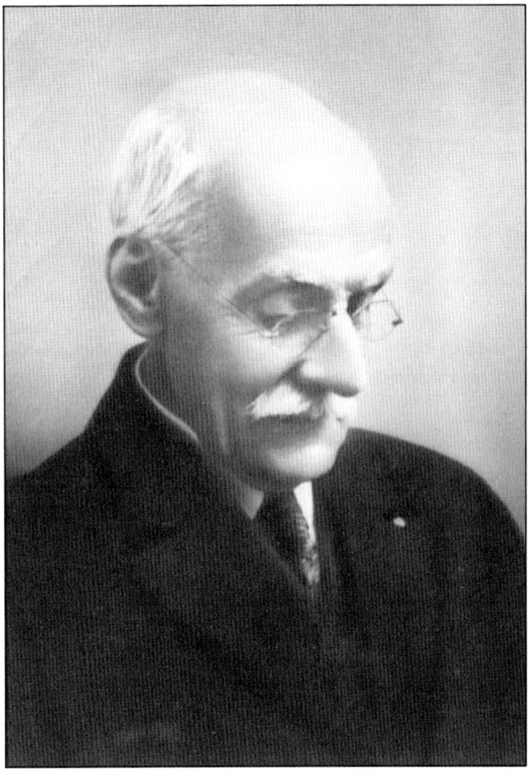

Gustavus Augustus Follin (1842–1927). Gustavus was born in Charleston, South Carolina, and served in the Civil War. He was captured in Columbia, South Carolina, by Sherman's army. He came to Winston-Salem in 1887 as a partner in the tobacco manufacturing firm of Lockett, Vaughn & Company. He saw the need for home building and financing institutions, so he organized the Winston-Salem Building and Loan Association. The venture was so successful that Gustavus devoted all his time to the work. When he retired around 1920, his son Marion G. Follin (1875–1948) took over the business. Gustavus was married to Ellen Estelle Marion (1846–1923).

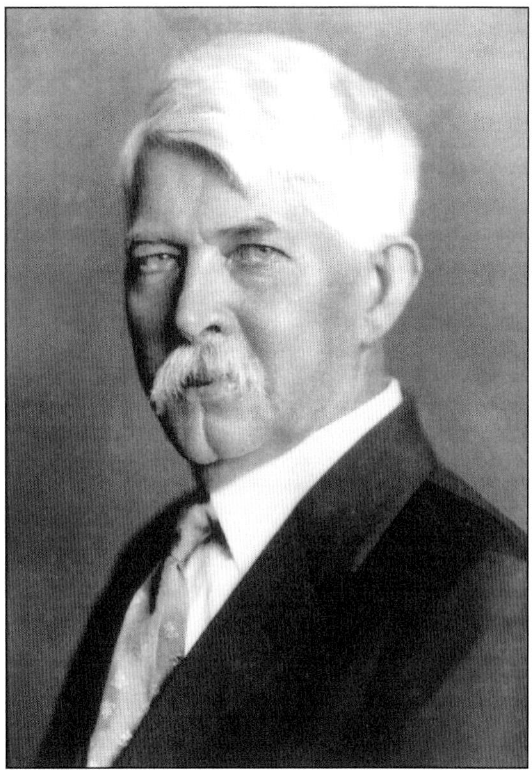

Andrew Jackson Farrell (1860–1924). Andrew, a Chatham County native, came to Winston-Salem around 1899 and lived on the corner of East Fourth Street and Woodland Avenue. He established a photography business, which he operated until 1919. For some of this time, it was located on the second floor of a Main Street building. Andrew served on the board of aldermen and was a charter member of Greenwood Avenue Baptist Church. Before he retired for health reasons, there were seven photography studios in town, and all of them were located in the downtown area. Andrew married Yadkin County native Lucy Belle Charles (1872–1958) in 1889.

UREY KEVIL RICE (1895–1965). Born in Kentucky, Urey attended Paducah High School and the Cleveland School of Art. He served as a chief petty officer in the Navy during World War I and came to Winston-Salem in 1921 to open the Robert E. Lee Hotel and to hire the first manager. The following year, he returned to his first love—the theater. He joined the Piedmont Amusement Company, operated by Sams and Moses, and became manager of the Forsyth Theatre. From 1922 to 1958, Urey managed the Carolina Theatre and other local theatres. He was married to Elsie Moses Rice (1900–1958).

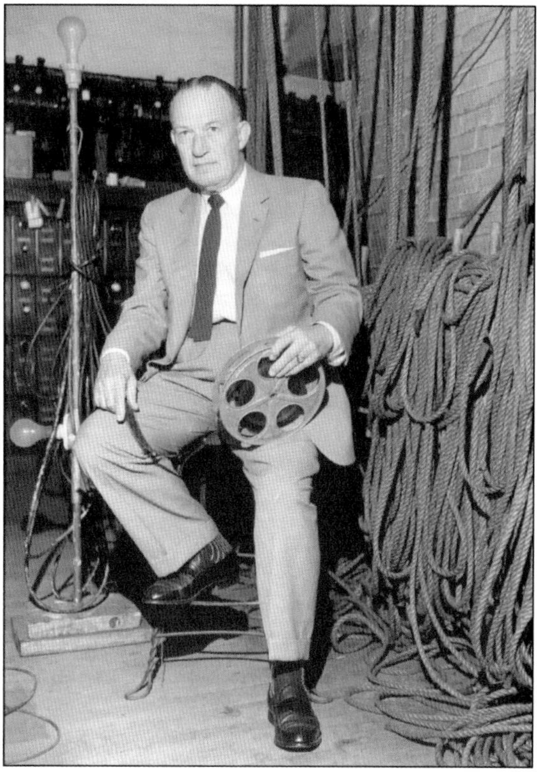

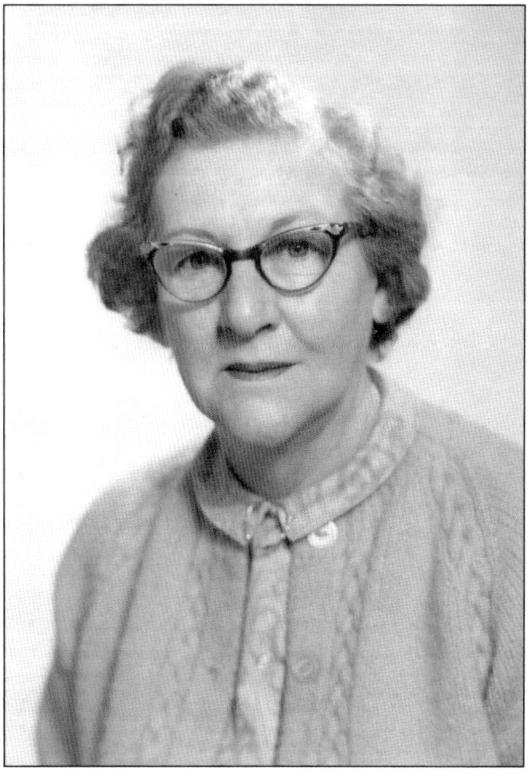

DORIS GERTRUDE CHIPMAN PARDINGTON (1904–1991). Doris was born in Maine to Alberto Lee Chipman (1878–1958) and Mertie Aimee Jordan Chipman (1879–1961). Doris was a charter member of the Little Theatre of Winston-Salem. Her participation in the Little Theatre led to other opportunities, such as hosting a radio program in which she reviewed books and becoming the first woman radio announcer in 1942. WAIR hired Doris because of her previous radio experience and her background in dramatics and speech. Doris was managing director of the Little Theatre from 1952 to 1972 and was married to Edward Davies Pardington (1901–1944).

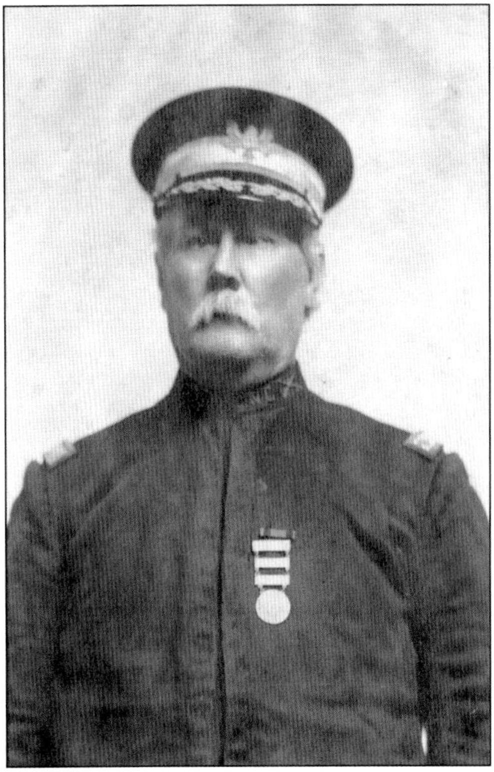

Col. Jesse Casper Bessent (1855–1924). A native of Mocksville, Jesse came to Winston-Salem in 1874. He was the city tax collector, justice of the peace, and fire insurance representative. Jesse was a Mason and a member of the Independent Order of Odd Fellows, where he held every office—both elective and appointive. He was captain of the Forsyth Riflemen and served his country in the Spanish-American War and in the National Guard. He married Laura White (1861–1947) and was father to Robert Booth Bessent (1883–1904). Robbie was a fireman for the Norfolk & Western Railway. He was killed when his train was derailed during an attempted robbery.

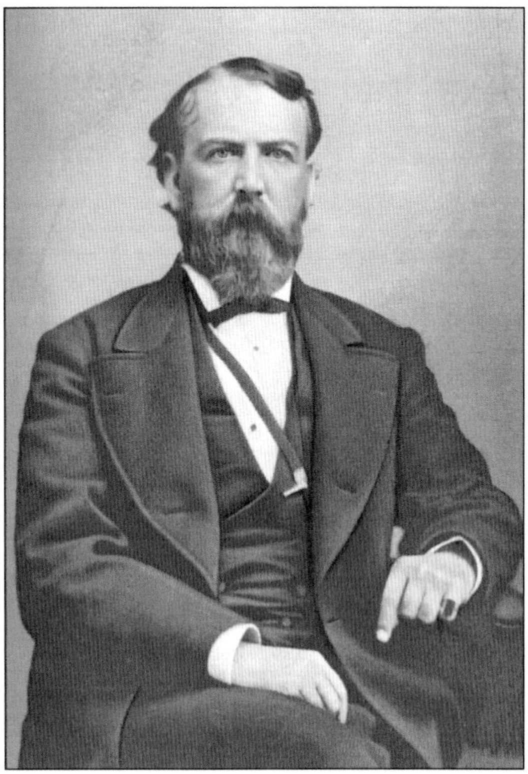

Rufus Lenoir Patterson (1830–1879). Rufus was born in Caldwell County. His father was a wealthy planter and prominent politician, North Carolina state treasurer, and president of the Raleigh & Gaston Railroad Company. Rufus grew up in Caldwell County and in Raleigh and graduated from the University of North Carolina. He was first married to Marie Louise Morehead (1830–1862), daughter of Gov. John M. Morehead, and secondly to Mary Elizabeth Fries (1844–1927), daughter of Francis and Lisetta Fries. Rufus owned and managed cotton, flour, and paper mills. He served as chairman of the Forsyth County Court and as mayor of Salem.

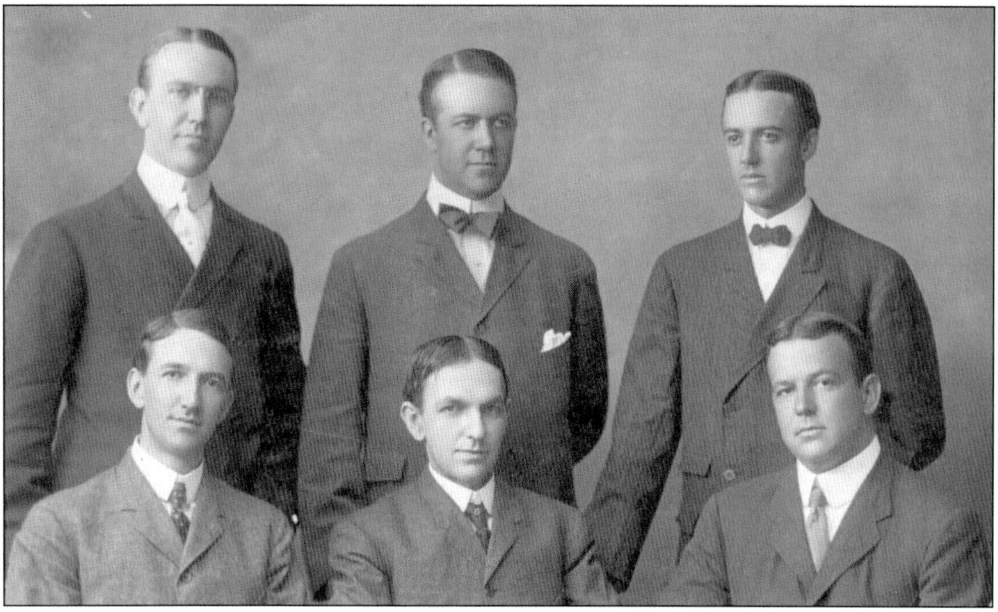

RUFUS AND MARY PATTERSON FAMILY. Rufus Lenoir Patterson and Mary Elizabeth Fries married in 1864 and had six sons, pictured above. While the names of the sons are known, they cannot all be identified in the photograph. However, Dr. Andrew Henry "Drew" Patterson (1870–1928) is identified far left on the first row, and Rufus Lenoir Patterson Jr. (1872–1943) is in the center on the second row. The other sons are Francis H. Fries Patterson (1865–1933), Samuel Finley Patterson (1867–1926), John Legerwood Patterson (1874–1935), and Edmund Vogler Patterson (1878–1934). Rufus Jr. and John Legerwood are buried elsewhere, but their names are on a monument in the center of the Patterson plot. The Rufus Patterson family plot, pictured below, sits on a hill, enclosed with a black cast-iron fence. (Below, MGR.)

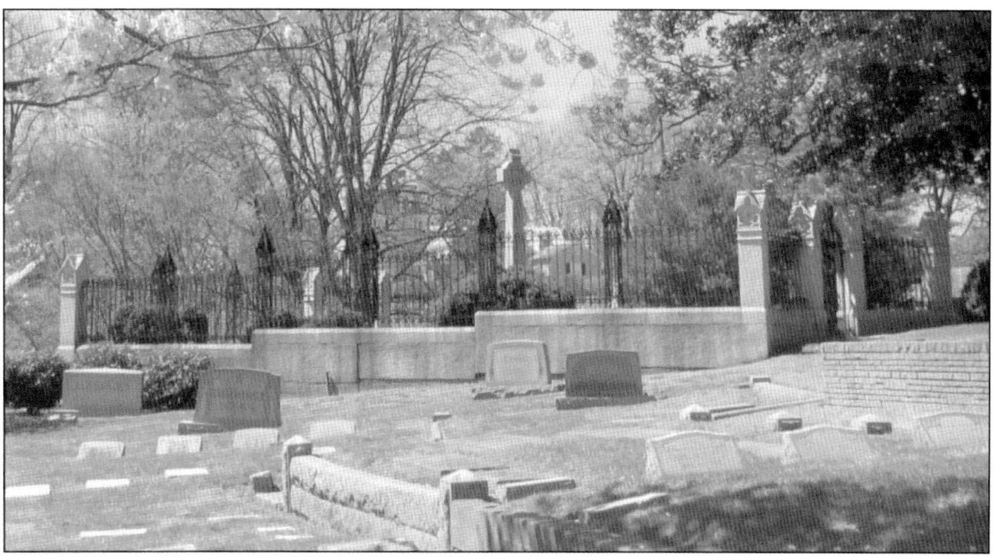

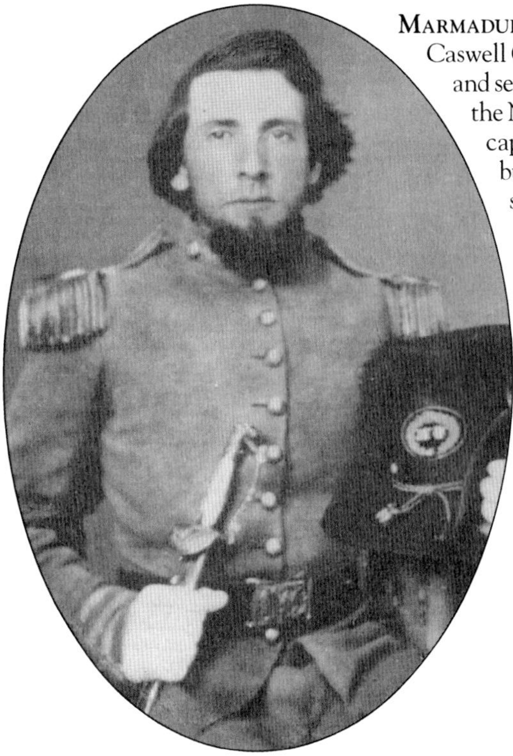

Marmaduke William Norfleet (1839–1890). Born in Caswell County, Marmaduke received a good education and served in the Civil War with the 42nd Regiment of the North Carolina Volunteers. He was wounded and captured at Gettysburg and subsequently paroled, but health problems prevented his return to active service. Marmaduke worked in the mercantile business in Yanceyville and then moved to Winston-Salem in 1873 to become a dealer in leaf tobacco. He founded Piedmont Tobacco Warehouse in 1875 and was in partnership with James S. Scales for a few years. His sons managed the business after his death. He married Mary Ellen Kirkpatrick (1842–1921) in 1864.

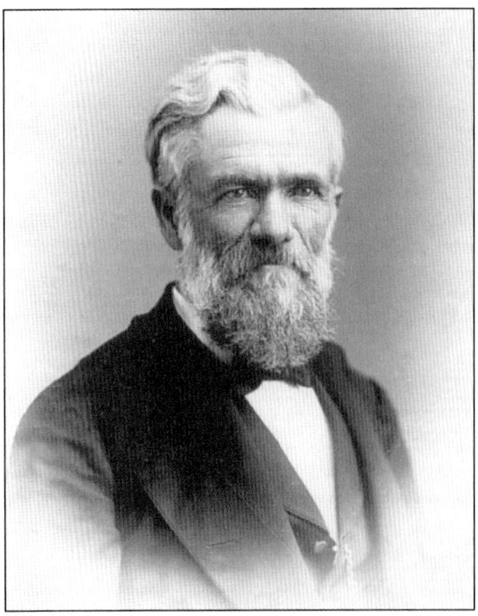

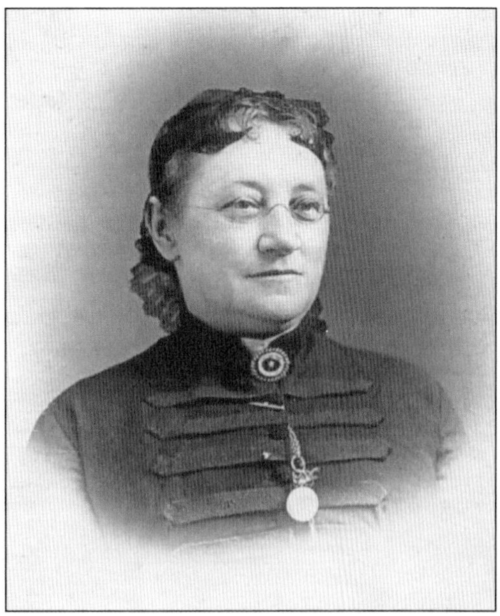

Gen. William Robertson Boggs (1829–1911) and Mary Sophia Symington Boggs (1831–1905). The lives of William and Mary are richly steeped in American military history. As a West Point graduate, William served his country in many locations, including Troy, New York, where he met and married his commanding officer's daughter, Mary. Together, they lived through the Civil War, with General Boggs returning to his engineering profession. They spent their last days in Winston-Salem.

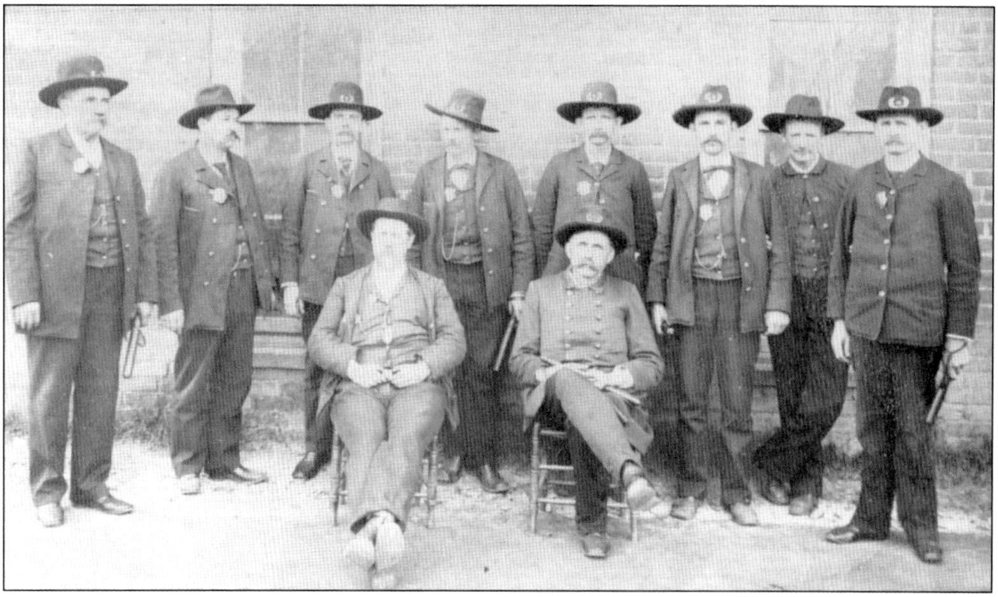

John Wesley Bradford (1846–1917). John was a North Carolina native and a Civil War veteran. He served in Company G, 47th Regiment of the North Carolina Troops. He was 16 years old when he enlisted and was a member of the Norfleet Camp of Confederate Veterans. John was a Forsyth County deputy sheriff and served as chief of police for Winston (seated front right in the photograph). He was married to Lou Ella Tucker.

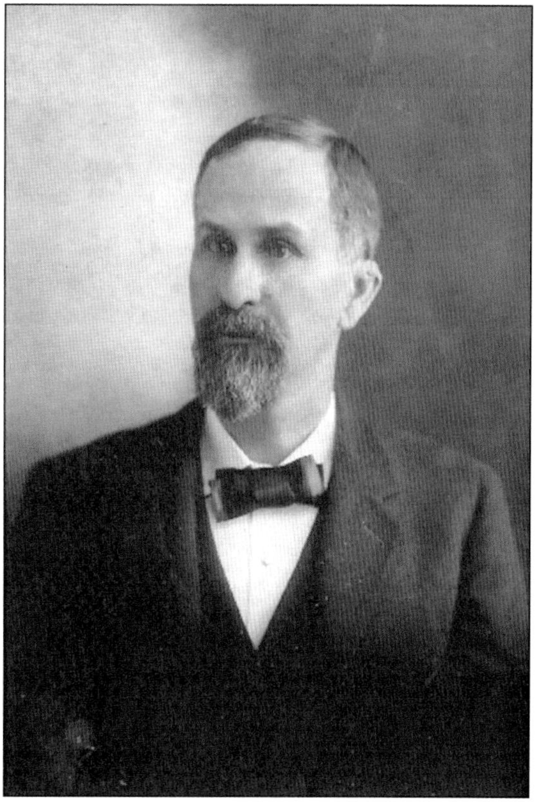

Capt. Daniel Patterson Mast (1842–1911). Born in Watauga County, Daniel came to Winston-Salem around 1870. Previously, he served in the Civil War in Company D, 9th Regiment, known as the First Calvary. He lost his right leg in the Battle of Chamberlain's Run in Virginia and was captured and hospitalized for several months. In Winston-Salem, Captain Mast was elected register of deeds in 1876 and held the position for 12 years. He was elected mayor in 1888 and served two terms. He practiced law, and his offices were over Thompson's Drug Store on West Fourth Street, where he also lived.

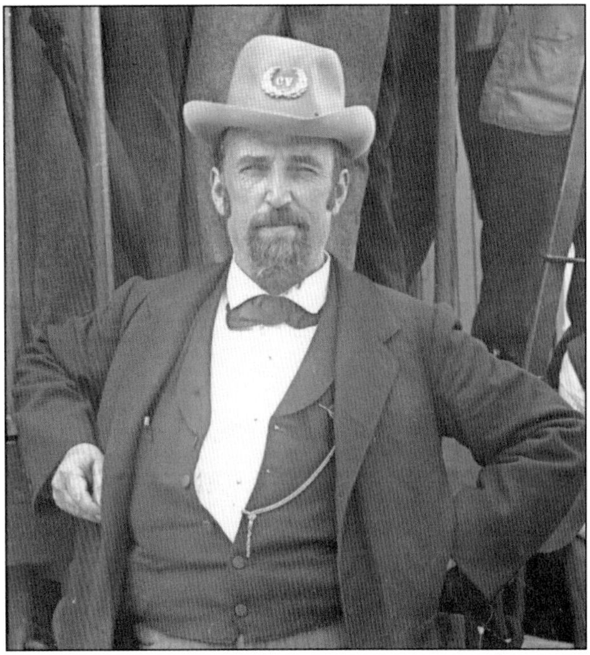

Cyrus Barksdale Watson (1844–1916). Born near Kernersville, Cyrus was educated at home and then at Kernersville High School. He enlisted in Company K, 45th Regiment of the North Carolina Troops during the Civil War. Hospitalized for wounds from two battles, he joined his command at Appomattox. He studied law and worked as a criminal lawyer with partners Robert B. Glenn and John C. Buxton. His son Thomas Wilson Watson (1871–1933) became a partner around 1901. Cyrus served in the state senate and worked to construct good roads in North Carolina. He married Amelia Henley (1847–1907), daughter of William Penn Henley (1817–1882) and Sarah Sabrina Lindsay Henley (1822–1910).

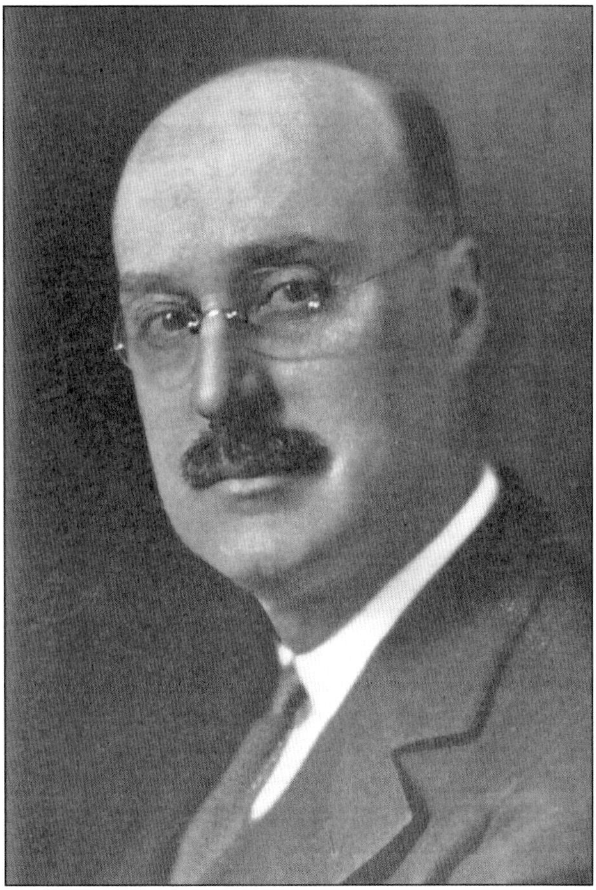

William Mayhew Hendren (1871–1939). William, a native of New Bern, came to Winston-Salem to practice law in 1894. He joined the Glenn, Manly & Hendren law firm, which became Manly, Hendren & Womble in 1896. He was the senior member at his death. In 1899, William married Annie Julia Rawley (1871–1929), daughter of Capt. Taylor Lindsey Rawley (1841–1927) and Sarah Pauline "Sallie" Lindsay Rawley (1844–1909). Captain Rawley worked in the leaf tobacco trade in Winston-Salem and was in charge of the city's waterworks for 10 years. He served in the Civil War and was at Appomattox for the final surrender.

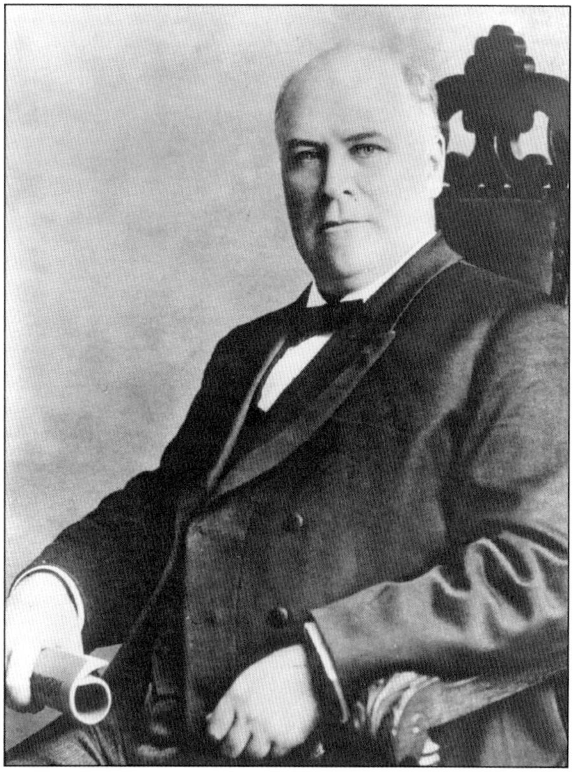

GOV. ROBERT BROADNAX GLENN (1854–1920). Robert's father, a Rockingham County tobacco planter and lawyer, died in the Civil War when Robert was eight years old. Robert studied law, came to Winston in 1885, and joined the law practice of William B. Glenn. He later worked with Clement Manly and William M. Hendren. He held several state government positions before serving as governor from 1905 to 1909. He died in Canada while attending an International Boundary Commission session, appointed by Pres. Woodrow Wilson. He married Nina Deaderick (1854–1926) in 1878. Robert B. Glenn High School was named in his honor.

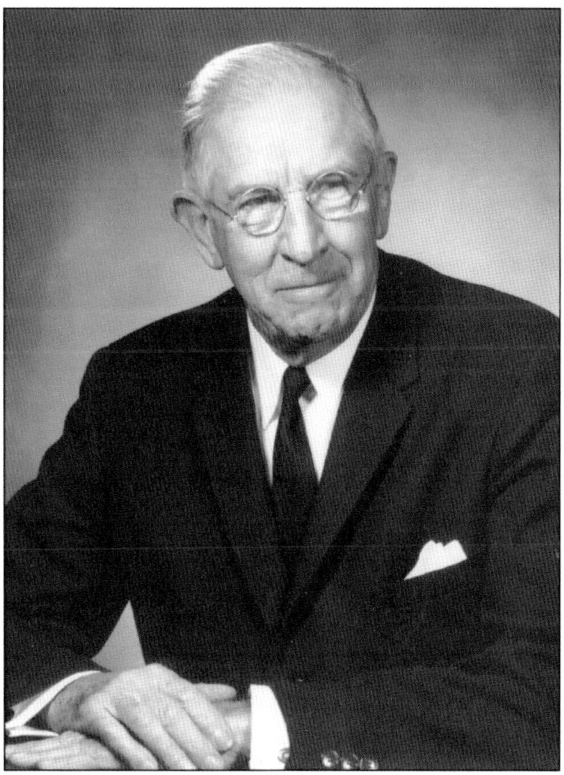

BUNYAN SNIPES "B.S." WOMBLE (1882–1976). B.S. was born in Chatham County to Rev. William Fletcher Womble (1859–1929) and Olivia Snipes Womble (1860–1948). He lived in several counties as a child, moving with his parents as his father served different Methodist churches. He studied law at Trinity College (Duke University), was admitted to the bar in 1905, and then came to Winston-Salem to practice law in 1907. He became associated with the firm of Manly, Hendren & Womble, which was known as Womble, Carlyle, Sandridge & Rice when he died. B.S. married Edith Willingham (1890–1980).

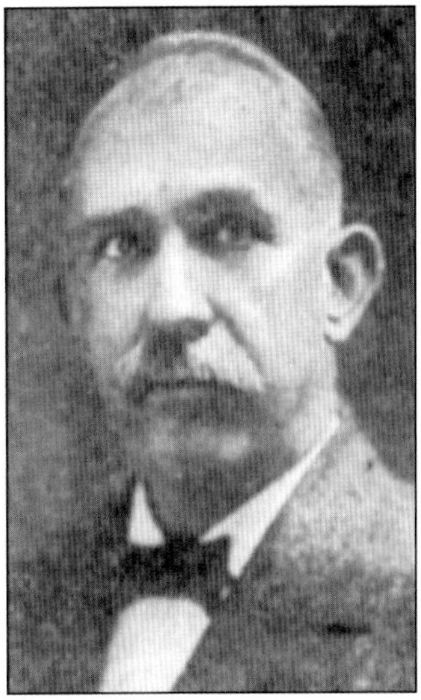

Col. H. Montague (1857–1939). Colonel Montague was born—and attended college—in Wake Forest. He studied law, which he practiced in Greensboro and Wadesboro before establishing his law practice in Winston-Salem. He was aide-de-camp to Gov. W.W. Kitchen, a member of his personal military staff, and a commissioned officer in the North Carolina National Guard with the rank of colonel. His favorite pastimes were reading, meditation, and walking. He established the annual Montague Medal for the high school senior with the highest average in each local high school. He married Estelle Nissen (1867–1954) in 1890.

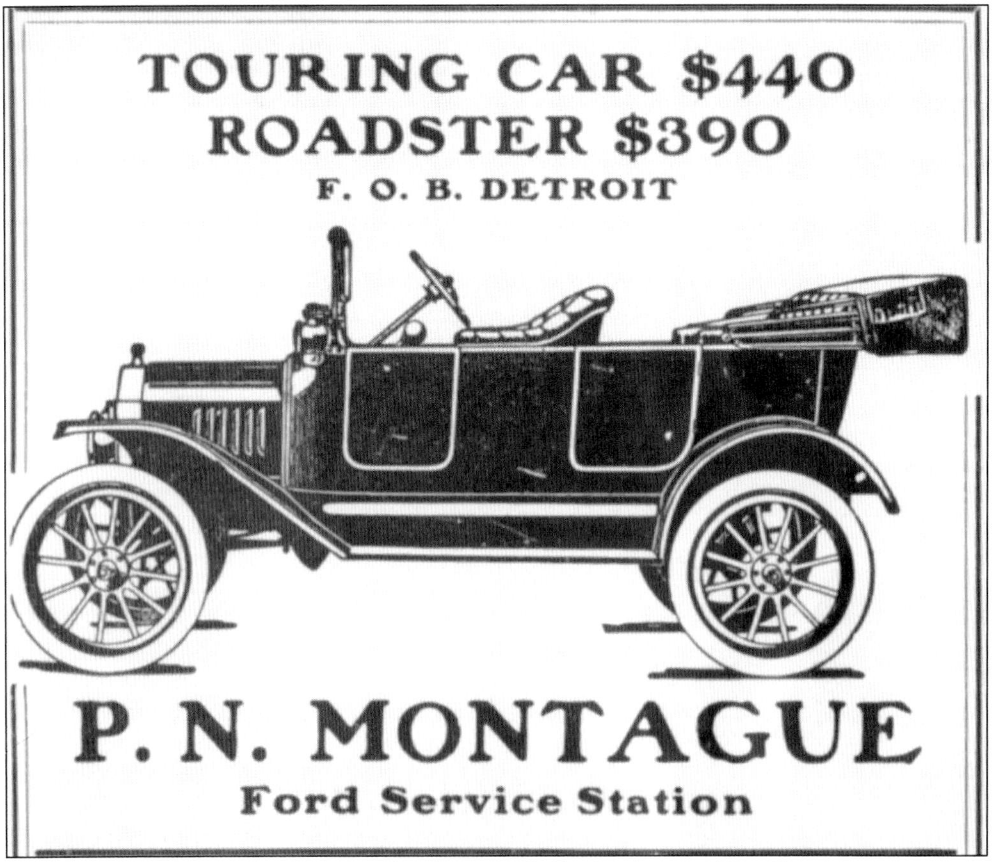

Paul Nissen Montague (1890–1959). The only child of Col. H. and Estelle Nissen Montague, Paul received a wide and varied education, which prepared him for military service and for business and legal professions. Paul served in World War I, during which he was a prisoner of war, and also served in World War II. Paul organized the Ford automobile agency in 1912 and worked for Wachovia Bank and Trust Company. He was married to Nita Davis (1899–1978.)

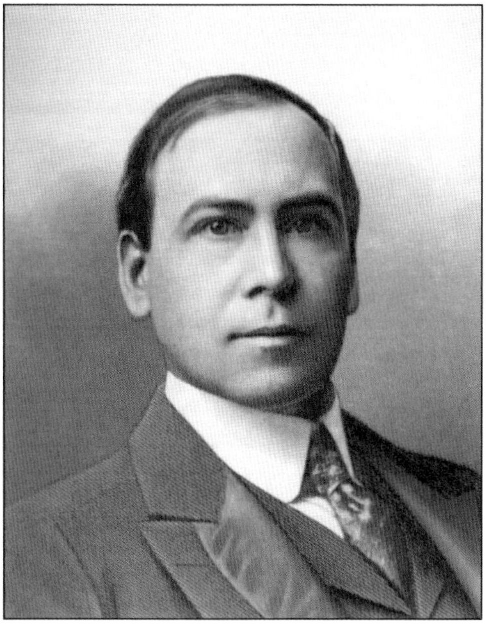

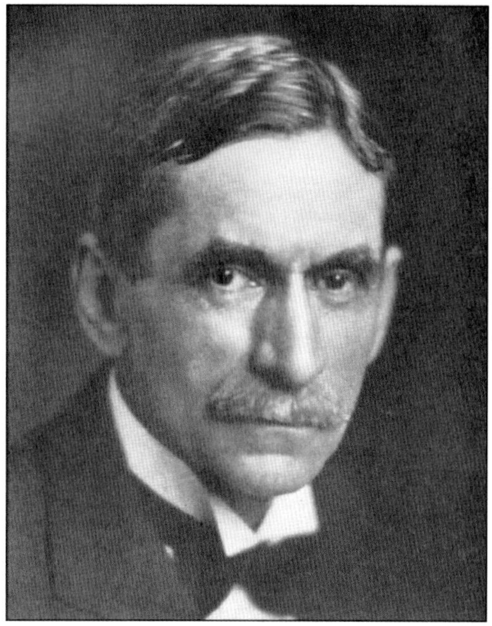

Adolphus Hill Eller (1861–1941) and Henry Reuben Starbuck (1866–1958). Born in Wilkes County, Adolphus studied law at the Folks Law School. Admitted to the bar in 1886, his first law practice was the firm of Eller & Starbuck in 1888. He assisted in the organization of Standard Building and Loan Association and served as president. He was a director and chairman of Wachovia Bank and Trust Company's trust committee. Adolphus married Laura Winifred Newland (1872–1938). Henry was born in Winston-Salem in the Starbuck home located on the site of present-day city hall. He also studied law in Caldwell County at the Folks Law School. He was one of the oldest practicing lawyers in Forsyth County and the first judge of Forsyth County Court. He also served in the North Carolina Senate. Henry was married to Nannie Lee Agurs (1867–1913).

A. H. ELLER. H. R. STARBUCK.

ELLER & STARBUCK,

ATTORNEYS-AT-LAW,

Winston, N. C.

WILL PRACTICE IN STATE AND FEDERAL COURTS, and give SPECIAL ATTENTION to COLLECTIONS, LOANS, INSURANCE, SALE OF LAND, MANAGEMENT OF ESTATES, ETC.

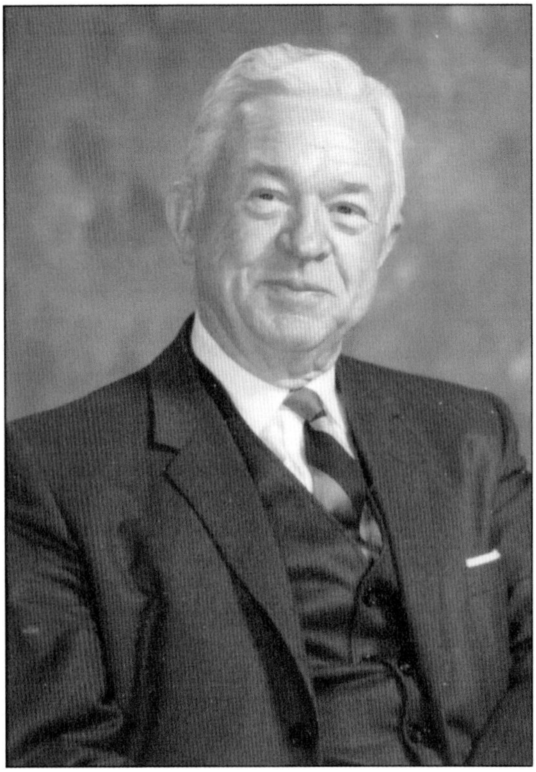

Irving Edward Carlyle (1896–1971). Born in Wake Forest, Irving attended Wake Forest College, taught school, coached baseball and basketball, and then studied law for two years. He came to Winston-Salem in 1922 and opened his law office; however, he joined the law firm of Manly, Hendren & Womble the following year. Later, he became a partner in the firm, which was then called Womble, Carlyle, Sandridge & Rice. Irving was active in civic and political affairs throughout North Carolina. Irving married Mary Belo Moore (1904–1996) in 1928. Mary was from New Bern and taught English at R.J. Reynolds High School.

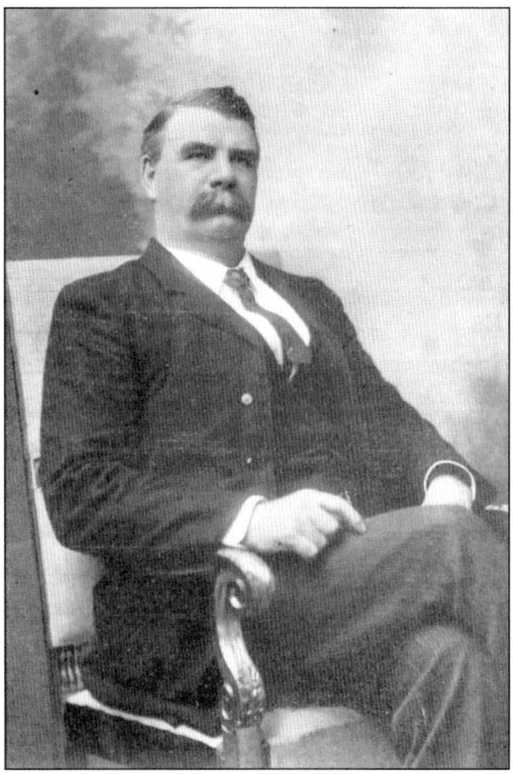

John Cameron Buxton (1852–1917). John was born in Asheville, attended several colleges, and was admitted to the North Carolina Bar in 1875. He came to Winston-Salem and practiced law a few years before he formed a firm with Cyrus B. Watson, which became Watson, Buxton & Watson when Watson's son joined the firm. John was elected mayor of Winston and a North Carolina senator. He served on the local school board for 27 years. He is credited with the development of local schools and with obtaining the city's Carnegie Library. John was married to Agnes Cornelia Belo (1852–1932), daughter of Frederick Edward and Carolina Belo.

CAPT. FREDERICK EDWARD BELO (1811–1883). Born in Salem, Edward attended Salem Boys' School and studied cabinetmaking under a local joiner named Peterson. He constructed a general store on South Main Street, made of red brick and decorated with Corinthian columns. The house also featured iron railings and grills that he made in his foundry. The first floor was for business, with family living quarters on the second level. A third floor was added later and used for staff housing. Edward helped build a railroad between Winston-Salem and Greensboro and was involved in farming and raising flowers. He was married to Carolina Amanda Fries (1817–1881).

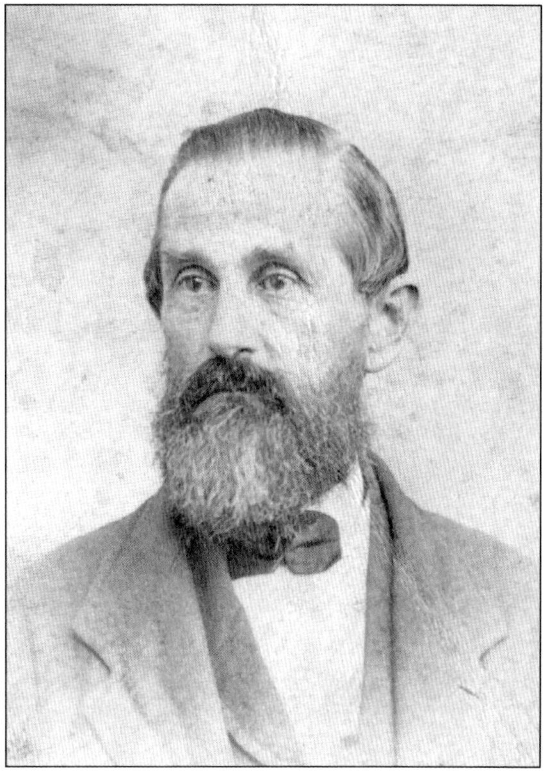

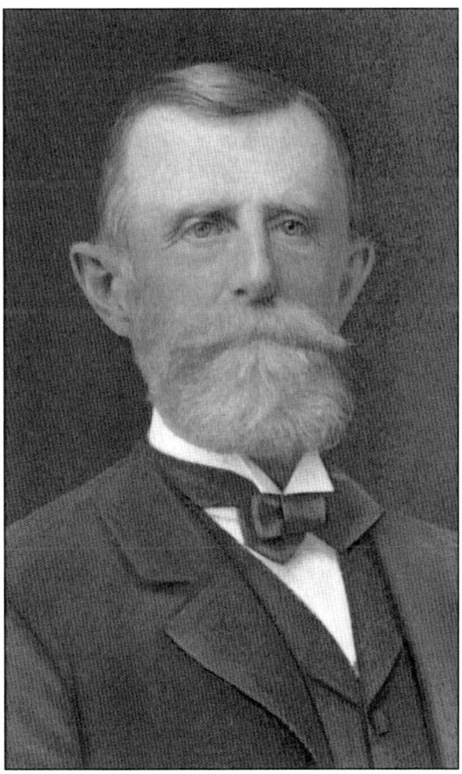

ALFRED HORATIO BELO (1839–1901). Alfred, son of Frederick Edward and Carolina Amanda Fries Belo, attended Salem Boys' School, Masonic Institute at Germanton, and Wilson's Academy in Alamance County. He worked in his father's store, in his linseed oil mill, and on his farm. He was commissioned a captain in the Forsyth Riflemen during the Civil War. Alfred moved to Texas, where he worked as a tutor, joined the *Galveston News*, and later purchased the company. He began the *Dallas Morning News*. Alfred was married to Jeannette Ennis (1846–1913). He donated the Belo House to be used as a home for self-supporting women.

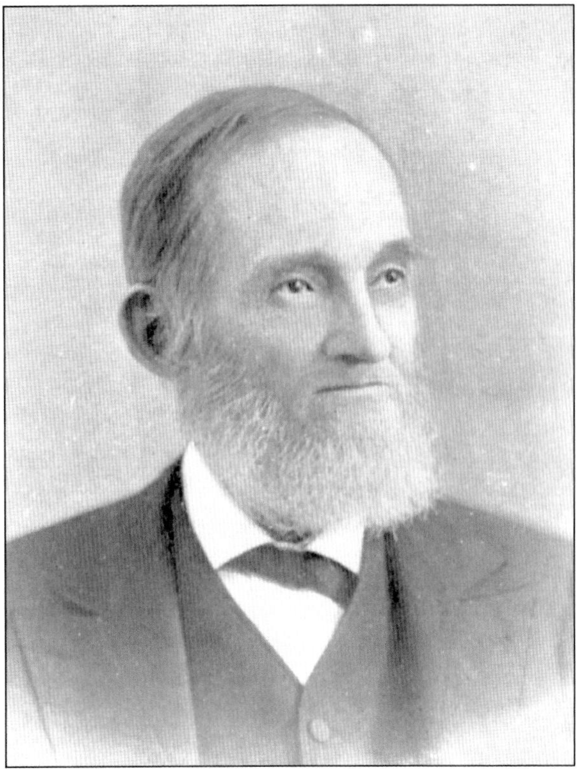

Dr. Calvin Henderson Wiley (1819–1887). Calvin's mother thought her son should be a minister, so she named him for John Calvin and her minister, Rev. Dr. Henderson. Calvin studied law and edited and published literary works. His concern about North Carolina's lack of a universal education system led to his appointment as the state's first school superintendent, where he worked to establish a public school system. After the Civil War, he studied theology and came to Winston-Salem, where he established a public school system. Calvin was married to Harriet Smith "Mittie" Towles (1841–1917). Calvin H. Wiley School was named in his honor in 1925.

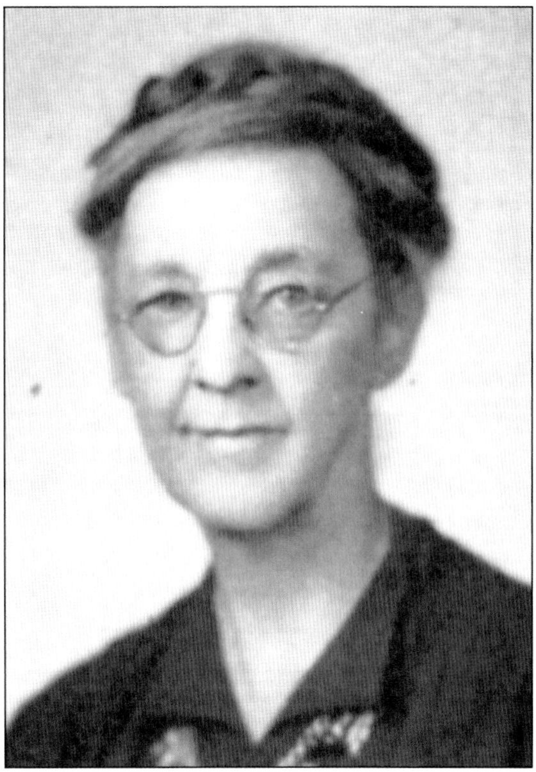

Mary Callum Wiley (1875–1965). Calvin and Mittie Wiley were parents to five children. Two of their daughters, Mary (pictured) and Annie, were teachers in the local school system. "Miss Mary" taught English at West End School, Cherry Street High School, and R.J. Reynolds High School. She wrote a daily historical column, "Mostly Local," in the *Twin City Sentinel* for 19 years. She also coauthored a Forsyth County history book for the county's 100th anniversary. Annie W. Wiley (1869–1947) was a school faculty member for 34 years, working as a teacher, a supervisor, and as principal of Central Park School for 23 years.

Daisy Lee Glasgow (1904–1986). Daisy Lee was born in Durham to Littleton James Glasgow (1867–1932) and Daisy Lee Adams Glasgow (1872–1924). She graduated from Winston High School and Salem College. "Miss Glasgow" was a fixture in room 207, teaching US history to thousands of Forsyth County students. She proudly taught in the same room for most of her career, though the name of the school changed from South Junior High School to South High School to Gray High School. Her teaching career spanned 41 years, and her reputation as a tough but engaging teacher is still remembered by former students.

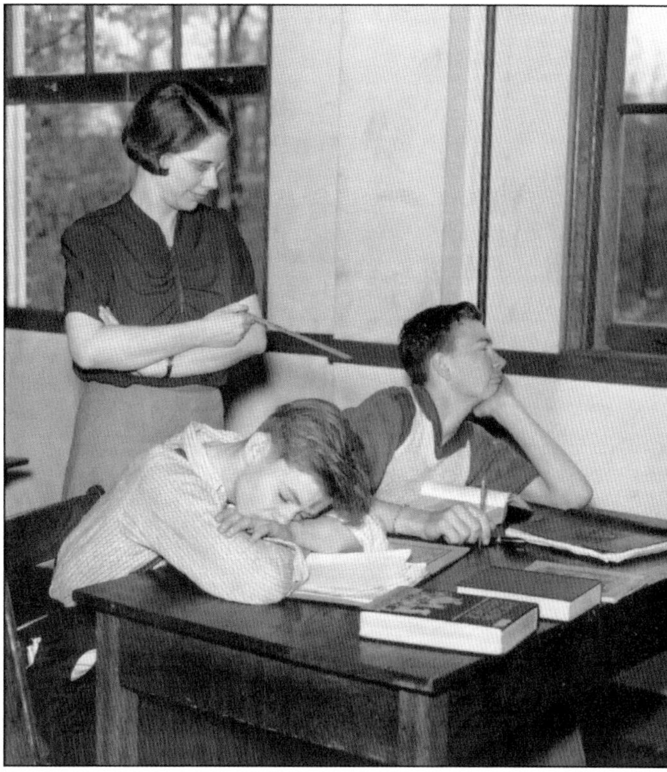

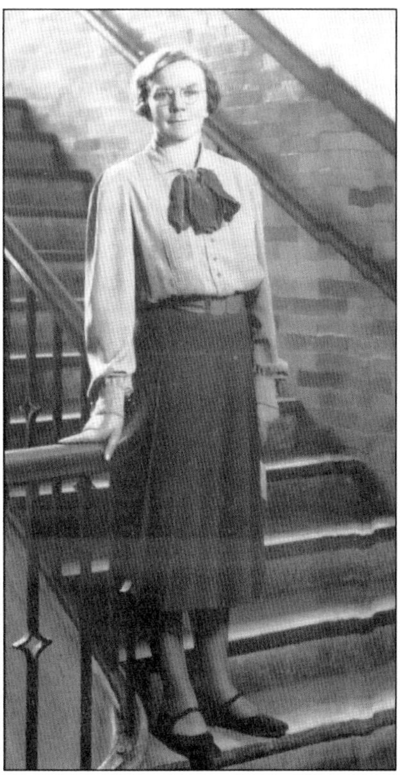

Kathleen Hall (1891–1983). Kathleen was born in High Point, and after college, she began her teaching career in Thomasville from 1913 to 1924. She came to Winston-Salem and taught at Forest Park School before transferring to Gray High School when the school opened in 1930. She retired from Gray in 1957, taught an additional 10 years in Stokes County, and then worked as a substitute teacher. Kathleen was honored in 1978 as the first public school teacher in Winston-Salem to have a school named for her. Hall-Woodward Elementary School was named for her and for Julius Woodward, principal at Gray High School and Kathleen's "boss."

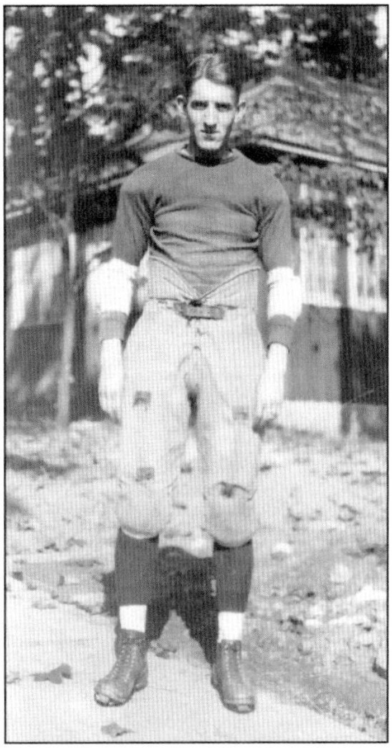

Leo James Caldwell (1903–1923). Leo was born to James Hughes Caldwell (1866–1942) and Lillian Eva Bowles Caldwell (1876–1946). He attended R.J. Reynolds High School during its first full year of operation and was a popular high school student and athlete. During a football game against Charlotte, Leo punted the ball and then tackled the receiver, who threw Leo to the ground. Leo died instantly from a broken neck. Devastated by his death, local citizens established the Leo Caldwell Memorial Student Loan Fund in his name. The fund formed the basis for the student aid program at the Winston-Salem Foundation. A portrait of Leo was presented to the school at the 1924 graduation exercises.

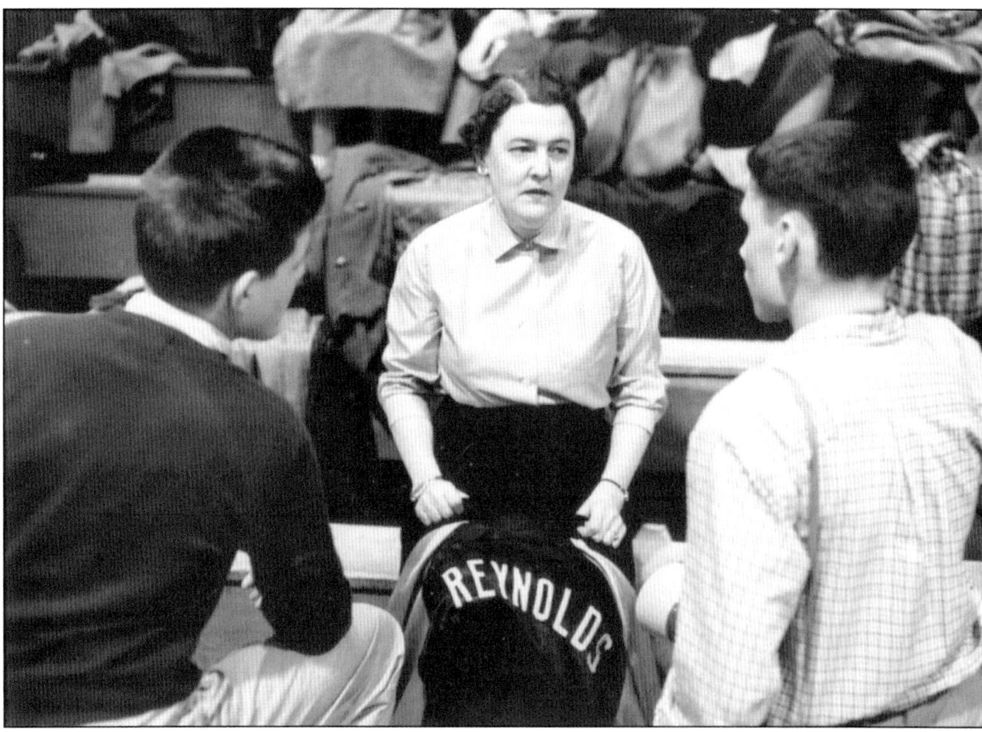

Annie Graham Caldwell (1907–1974). Annie was a sister to Leo James Caldwell, discussed above. Their father was an ardent sports fan and passed his love of sports to his children. Annie was a graduate of R.J. Reynolds High School and worked as librarian and history teacher for Ardmore School and R.J. Reynolds from 1929 to 1971. She coached the Reynolds cheerleaders and was the football team's top booster.

MARGIE MAE HASTINGS HOPKINS PRATT (1898–1969). Margie was born in Winston-Salem to John Raymond Hastings (1867–1926) and Evie Lambe Hastings (1874–1966). She graduated from R.J. Reynolds High School in 1915, from Salem College in 1919, and then from Columbia University. She taught high school mathematics and then taught mathematics at Salem College from 1930 to 1933. Margie was one of the organizers of Summit School, and she taught there for four years. Margie was first married to Clifford Stedman Hopkins (1882–1949) and secondly to Carl Day Pratt (1891–1981).

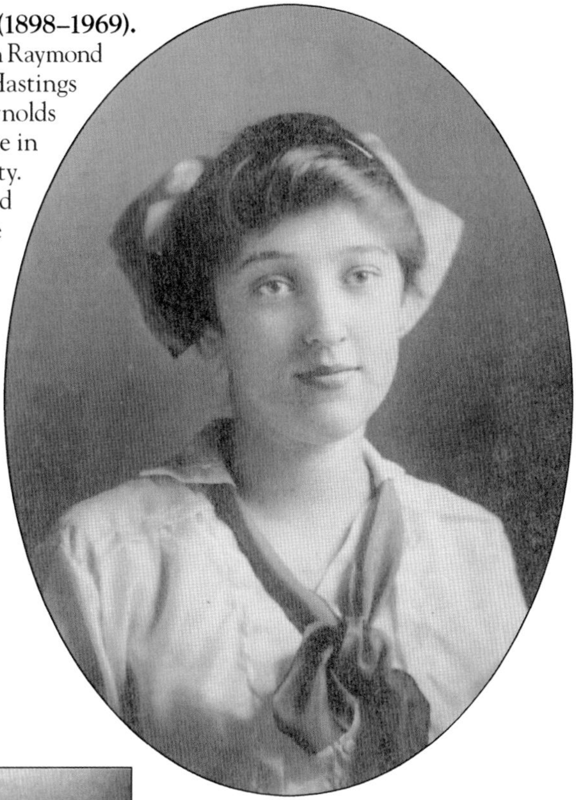

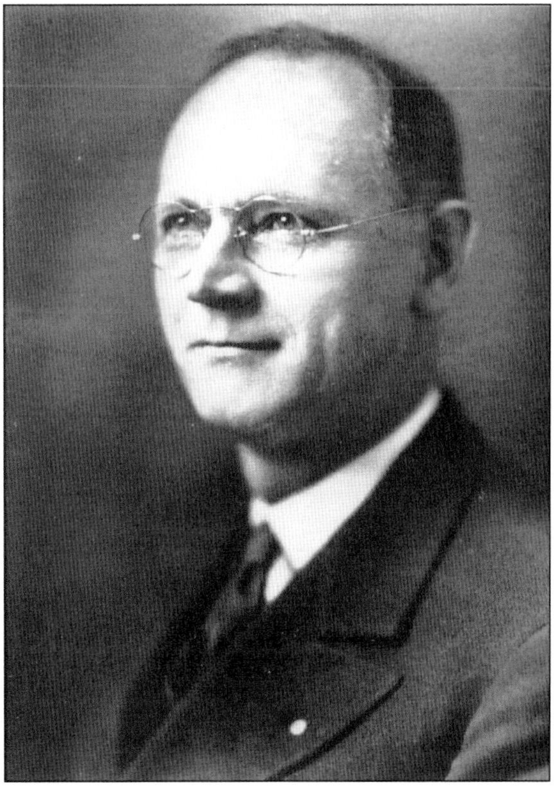

ROWLAND HILL LATHAM (1880–1948). Rowland was born in Plymouth and moved to Virginia as a child. He graduated from the University of Virginia with bachelor's and master's degrees in education. Rowland married Mamie Pollard Brown (1882–1973) and worked as superintendent of schools in Weldon before coming to Winston-Salem in 1910 to be superintendent of Winston-Salem city schools. He held this position until 1933, when he resigned over a disagreement with the board of aldermen. He then worked as school superintendent in Asheville, retiring in 1946. Latham Elementary School was named in his honor.

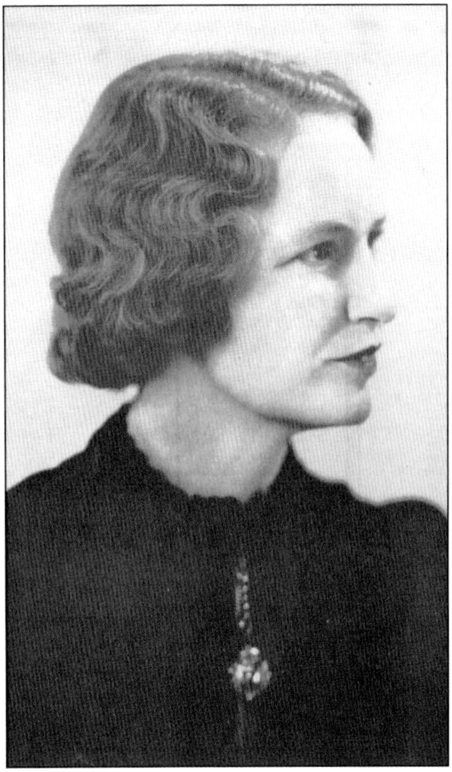

Annie Moselle Stephenson (1906–1972). Born in Milton to James B. Stephenson (1879–1938) and Cora A. LeGrand Stephenson (1883–1966), Moselle moved to Winston-Salem in 1913. She graduated from R.J. Reynolds High School and Winthrop College and began her 40-year teaching career as director of female athletics at Forest Park School in 1928. Moselle was head of the English department at Gray and Parkland High Schools, taught journalism, and was the yearbook advisor. Gray High School seniors dedicated the 1941 yearbook to Moselle "for her faithfulness, sincerity, willingness, and friendliness toward all, and her sympathetic nature in helping with our problems."

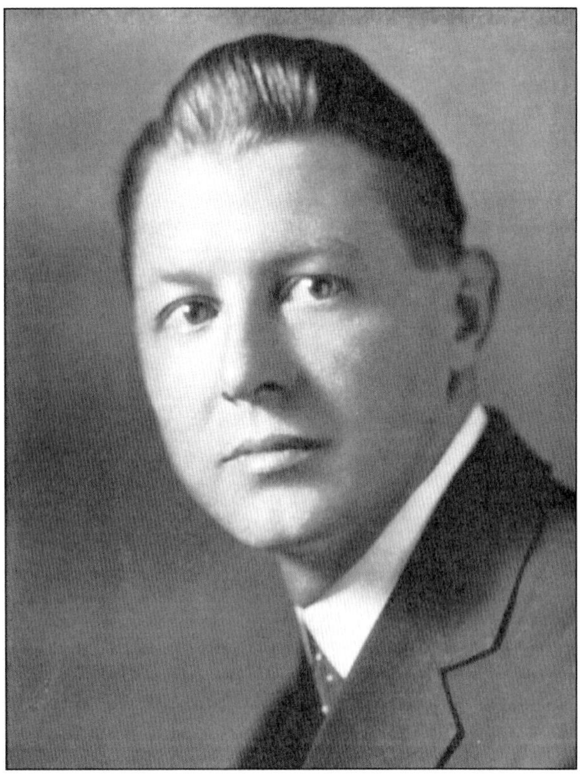

Robert Sidney Haltiwanger (1893–1986). Born on a 300-acre South Carolina cotton farm, Robert planned to study medicine at Davidson College but fell in love with teaching. He served in the Navy during World War I and then joined the Winston-Salem school system, where he organized athletic programs and scientific courses. Robert and his wife, Jane Couch Haltiwanger (1894–1976), built a home near the site of the new R.J. Reynolds High School. When Reynolds opened in 1923, Robert, nicknamed "Halty," was one of the original faculty members. Hanes Junior High School became Hanes High School, and he served as principal of both, retiring in 1959.

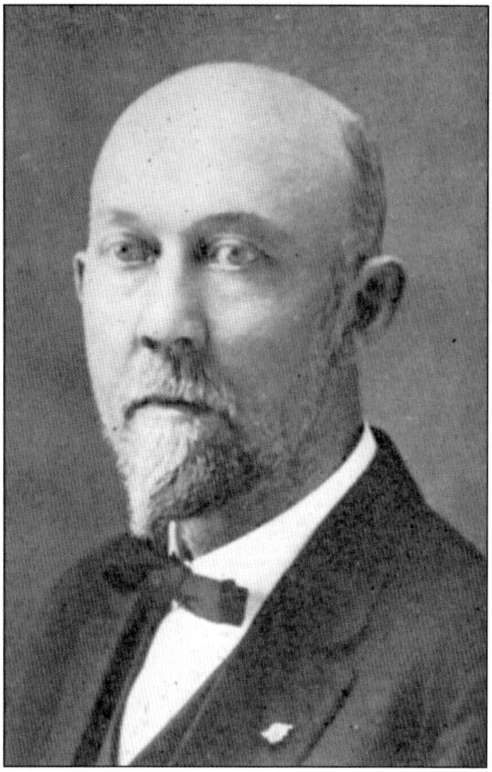

Leon Cash (1866–1937). Leon attended schools in several counties and began teaching at age 16. He was school superintendent for Davie County, taught at Salem Boys' School, and served as North Winston Graded School principal. After devoting 27 years to a career in education, he worked for Forsyth Chair Company and then became president and treasurer for Standard Building & Loan Association. Leon was chairman of the board of commissioners and the first Forsyth County auditor. He was called "the grand old man of Masonry" for his work with the Masonic Order. Leon married Frances Hartsell (1867–1903) in 1889.

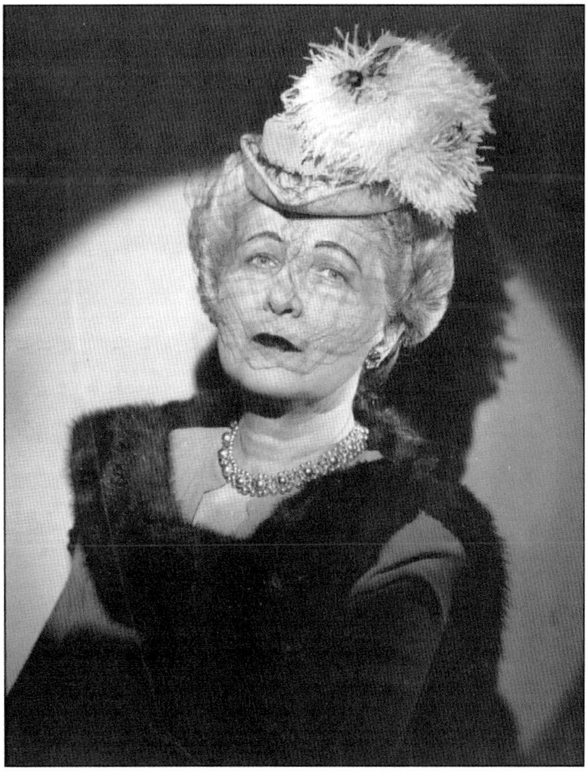

Audrey Clore LeGrand (1895–1983). Virginia-native Audrey graduated from Virginia College, where she majored in organ and voice. She attended Salem College and taught voice there for eight years. Audrey toured North Carolina as a recitalist and was a soloist for musical events, such as Handel's *Messiah*, and for Centenary Methodist Church and Brown Memorial Baptist Church. Audrey taught voice and piano at Rural Hall School for 40 years and taught voice and piano in her home. She also modeled for various department stores and modeled hats particularly well, as pictured. She was married to Eugene Foote LeGrand (1887–1960).

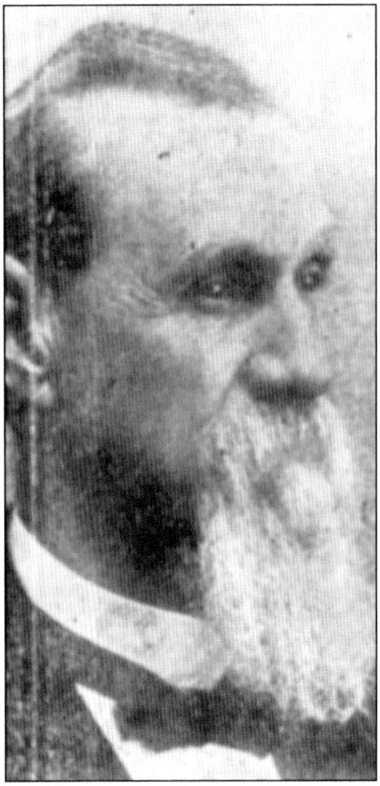

Maj. Thomas Jethro Brown (1833–1914). Thomas Jethro was born in Caswell County, studied at the Dan River Institute, and moved to Davie County, where he farmed until the outbreak of the Civil War. He formed a company of volunteers, and they were assigned to the 42nd Regiment of the North Carolina Volunteers, where he was promoted to major and engaged in several battles. He moved to Winston-Salem in 1872 and opened the first tobacco warehouse, marking the beginning of the prosperous tobacco industry in the city and region. He was also involved in the Brown-Rogers Hardware business. He was married to Delphine Hall (1847–1889).

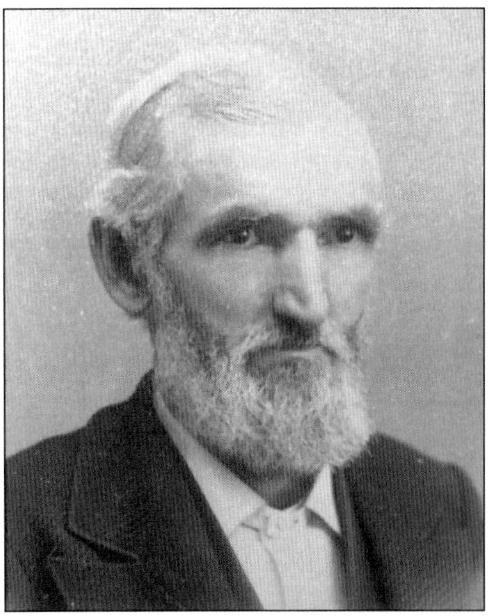

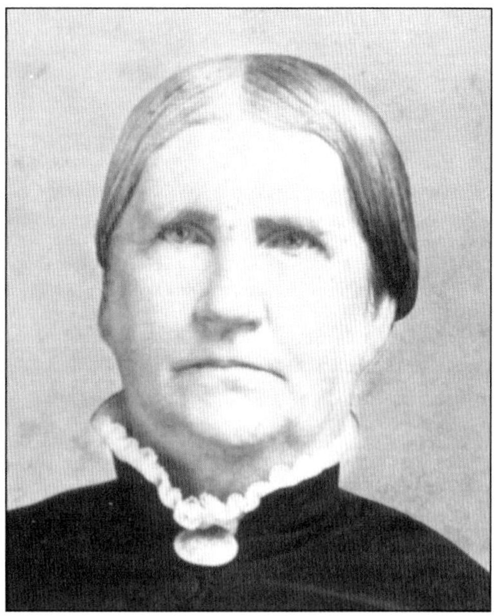

Peter Adams Wilson Sr. (1825–1892) and Lucretia Sullivan Wilson (1823–1900). Peter and Lucretia were early settlers of Winston. They operated the first hotel in town, the Wilson Hotel, where they also lived. A tailor by profession, Peter served the city as mayor and commissioner. He was a representative in the General Assembly and a senator from Stokes and Forsyth Counties. A charter member of the Masonic Lodge, Peter was the first grand master.

THOMAS JAMES WILSON (1859–1942). Thomas was the son of Peter and Lucretia Wilson. He was just a boy when he attended the first tobacco auction in Brown's first tobacco warehouse. He and his brother Nathaniel Sullivan Wilson (1854–1934) became tobacco manufacturers and made plug tobacco. At one time, there were many small tobacco manufacturers in Winston-Salem, but the smaller companies eventually found it difficult to compete with the larger companies. Thomas later worked for the Northwest Mutual Life Insurance Company, and Nathaniel was clerk of Forsyth County Superior Court. Thomas married Bettie Sadler Harris (1860–1936), and Nathaniel married Bettie Spicer (1865–1955).

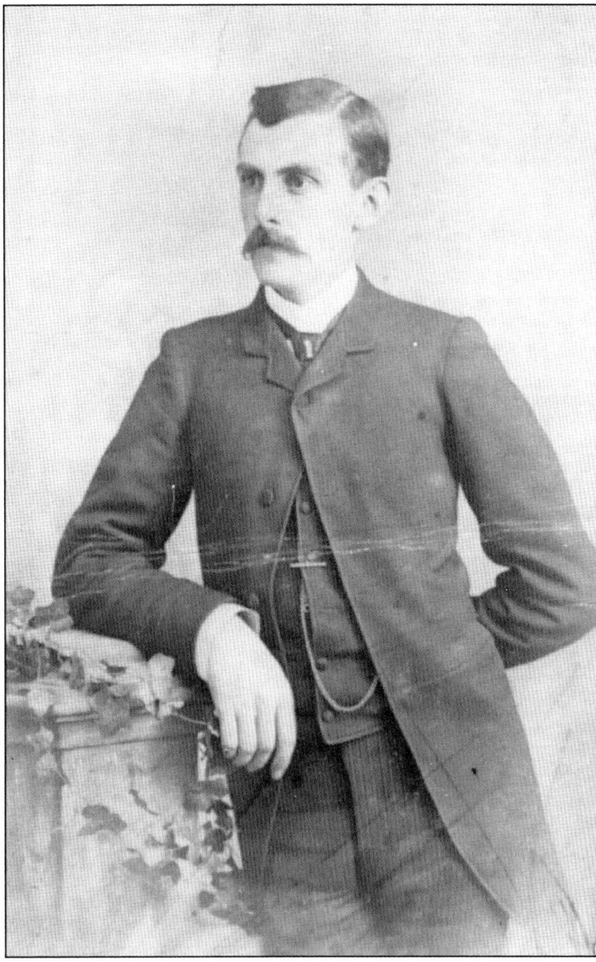

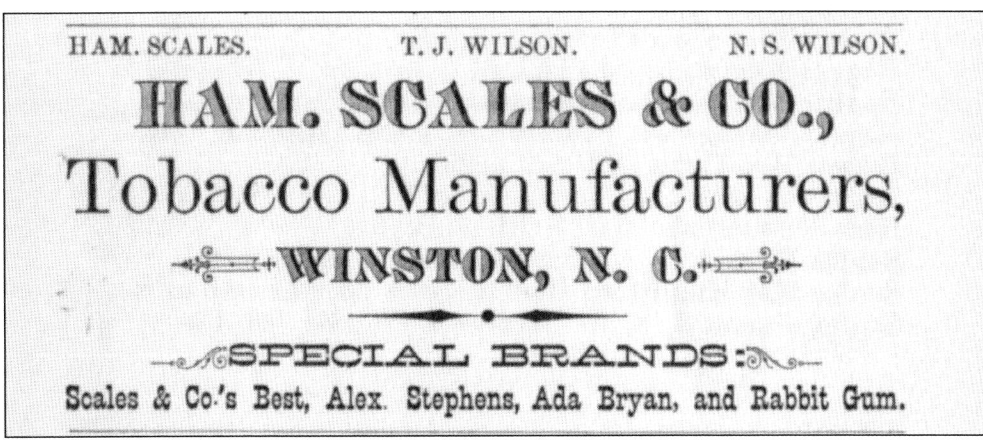

MAJ. HAMILTON SCALES (1821–1890). Born in Rockingham County, Hamilton earned his living by making plug tobacco. He served in the Civil War but withdrew because of poor health. He later served in the Home Guard. Hamilton came to Winston-Salem in 1870 and opened the city's first tobacco manufactory. Thomas and Nathaniel Wilson became his partners in 1888, and he sold his interest to them shortly before his death.

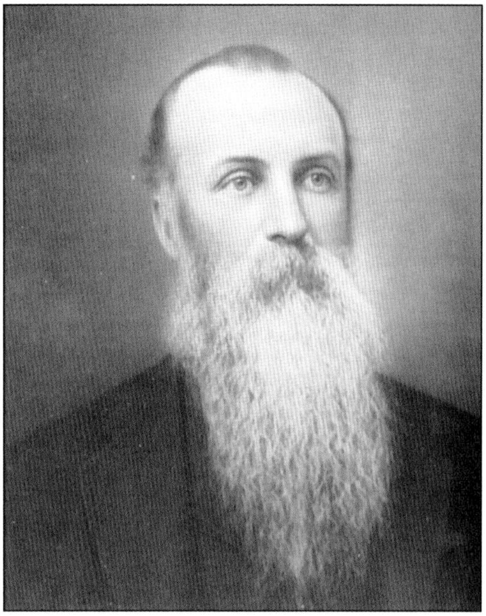
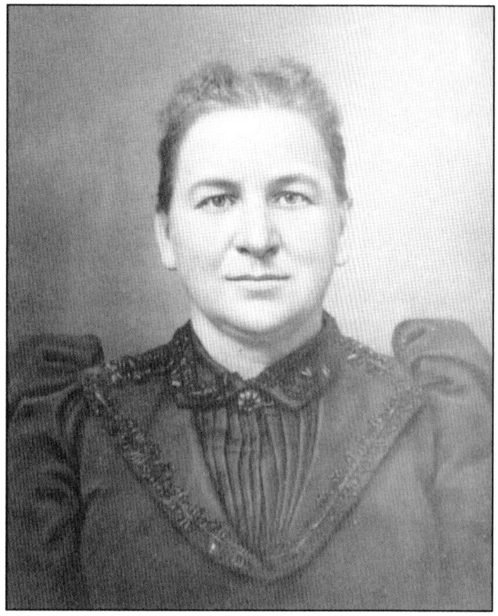

SIHON ALEXANDER OGBURN (1840–1927) AND MARY JANE TISE OGBURN (1847–1930). Sihon was born in Stokes County before Forsyth County was formed in 1849. He grew up on his father's farm and helped him raise tobacco. Sihon served in the Civil War and was wounded at the Battle of Fredericksburg. In 1865, he married Mary Jane Tise, daughter of Jacob Tise (1817–1904) and Margaret Kiser Tise (1825–1915). They were married 62 years and had 13 children. Sihon worked in merchandising with his father-in-law, then farmed, and eventually bought land and worked in the grocery trade. He formed a partnership with his brother Charles J. Ogburn (1842–1927) and William P. Hill (1847–1920) and manufactured tobacco. He later withdrew from the partnership and manufactured tobacco independently for 18 years. Sihon helped to establish the Ogburn Memorial Methodist Church.

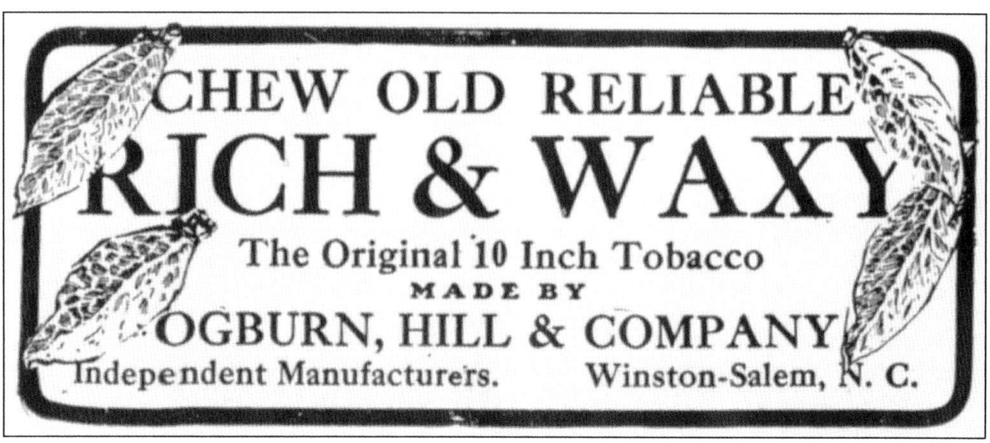

William Barrett Taylor (1851–1933). William was born in Virginia and came to Winston-Salem in 1883. He and his brother Jacqueline Plummer Taylor (1858–1916) established Taylor Brothers Tobacco Company. William knew his employees by name and inaugurated morning prayer services in the factory. He was president of the company at his death. William married Elizabeth McCaw Boggs (1858–1922), daughter of Gen. William Robinson and Mary Symington Boggs. Elizabeth helped establish the Twin City Hospital and was president of Associated Charities for many years. She was a member of the YWCA board and a charter member of the Women's Club.

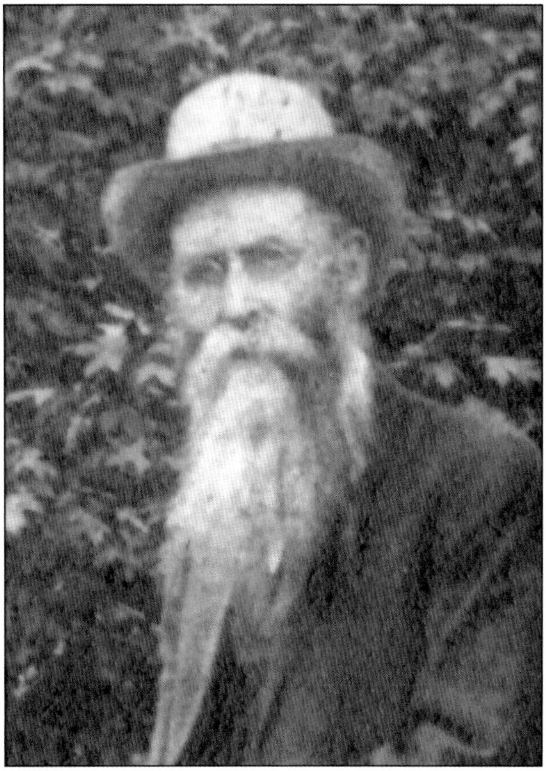

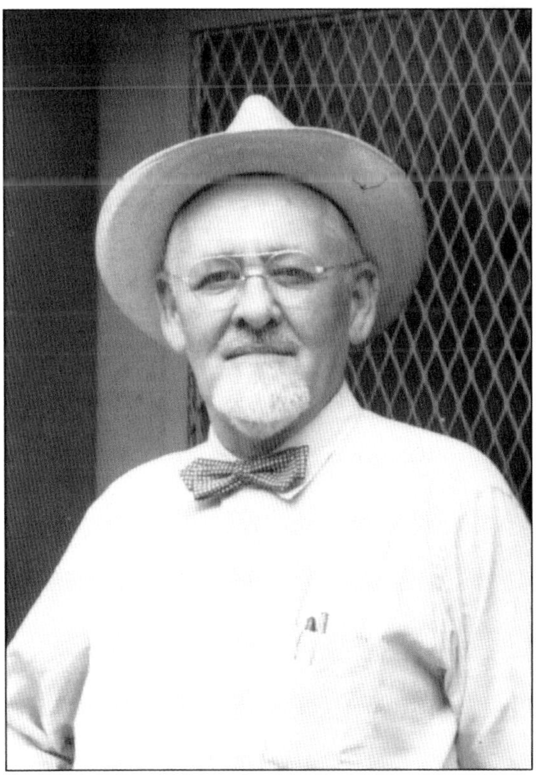

Archibald "Arch" Boggs Taylor (1892–1962). Arch was born in Salem to William Barrett and Elizabeth McCaw Boggs Taylor. He graduated from West End School and Davidson College and then worked for Taylor Brothers. Arch joined the Army and worked at a base hospital during World War I. He must have been homesick, because in a letter to friends in 1918, he said that he missed his friends in the factory, their great songs, and the smell of tobacco. He rejoined Taylor Brothers and became president in 1947, earning his nickname "Mr. Tobacco." Arch married Margaret Louise Webb Taylor (Williams) (1898–1981).

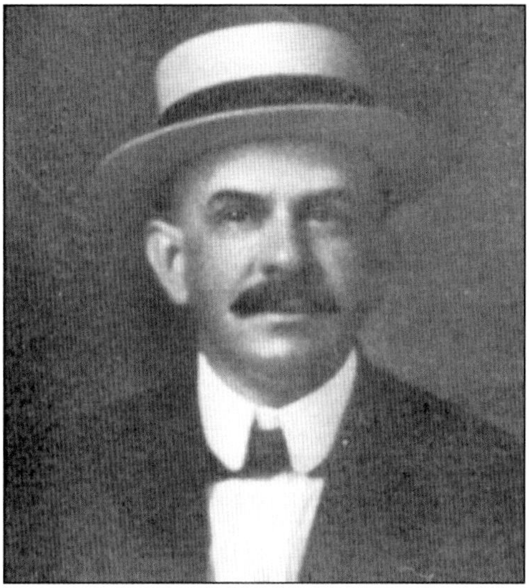

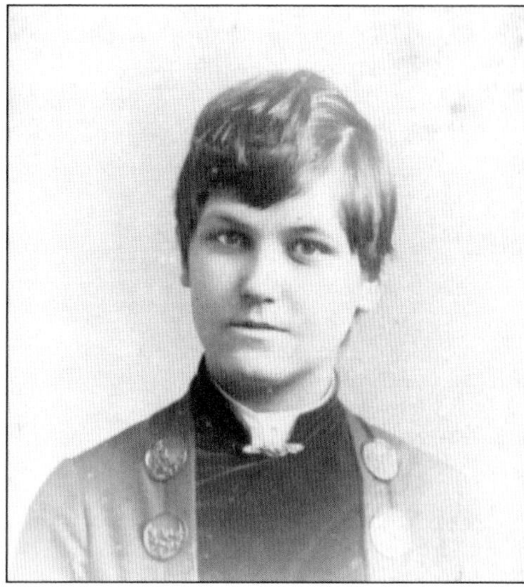

George T. Brown (1869–1913) and Robert Lynn Williamson (1860–1934) Families. George Brown (above, left) was born in Mocksville to Rufus D. Brown (1836–1893) and Sarah Gibbs Brown (1850–1892). Rufus and his brother William Lafayette Brown (1831–1899) were partners in Brown Brothers Tobacco Company. George studied business in college and began working in the tobacco industry. He met Robert Lynn Williamson, originally from Caswell County, in Winston-Salem. They formed a partnership to manufacture plug and smoking tobacco, which was called Brown & Williamson Tobacco Company. Some of their brands and parts of their business were purchased from Robert's father, who owned the T.F. Williamson Tobacco Company. Robert married Minnie Thompson (1869–1893) in 1889. George married Elsie Thompson (1876–1957), pictured above right. Elsie and Minnie were daughters of Dr. Vines Oscar Thompson (1835–1903) and Lina Dillard Joyner Thompson (1840–1914).

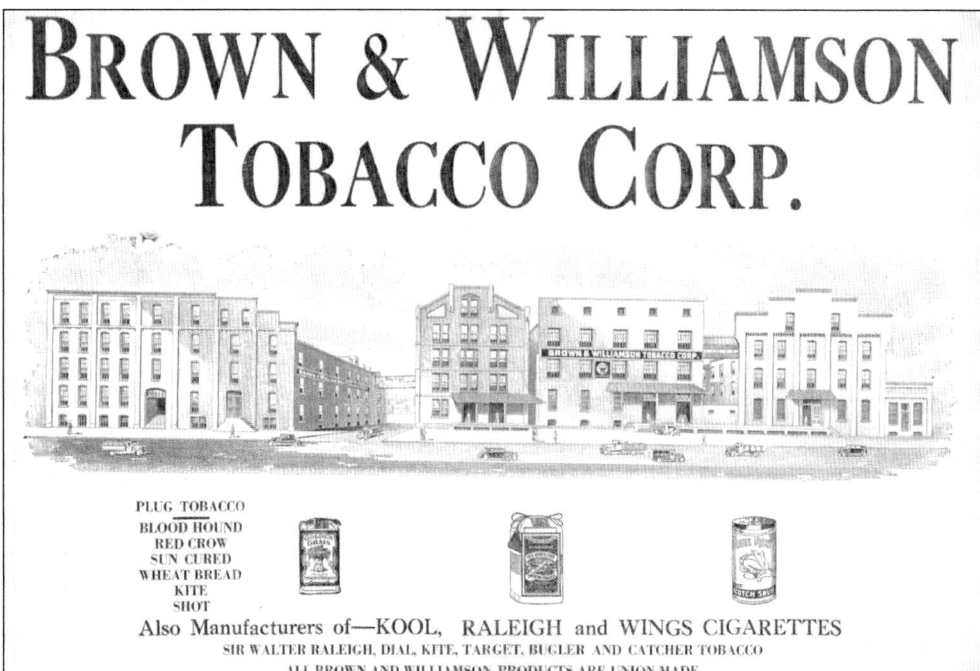

REV. DR. HENRY A. BROWN (1846–1929). Henry was born in Rockingham County and served with Company K, 3rd Regiment of Junior Reserves during the Civil War. After the war, he resumed his studies and graduated from Wake Forest College. He was ordained a Baptist minister and began his ministry as a home missionary with a circuit of five churches in three counties. In 1877, he became the pastor of First Baptist Church and served the church and the community for 40 years. Brown Memorial Baptist Church was named in his honor. He married Julia Z. Cain (1854–1914) in 1878.

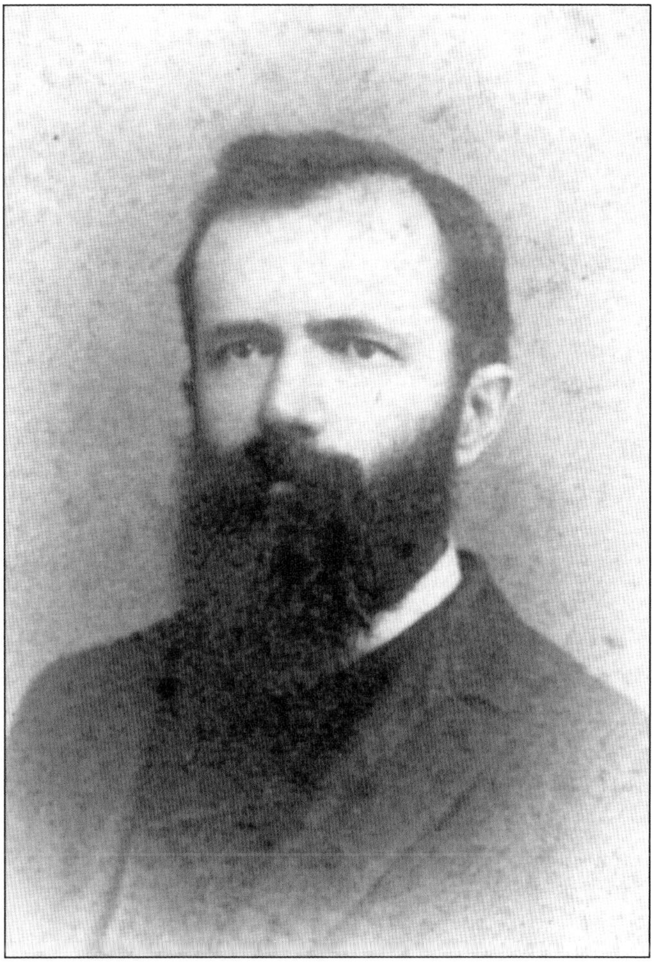

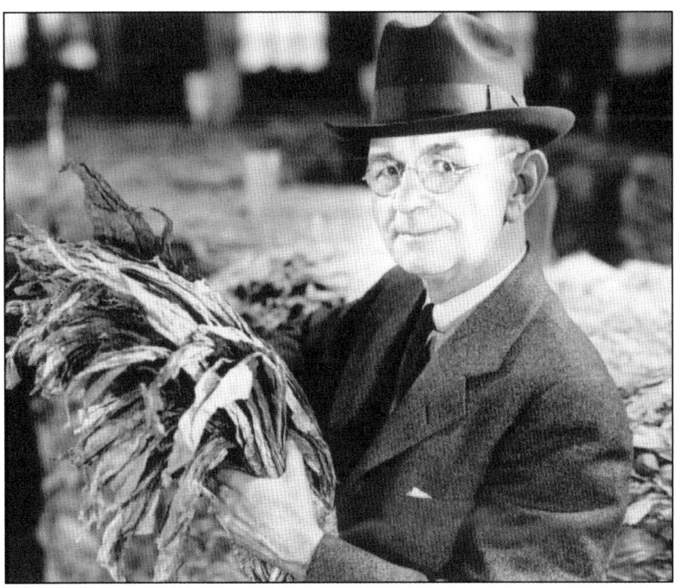

HENRY STRAUGHAN STOKES (1880–1962). Richard Joshua Reynolds hired Virginia-born Henry in 1900 to work for his company. "Mr. H.S.," the first college graduate hired, was in charge of leaf processing and was a member of the board of directors when he retired in 1947. Henry was a founder of First National Bank, serving as president and chairman of the board. He married Eloise Brown (1886–1980), daughter of Dr. Henry and Julia Brown, in 1911.

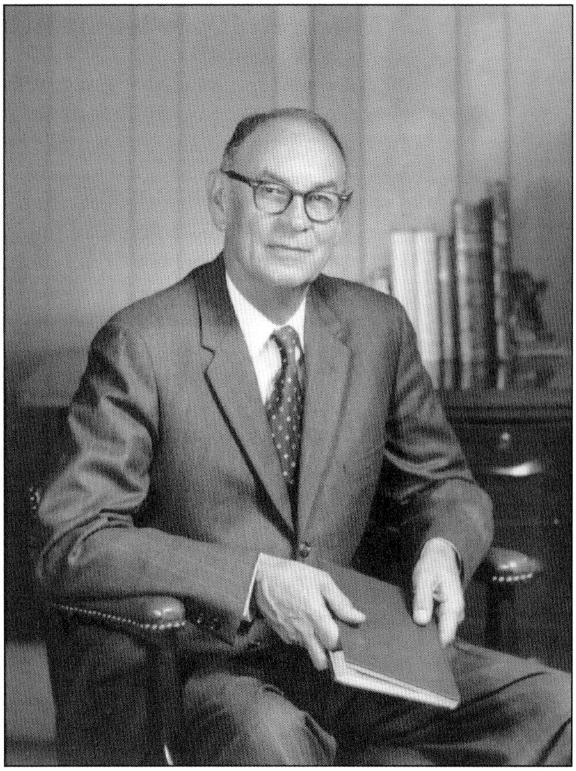

Colin Stokes (1914–1984). Colin followed in the career footsteps of his father, Henry S. Stokes, by joining R.J. Reynolds Tobacco Company in 1935, after graduating from college. He first worked as a foreman in Factory No. 12 and then was named superintendent of manufacturing. He was elected to the board of directors and became chairman and chief operating officer as well as chairman of the executive committee of R.J. Reynolds Tobacco Company. After R.J. Reynolds Industries was formed, Colin became president, chairman, and chief executive officer, retiring as an officer in 1979. He was married to Mary Louise Siewers Stokes (1918–1996).

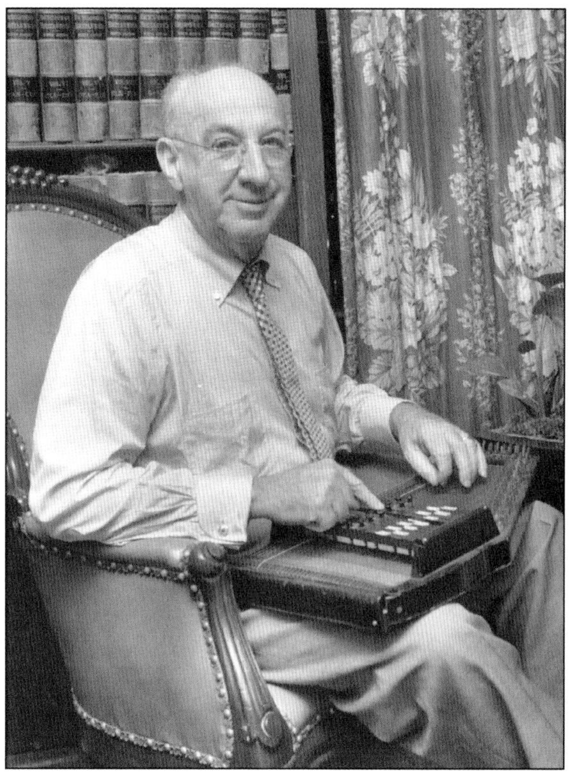

John Clarke Whitaker Sr. (1891–1978). Born in Winston-Salem to William Asbury and Anna Bitting Whitaker, John went to work in the factory at R.J. Reynolds Tobacco Company after college, in 1913. John was the first operator of the first machine to make a Camel cigarette. He served in the Navy during World War I. John returned to Reynolds, where he was personnel manager and later was elected president and chairman of the board. The Whitaker Park Cigarette Plant was named for him, as was the Forsyth Memorial Hospital Rehabilitation Center. John was married to Elizabeth Parker Norman Whitaker (1913–2000).

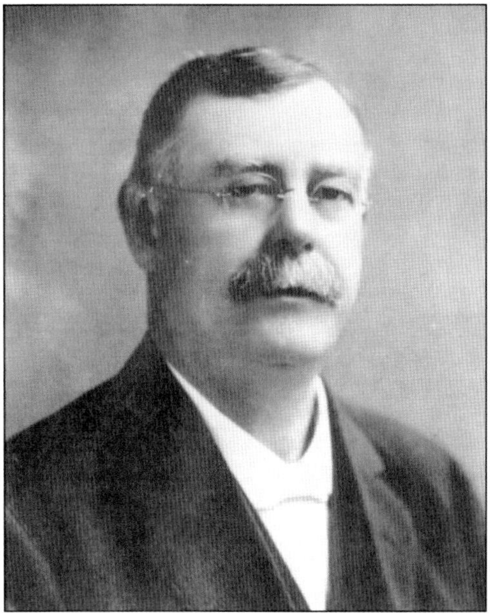

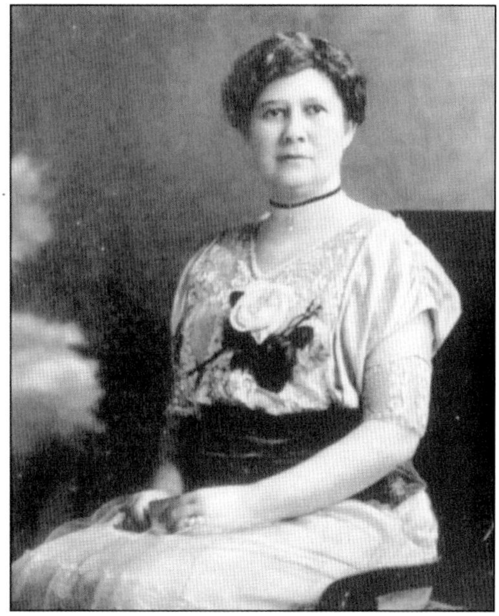

D. Rich (1862–1924) and Carrie Watkins Rich (1864–1916). D. Rich was born in Davie County and came to Winston-Salem about 1880. He was employed by R.J. Reynolds Tobacco Company before it was incorporated in 1890. He worked in the bookkeeping department and advanced to the positions of treasurer and director of the company. He and his first wife, Carrie, gave their time and money to further the work of First Baptist Church.

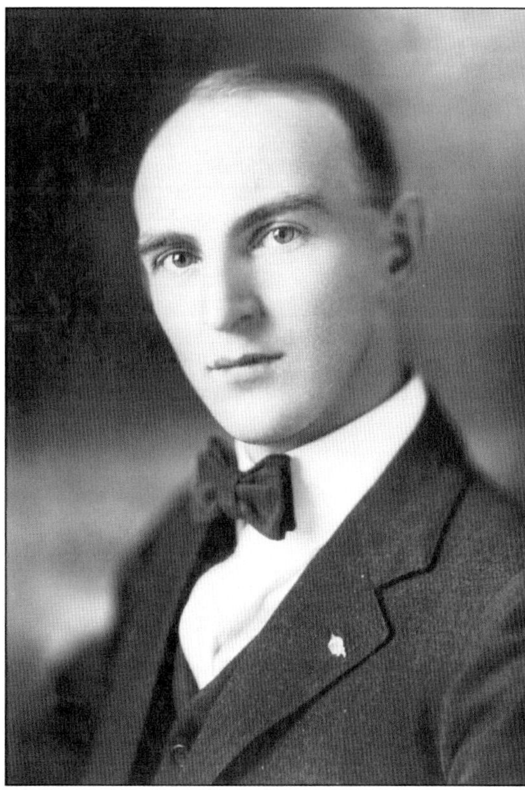

Robert Dicks Shore (1889–1937). Robert was born in Yadkin County and came to Winston-Salem as a child. He joined R.J. Reynolds Tobacco Company in 1906, was promoted to treasurer in 1923, and elected to the board of directors in 1929. Robert married Marie Merritt Rich (1888–1968) in 1926. Marie was previously married to D. Rich, who died in 1924. Marie was born in Charlotte to Thomas Harvey Merritt (1862–1940) and Minnie Smith Merritt. By her marriages to D. Rich and Robert Shore, Marie was the wife of two treasurers of R.J. Reynolds Tobacco Company.

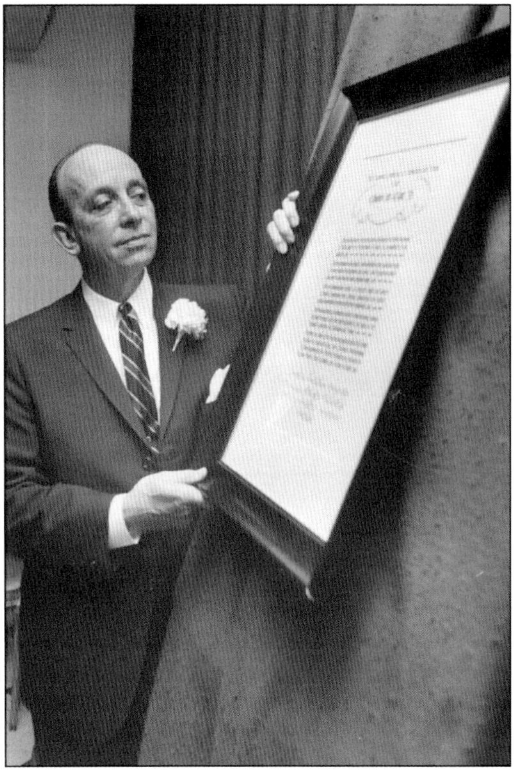

Charles Byrd Wade Jr. (1915–1994). Charlie Wade was born in Morehead City and graduated from Duke University, majoring in history. He joined R.J. Reynolds Tobacco Company in 1938 and served in World War II. He returned to R.J. Reynolds Tobacco Company and became personnel manager, served on the board of directors, and was senior vice president of R.J. Reynolds Industries. Charlie married Charlotte-native and Salem College graduate Margaret Patterson (1919–2008) in 1942. He served as chairman of the North Carolina Symphony and helped raise money to build the *Queen Elizabeth II*, a replica of a 16th century English ship.

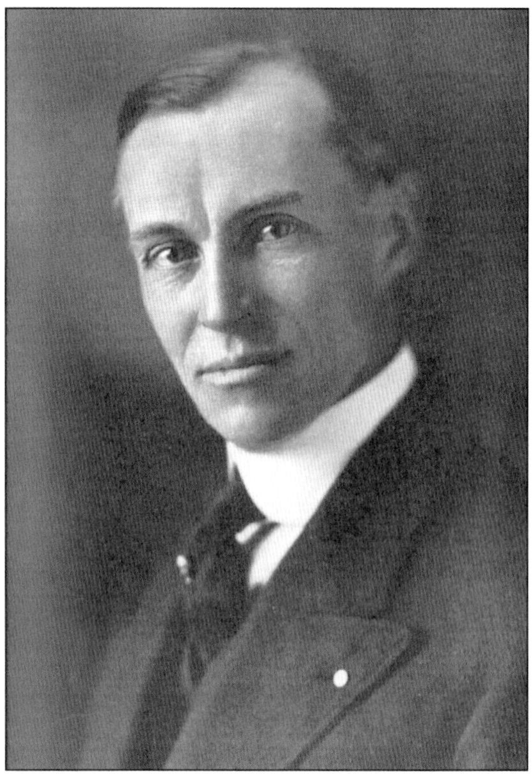

Kerner Evan Shore (1882–1961). Kerner's maternal roots were in Kernersville, the town named for his mother's family. His fraternal roots were in Yadkin County, where his grandfather Wiley Shore served several years as sheriff. In 1906, Kerner married Salem College graduate Bessie May Nissen (1881–1946) and began his career in the transportation business. He worked for Nissen Wagon Works, the company that made wagons and other vehicles. With the advice and assistance of his father-in-law, Kerner embarked on a new career with the automobile. In 1910, he organized the Carolina Cadillac Company and ran it until 1930.

Jonathan Lewis Casper Sr. (1866–1921). Born in Rowan County, John came to Winston-Salem around 1888 and married Sarah Ann Nading (1868–1923), daughter of Francis A. Nading (1840–1902) and Martha Fulp Nading (1838–1904). John operated a heavily advertised wholesale and mail-order hard liquor business in the pre-Prohibition days. The former alderman, who was known for his charitable works, moved his business to other states and served one year in Leavenworth Prison for "moonshine conspiracy." After his pardon, he returned to Winston-Salem and established the Basketeria in 1918, the city's first self-service grocery store, then sold it to a local businessman.

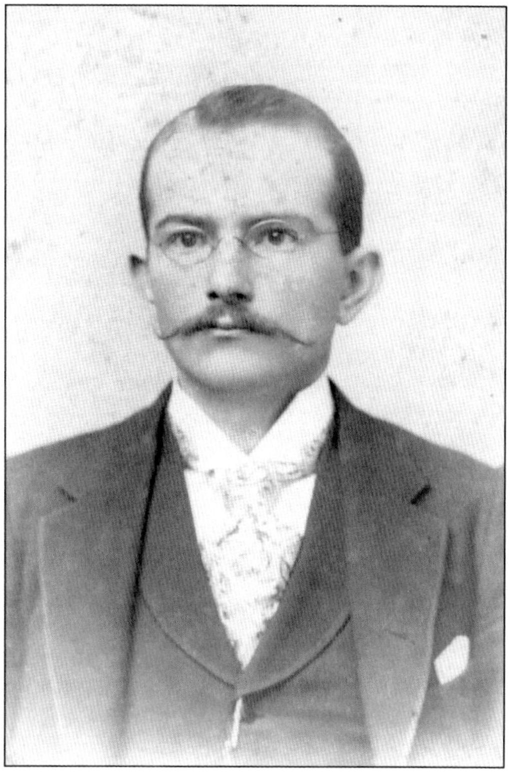

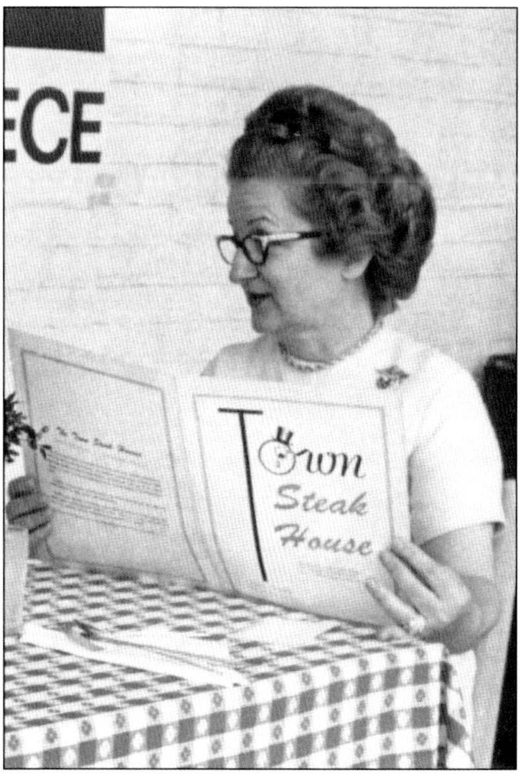

Mary Sapos Chamis (1912–1971). Born in Greece, Mary came to the United States when she was three years old. She lived first in Colorado and then came to Winston-Salem in 1927. Mary married William John Chamis (1906–1965) in 1940, and they both became naturalized US citizens shortly afterward. William operated the Piccadilly Restaurant on West Fourth Street. Mary and William established Town Steak House No. 1 on Lockland Avenue, followed by Town Steak House No. 2 at the Thruway Shopping Center. The popular Town Steak House Restaurants served a variety of delicious dishes in a comfortable, yet elegant, atmosphere.

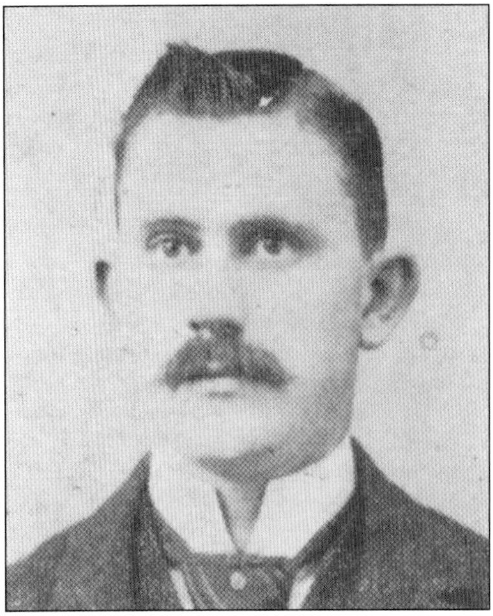

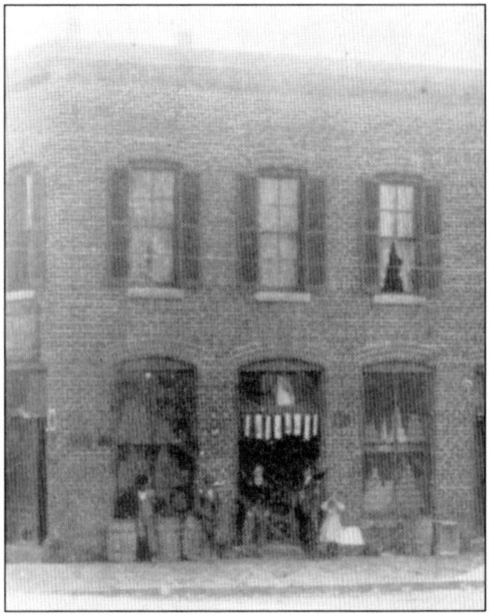

John Thomas Joyner Sr. (1867–1954) and Julius Clay Kreeger (1870–1959) Families. Born in Yadkin County, John came to Winston-Salem after graduation from Oak Ridge Military Academy. He opened a grocery business on the corner of West Fourth and Burke Streets around 1891. He and the store are pictured above. Children from the West End School, located just across the street, were frequent customers. In 1892, John married Phoebe Rominger (1856–1939), daughter of Elias Cornelius Rominger (1819–1897) and Elizabeth Catherine Hauser Rominger (1828–1910). Phoebe headed the missionary box committee at First Baptist Church for over 40 years. Her sister Elizabeth Rebecca "Bettie" Rominger Kreeger (1866–1920) was also active in missionary work at Brown Memorial Baptist Church. Bettie married Julius Clay Kreeger (center in below photograph), who was a 36-year post office employee, North Carolina legislator, and family genealogist. Julius's second wife was Minnie Phillips (1883–1973).

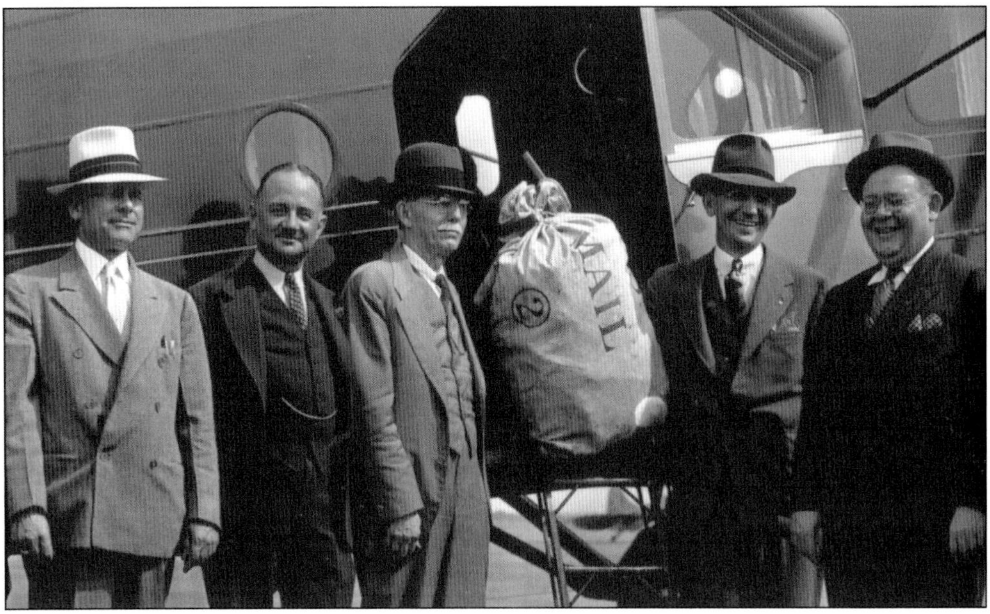

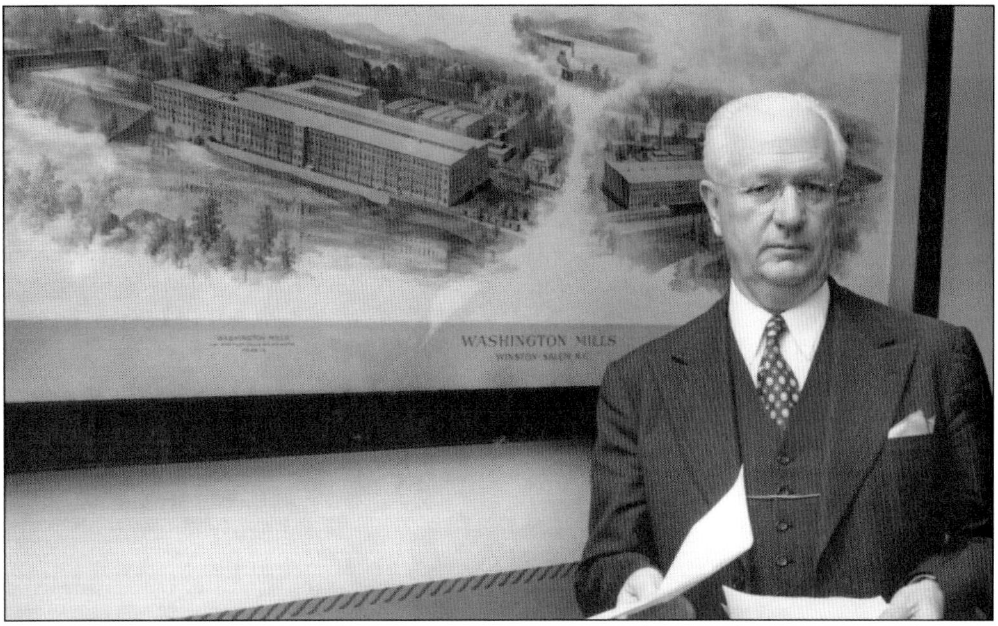

Agnew Hunter Bahnson Sr. (1886–1966) and Family. The son of Dr. Henry T. and Emma Fries Bahnson, Agnew (pictured above) was named for the doctors who saved his father's arm from amputation when it became infected during the Civil War. Agnew worked and advanced in several mills, including Washington Mills, where he was president and chairman of the board. He organized the Normalair Company (later Bahnson Company) and married Elizabeth Moir Hill (1892–1966). Agnew Hunter Bahnson Jr. (1915–1964) followed his father in the management of the Bahnson Company and was an author, adventurer, pilot, and musician. His wife, Katharine King (1921–2007), Salem College graduate and 1941 May Queen, helped in the creation of the School of the Arts and the local arts council. Later married to John de Breganza and John Griffith "Gick" Johnson (1915–2010), Katharine is shown with Agnew Jr. in the photograph below.

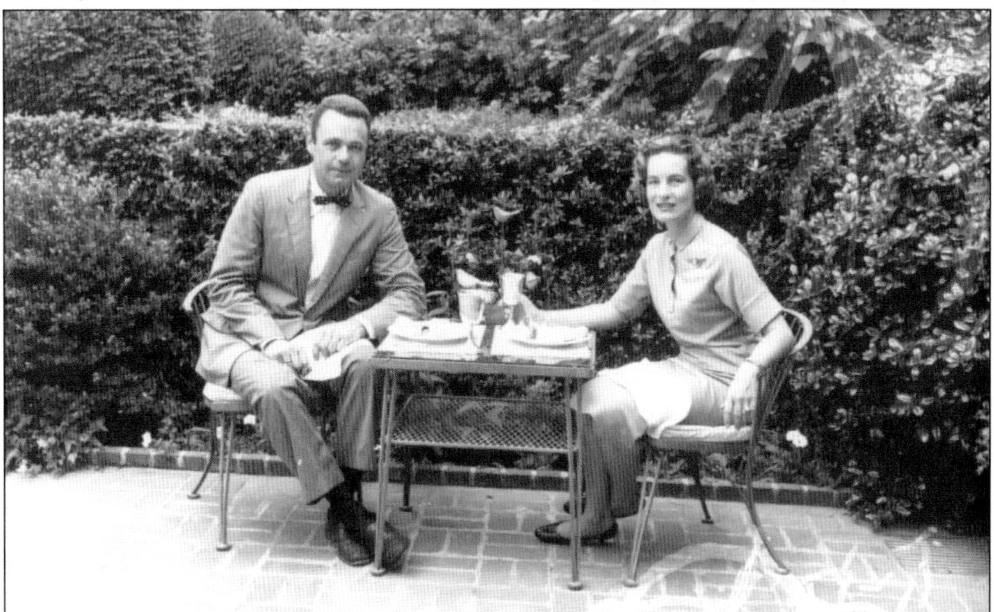

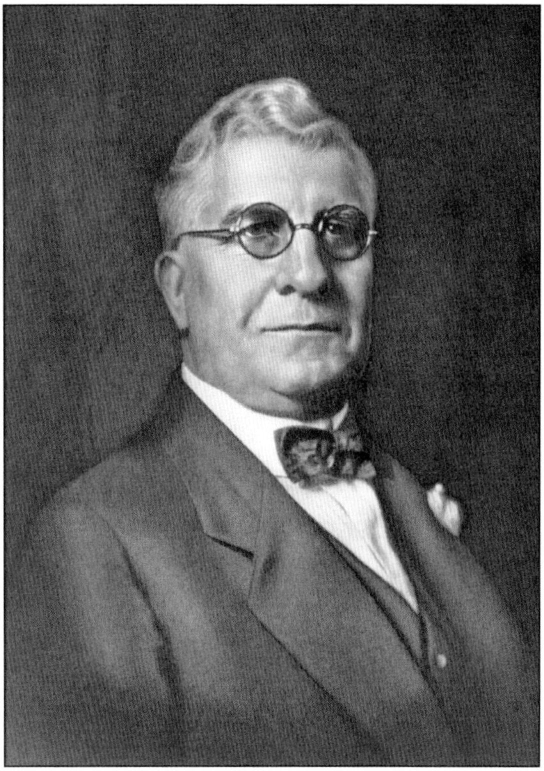

Col. Jacob Lott Ludlow (1862–1930). Jacob was born in New Jersey and earned degrees in civil engineering. In Winston-Salem, he established a civil engineering practice, which was a new field, particularly as it related to municipal engineering. He was an advocate for the city's public water and sewage system and was in favor of paving roads and certain public places. He designed the West End section of town, based on the contour of the land. He established a specialized engineering firm in 1919 called Ludlow Engineers, which worked throughout the South, with its home base in Winston-Salem. Jacob married Myra Hunt (1863–1938) in 1887.

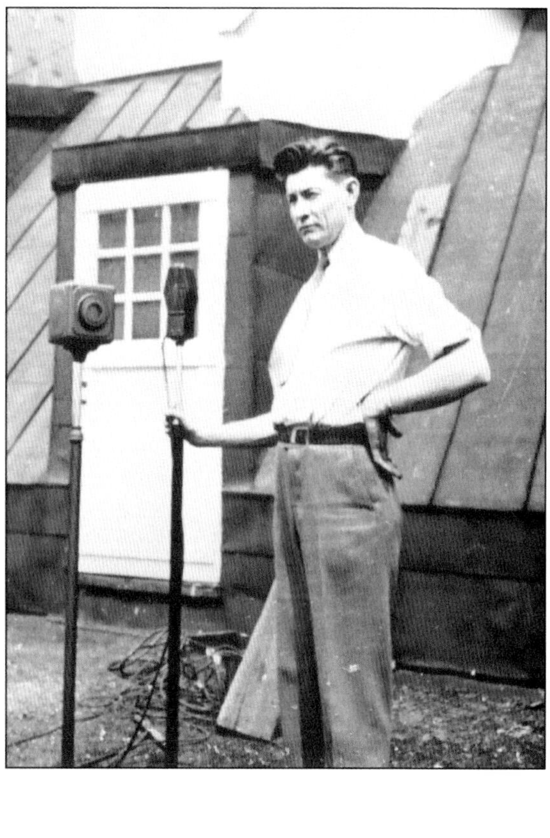

Douglas Julian "Doug" Lee Sr. (1898–1992). Doug Lee was born in Winston-Salem and became interested in radio at an early age. He collected electronic parts to make his own radio set. He was an advocate for starting a radio station in Winston-Salem when other cities were going on the air. His ideas finally became a reality in 1930 when WSJS radio debuted on Good Friday. The first broadcast of the Easter sunrise service in Old Salem two days later began a tradition that continues annually and was supervised by Lee until 1985. Doug was married to Mary Lee Davis (1901–1986).

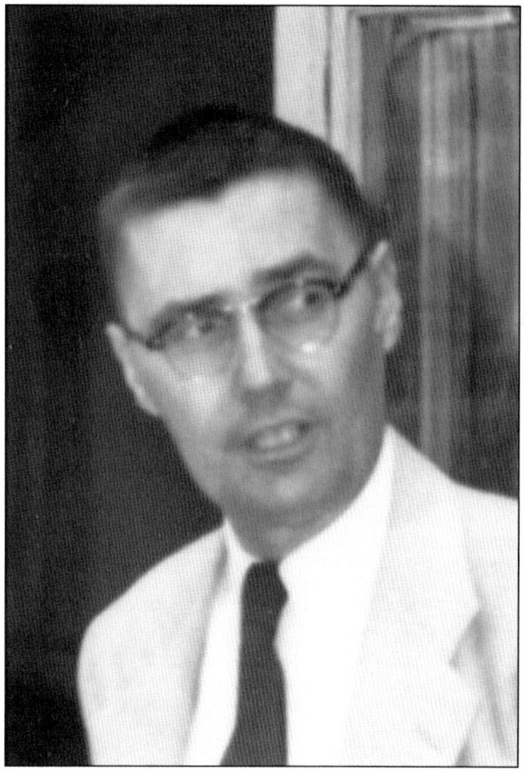

Frank Liipfert Horton (1918–2004). Born in Wake County to Dr. Miles Christopher Horton and Theodosia Liipfert Horton Taliaferro (1891–1971), Frank served in the Navy during World War II. Frank and his mother settled in Winston-Salem and operated an antiques store. Frank was named secretary of the Old Salem Restoration Committee and stated that "we plan to restore the old town as it was and not as we imagine it should be." The Frank L. Horton Museum Center was named to acknowledge Frank as the founder of the Museum of Early Southern Decorative Arts (MESDA) and the first director of restoration for Old Salem.

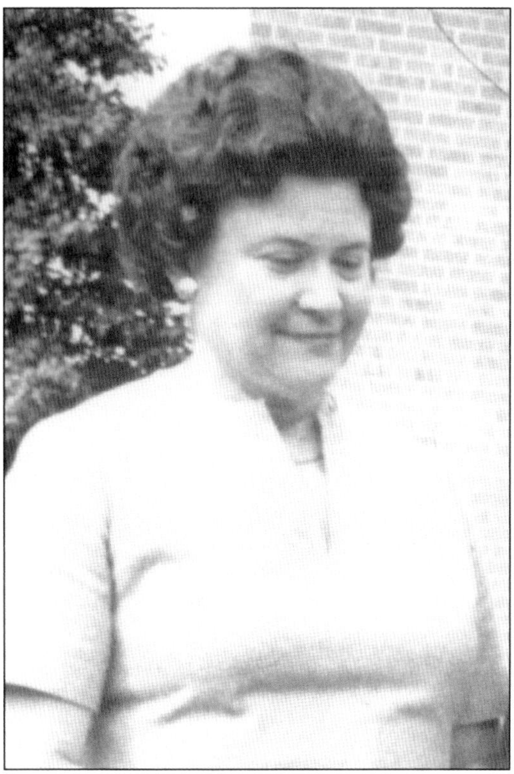

Flora Ann Lee Bynum (1924–2006). Flora Ann was born in Guilford County, graduated from Meredith College, and worked for the Winston-Salem Chamber of Commerce. Flora Ann was best known for her work as chairman of the Old Salem Landscape Restoration Committee and as a member of the Old Salem Board of Trustees. She was recognized as an authority on Moravian horticulture and as a plant historian. She published books and pamphlets on Old Salem and historic landscapes, and she graciously invited Old Salem visitors to tour her 19th-century perennial garden on South Main Street. She was married to Zachary Taylor Bynum Jr. (1922–2002).

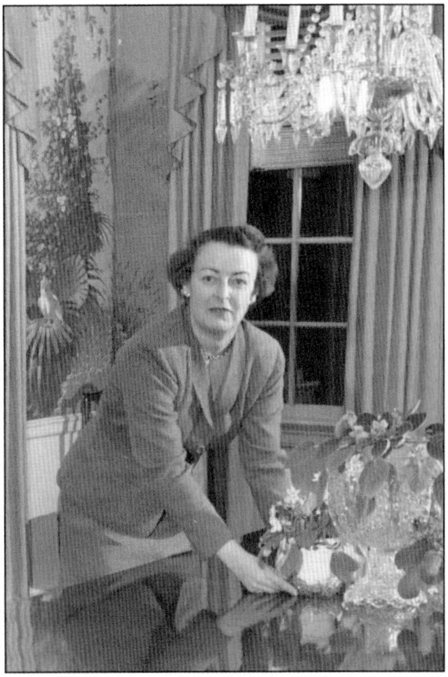

Virginia Lash Dunklee Rice (1907–1962). Virginia was born in Virginia and came to Winston-Salem with her parents, Frank Guenter Dunklee (1876–1923) and Letitia Lash Hairston Dunklee (1879–1943). Virginia graduated from R.J. Reynolds High School and Hollins College. She married Jonas Shearn Rice Sr. (1902–1974) in 1934. Jonas, or "Joe," came to Winston-Salem from Texas about 1930 and, with his brother Thomas Botts Rice (1905–1991), established the Dr. Pepper Bottling Company, which later became Northwest Beverage Company. Thomas married Mary Louise Moore (1910–2008) in 1931. Joe married his second wife Rosalie Hanes Moore (1910–1982) in 1965.

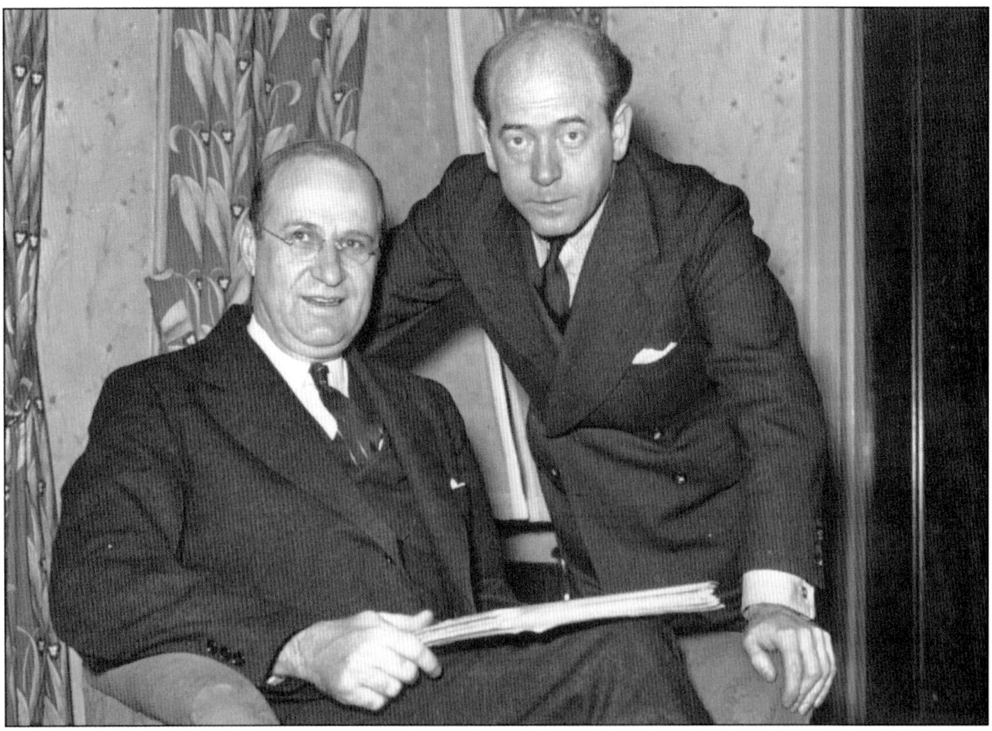

Dr. Charles Gildersleeve Vardell Jr. (1893–1962). Charles, pictured at left with Eugene Ormandy, was born in Salisbury and received early musical training from his mother. He continued his musical studies at Princeton University and Juilliard School of Music. Charles taught music at Salem College and served as dean of the School of Music from 1928 to 1951. He was well known for his symphony composition "Carolinian." Charles was married to Eleanor Ferrill (1893–1969).

KATHARINE "KATE" GROGAN PULLIAM (1874–1972). Kate was born in Rockingham County to James Madison Grogan (1826–1899) and Mary Catherine Dodd Grogan (1849–1933). Her father was a tobacco merchant with extensive real estate holdings. James Madison married Mary Catherine Dodd in 1868. Both parents were born in Rockingham County and moved to Winston-Salem in 1871. James Madison's first wife, Paulina Smith, died in 1867. In 1900, Kate married Henry Byrd Pulliam (1864–1934), the widower of her sister Mattie D. Grogan Pulliam (1870–1897). Henry was born in Caswell County and was secretary of the Orinoco Supply Company.

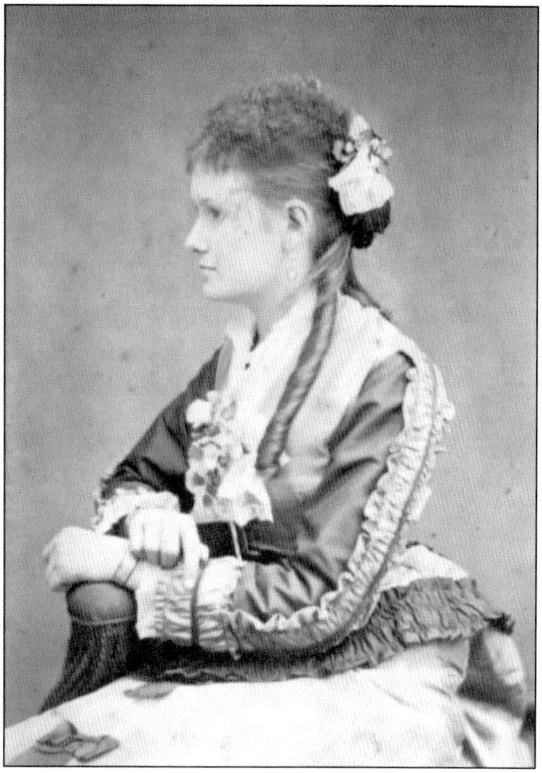

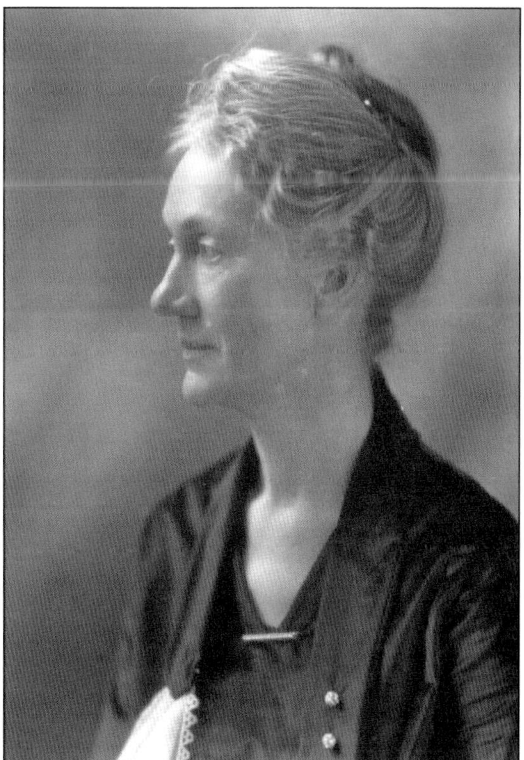

ANNIE WILEY GROGAN (1878–1957). "Miss Annie" was born in Winston-Salem to James Madison and Mary Dodd Grogan. Annie's first job was as a telephone operator. She made a dramatic career change in 1905 when she became secretary of Associated Charities, a forerunner of Family Services. Mayor George W. Coan Jr. suspended business at city hall during her mother's funeral in 1933. Annie retired in 1936, after 31 years of feeding, clothing, and sheltering the city's poor and sick residents. For her untiring devotion to the needs of the less fortunate, she was called "Mother of Charity."

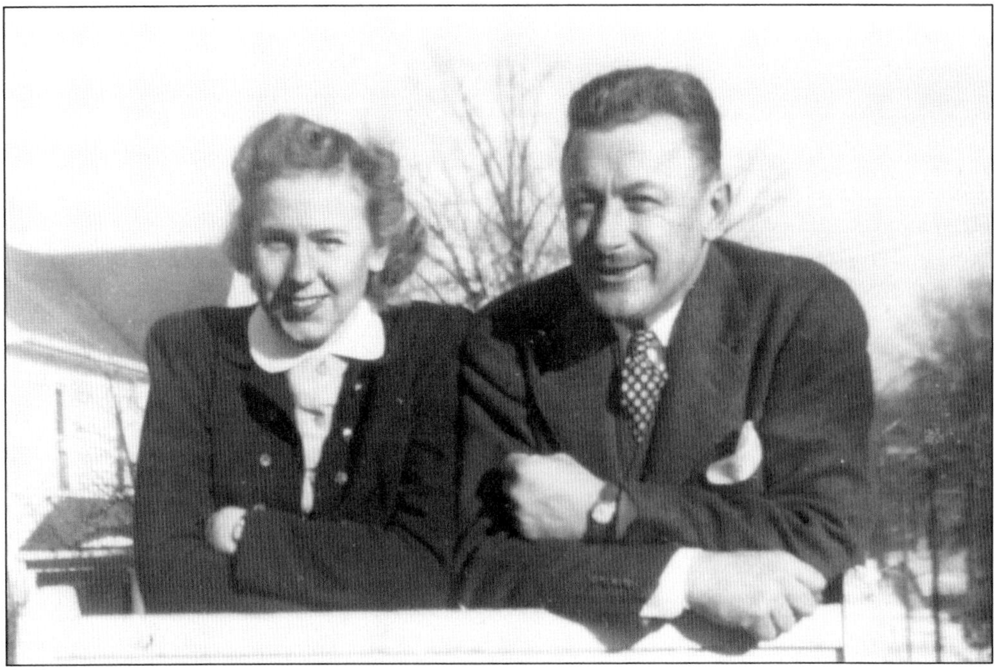

Addie Bell Grogan Wiese (1920–1971) and Milton Valentine Wiese (1893–1970). Born in Winston-Salem to Irvin Washington and Eva Bell Cherry Grogan, Addie Bell graduated from R.J. Reynolds High School. She married New York–native Milton in 1942. Milton came to Winston-Salem in 1939 to operate the Royal Crown Bottling Company. He purchased Forsyth Frozen Foods and perfected the hickory-smoked country ham process, resulting in the award-winning "Olde Salem Ham." (MGR.)

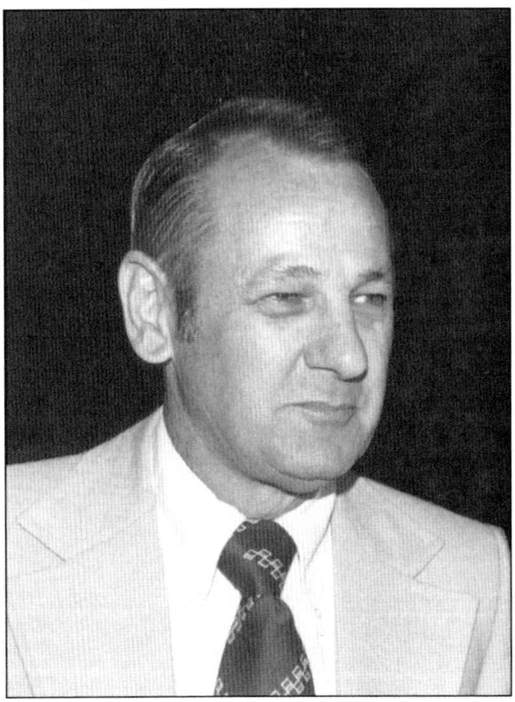

John Gray Grogan (1924–2003). John was born in Winston-Salem, the youngest of eight children born to Irvin Washington and Eva Bell Cherry Grogan. He was a brother to Addie Bell, discussed above. John graduated from R.J. Reynolds High School in 1942 and Guilford College in 1950. He served in the US Air Force during World War II and was a prisoner of war. Talented in woodworking, John made furniture for members of his family. He was also a skilled mechanic and worked for several years at Medical Park Hospital. John married Jean Shelton Shoemaker in 1949. (JSG.)

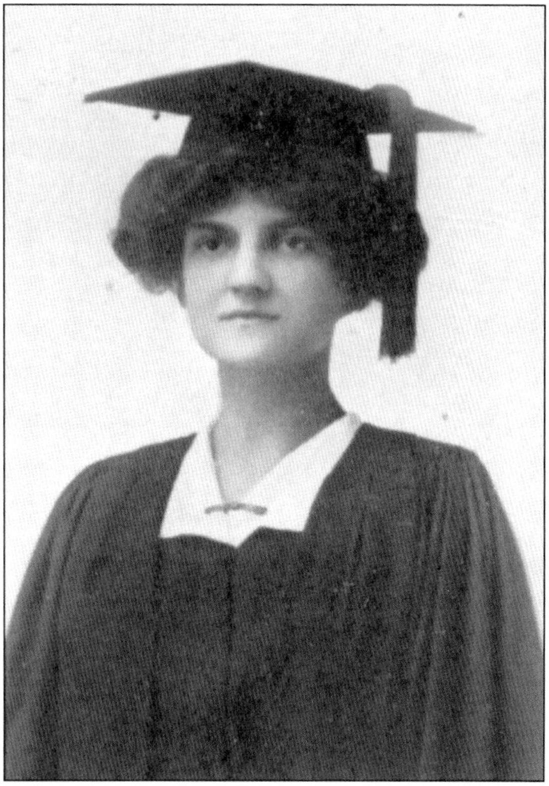

Elizabeth Leary Grogan Trotter (1893–1980). Elizabeth was born in Winston-Salem to Jeffrey Scales Grogan (1862–1911) and Mary Lee Perkins Grogan (1869–1934). Jeffrey came from Rockingham County, as did his father, Martin Grogan (1828–1891) and his stepmother, Nancy Kinner Dalton Price Grogan (1830–1894). Martin was a magistrate, mayor, and US commissioner. Elizabeth graduated from Salem College in 1912 and married Alexander Graham Trotter Jr. in 1919. She and Alexander lived in Charlotte, where he worked in a bank. After Alexander's death in 1929, Elizabeth and their daughter Betsey Graham Trotter returned to Winston-Salem and lived with her mother and sister.

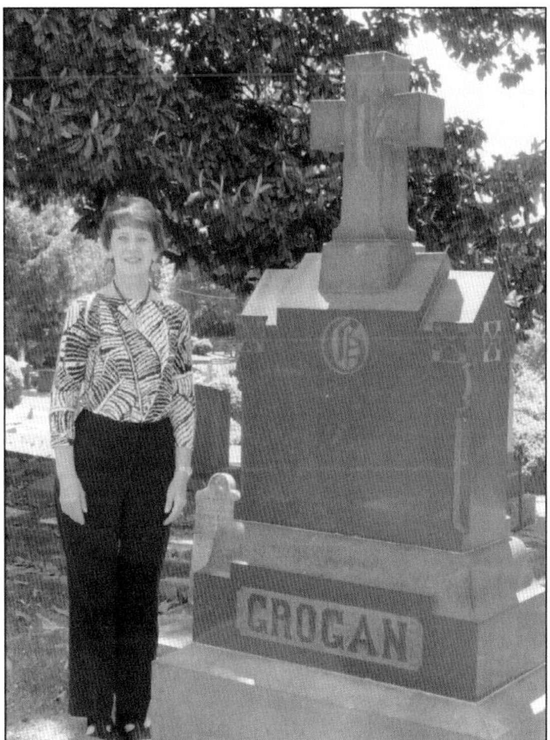

Meet the Author. Molly Grogan Rawls was born in Forsyth County to Winston-Salem native Joseph Cherry Grogan Sr. Molly is standing beside the marker for the Jeffrey Scales Grogan family members, many of whom are mentioned in the preceding pages and are distant relatives through her father's lineage. Jeffrey came to Winston-Salem around 1876 with his father, Martin Grogan. His mother, Martha Ann Scales, died in 1864, and his father married Nancy Kinner Dalton Price in 1865. After his graduation from Davidson College, Jeffrey attended law school, was admitted to the bar, and practiced law in Winston-Salem for 23 years. (JDR.)

Index of Names